Rich,

Charlie's example and lessons fill these pages. I wouldn't be here today if not for him and all I learned from him. I hope it is a fitting tribute to him.

Thanks for your leadership and support.

"In *Everyone Leads*, Schmitz provides leaders and organizations with innovative ideas about how to make a greater difference in their communities, as he has done with Public Allies."

—**Sonal Shah,** former director, White House Office of Social Innovation and Civic Participation under President Barack Obama

"Grounded in our core American values and informed by current technological and social trends, *Everyone Leads* makes a powerful call for citizen leadership, with inspiring stories and practical steps we all can take on the issues we care about."

—**David Eisner,** CEO, National Constitution Center, and former CEO, Corporation for National and Community Service under President George W. Bush

"*Everyone Leads* challenges leaders and organizations to think in new ways about how we lead. It calls on us to see our effectiveness not just in the achievement of goals, but in the values we practice and the people we engage as we achieve them. Schmitz has issued a call to action well worth heeding—bravo!"

—**Dr. Cheryl Dorsey,** CEO, Echoing Green

"We have long admired how Public Allies discovers one of our community's most untapped assets: young people, especially those not often seen as potential leaders. We hope many more will join them in building these assets."

—**John McKnight and Jody Kretzmann,** co-founders, Asset-Based Community Development Institute at Northwestern University

"Public Allies has proven again and again that young people have tremendous potential to lead when given the opportunity. This book will be an indispensable resource for campus programs and students who want to get involved in working for community change."

—**Liz Hollander,** former CEO, Campus Compact, and senior fellow, Tufts University

"Universities are essential to 'building leadership from the community up.' As community stakeholders, educational institutions must be contributors, collaborators, problem solvers, and learners. There is no room for ivory tower musing; rather, we educators must put our privilege to work and engage in action research that invites co-creating solution-oriented pathways with community members. *Everyone Leads* provides the inspiration, optimism, and hopefulness needed to mobilize community assets. The message is that together, people can and must be change agents."

—**Dr. Patricia Arredondo,** associate vice chancellor and dean of the School of Continuing Education, University of Wisconsin–Milwaukee

Everyone Leads

Everyone Leads

Building Leadership from the Community Up

Paul Schmitz

Published by Jossey-Bass
A Wiley Imprint
989 Market Street, San Francisco, CA 94103-1741—www.josseybass.com

Jossey-Bass books and products are available through most bookstores. To contact Jossey-Bass directly call our Customer Care Department within the U.S. at 800-956-7739, outside the U.S. at 317-572-3986, or fax 317-572-4002.

Jossey-Bass also publishes its books in a variety of electronic formats. Some content that appears in print may not be available in electronic books.

Library of Congress Cataloging-in-Publication Data

Schmitz, Paul, date.
Everyone leads: building leadership from the community up/Paul Schmitz.—1
p. cm.
Includes bibliographical references and index.
ISBN 978-0-470-90603-3 (hardback); ISBN 978-1-118-12072-9 (ebk);
ISBN 978-1-118-12073-6 (ebk); ISBN 978-1-118-12074-3 (ebk)
1. Leadership. 2. Community leadership. I. Title.
HM1261.S365 2012
303.3′4–dc23

2011033498

Printed in the United States of America

FIRST EDITION
HB Printing 10 9 8 7 6 5 4 3 2 1

Contents

Preface

Writing this book has been one of the greatest professional experiences of my life. Several other authors told me how hard it would be, and they were right. The book has taken much more time than I thought it would, and the writing has evolved in ways I did not imagine when I wrote the original outlines. I've spent countless hours reflecting on and processing years of lessons about leadership, communities, values, and my own leadership journey.

At the end of each program year, our Allies participate in a Presentation of Learning, where they demonstrate before an audience of peers, Public Allies staff, and other leaders how they have learned and practiced our leadership values and describe how they will continue doing so in the future. This book is my Presentation of Learning after eighteen years with Public Allies. And these eighteen years have been an incredible learning experience.

I love my job. Every day, I get to help a diverse and talented group—young people who have a passion for making a difference—begin their careers working for community and social change. I know that as Public Allies helps them step up and lead, they will help others step up, too. Our alumni cascade our impact through communities. Our staff has firsthand knowledge of what an incredible privilege it is to participate in this transformation. And of course we ourselves are transformed.

Just as Public Allies has been my university, our staff, our Allies, our partners, and our mentors have been my teachers.

Note: All author proceeds from this book will support the work of Public Allies.

To the Allies—past, present, future—and staff of Public Allies, who inspire me and offer us all hope for the future

To those who have contributed to my own leadership journey, especially to the memory of those beloved mentors who have passed—Jimmy, Charlie, Lisa, and Uncle Jim

And to Olivia, Maxwell, Maya, and Jennifer, whose love inspires me to be my best and do my best each day

Acknowledgments

As I conducted research for this book, I increasingly realized that the philosophy, practices, and stories behind the Public Allies program have been handed down by oral tradition. Much of the practical information about how to deliver our program has been documented, but our reasons for delivering our program the way we do have not been well documented. As a result, I needed more time to prepare the book—and was presented with an amazing opportunity. I got to interview dozens of Allies, staff, and alumni across the country, and to read many stories and examples compiled by others. Therefore, I first must thank all of you whose stories have shaped this book and animated our approach. Thanks also to those of you whose stories do not appear here—trust me, your stories will be told in other ways. All of you have inspired me, again and again, and made me so proud to lead Public Allies.

The great historian Sean Wilentz, describing how Bob Dylan has taken melodies, quotes, stories, and images from various literary, artistic, and musical traditions and transformed them into something new, defends this practice, saying that "every artist is, to some extent, a thief; the trick is to get away with it by making . . . something new."[1] Our staff has done the same thing over the years, and I thank all the people, named and unnamed, who influenced, inspired, and taught various members of the Public Allies community as we built our leadership approach and curriculum. Our unique approach is grounded in the work of many amazing leaders.

I was able to write this book because of the support of Public Allies' board of directors, management team, and staff. I must begin by acknowledging that my growth as a leader, along with the growth of Public Allies, has been most enabled by the leadership of our board chair, Bill Graustein. Bill is a community builder and philanthropist in Connecticut, and he is perhaps the greatest exemplar I know of our values and our community-building approach. I am truly blessed to have this thoughtful, humble, intellectually deep, loving leader as Public Allies' chair, largest donor, and role model. He put the "angel" in "angel investor."

Along with Bill, I also thank the other board members whose support of this project allowed me to dedicate the immense time and patient attention it required: David Benjamin, Claire Bennett, Melia Dicker, David Eisner, Leif Elsmo, Katherine Gehl, Liz Hollander, Richard Murphy, Julian Posada, Christa Robinson, Jason Scott, Kanwar Singh, Michael Smith, Dorothy Stoneman, and Jaime Uzeta. I am so grateful to work for you.

There is no way I could have even started this book without having Cris Ros-Dukler as my COO. Cris and I lead the organization in a partnership that has been very positive for the organization. In Chapter Eight, I share a list of things that I suck at. Cris is really good at most of those things, and her leadership has strengthened the organization. We work with a terrific management team: Enrique Ball, vice president of marketing and development; Tim Hosch, vice president of finance and administration; and David McKinney, vice president of programs. Together, they have led Public Allies to quality, growth, and learning while staying true to our mission and values. I also thank Nelly Nieblas, our director of external relations and public policy, and, again, Enrique Ball for their patience and the extra effort they made in areas where we work together while I was writing this book. And I must especially thank my super assistant, Melinda Rodriguez. I am so fortunate to have her steady, positive, warm, professional support; her own life and leadership inspire me. It is so great to have Cris and Melinda, such powerful, smart, caring, fun women, as my closest co-workers.

Diane Bacha, our director of communications, worked with me on every aspect of the book, and her contributions are everywhere. She helped me edit every page, brainstorm ideas, collect stories, coordinate edits and feedback from early readers, master the publisher's style guide, and do the difficult work of securing permissions from all the sources cited here. This book is much better because of her incredible help.

I must also thank all the readers who reviewed early drafts of the chapters and sent us useful edits, feedback, and suggestions that have made the book better and will make it more relevant to its audience. Thanks to MacArthur Antigua, Heidi Brooks, Dana Burgess O'Donovan, Max Chang, Bob Francis, Bill Graustein, Ava Hernandez, Liz Hollander, Asha Loring, Marc McAleavy, David McKinney, Jeanette Mitchell, Joanne Murphy, Richard Murphy, Cris Ros-Dukler, Jason Scott, Michael Smith, Jaime Uzeta, Fahd Vahidy, James Weinberg, Todd Wellman, and Harris Wofford.

I thank and forgive Jesse Wiley, and I hope he forgives me, too. Jesse is the editor responsible for initiating this project, and occasionally during the last nine months, when I was at the height of frustration or stress, I took his name in vain. I must also thank the people for whom I caused stress and frustration: Vince Hyman, Dani Scoville, and Alison Hankey. Vince was my coach and editor, and he stayed patient and persistent as a four-month project extended to nine months. He used my guilt as a tool but never exploited it, and his edits, feedback, and suggestions were enormously helpful; he is a real pro. Dani Scoville helped us get all our ducks in a row on the way to the finish line. Xenia Lisanevich and Xavier Callahan caught all my mistakes and made very thorough and helpful edits. Alison Hankey, another real pro, managed the project in a way that allowed me to revise the timeline and the project itself to make this, I believe, a much better book.

It would be impossible to thank everyone who has ever been associated with Public Allies and made a difference in my life and my leadership. Nevertheless, along with my current team, I must also thank Tony Allen, Sheila Bernus-Dowd, Craig Bowman, Tony Brown, Katrina Browne, Omar Brownson, Mike Canul, Patrick Carroll, Dan Condon, Julius Davis, Michelle Dobbs, Magda Escobar, Ian Fisk; Merilou Gonzales, Patricia Griffin, Patrick Griffin, Peter Hart, Chris Hero, Jay Kim, Vanessa Kirsch, Wendy Kopp, Edward Minter, Karen Mulhauser, Jojopa Nsoroma, Michelle Obama, Jason Scott, Trabian Shorters, Tavis Smiley, Chuck Supple, Suzanne Sysko, Kimberly Tuck, Kristin Venderbush, David Weaver, Tim Webb, Brian Young, and Josh Zepnick.

I stand on the shoulders of many giants. I have been mentored and supported by so many leaders, and I have benefited greatly from their wisdom, love, and support. Again, it is hard if not impossible to thank everyone, but I'll try. Thanks to Dan Bader, Bill Boletta, Charlie Bray, Dana Burgess O'Donovan, Daniel Cardinali, Patrick Corvington, Cheryl Dorsey, Jim Forbes, Bob Francis, Katie Gingrass, Leslie and Mike Grinker, Darrell Hammond, Reuben Harpole, Father James Hoff (Uncle Jim), Michele Jolin, Jody Kretzmann, Wayne Lawrenz, John McKnight, Jeanette Mitchell, Beth, Jim, and Joanne Murphy, Brent Rupple Jr., Sonal Shah, Jerry Shepard,Tom Sheridan, Jo and Mimi Spiro, James Stearns, Linda Stephenson, Lisa Sullivan, Marta Urquilla, James Weinberg, the Welland family, Shelley Whelpton, Harris Wofford, and my old friends from the Cosmic Corner.

I must also thank my parents and my family. As you will see in Chapter Two, I was a difficult child, and we had many conflicts, but we pulled through it all together. I want especially to thank my mom for reading Chapter Two, discovering many things for the first time, and telling me she was proud of me for sharing my story.

My time and my work on this book were supported by the W.K. Kellogg Foundation. Thank you to Anne Mosle and Kara

Carlisle for their generous support and their belief that Public Allies' work is worth sharing. I also must thank some of those whose support has been most important to our growth. Suzanne Aisenberg, formerly of the Atlantic Philanthropies, and Robert Sherman, formerly of the Surdna Foundation, were instrumental in helping me as a new CEO lead Public Allies' second wave of growth. Thanks also to Christine Kwak, Tom Reis, and Lisa Flick Wilson of the W.K. Kellogg Foundation; to David and Cheryl Einhorn and Jennifer Hoos Rothberg of the Einhorn Family Foundation; to Josh and Anita Bekenstein; to Kippy Joseph of the Rockefeller Foundation; to Alison Yu of the William Randolph Hearst Foundation; to Shawn Dove and Mimi Corcoran of the Open Society Institute; to Richard Brown and Christine Rhee of American Express; and to Doug Jansson and Jim Marks of the Greater Milwaukee Foundation (my first believers).

Most of this book was written at Alterra Cafes in Milwaukee. I thank their great employees for giving me a place to plug in, drink, and eat. As I comfortably wrote for hours and hours while blasting Wilco, Radiohead, the Beatles, Bob Dylan, and others through my headphones, I always felt welcome.

And, finally, my children—Olivia, Maxwell, and Maya—bring great joy, love, and magic to my life every day. I couldn't possibly love them more or be more proud of them. I am the luckiest dad in the world. And I am also very lucky to have found Jennifer Frank and her wonderful children, Eli and Nora. I'm passionate about work-life balance, and I had to make sacrifices on each side as I completed the book. I am better at my work because I take the time to treasure the love, care, and support I have from Jennifer, my kids, and so many family members, friends, and mentors. Growing up, I never could have imagined the career I have or the love and support I have in my life today. I am very grateful.

Milwaukee, Wisconsin Paul Schmitz
August 2011

Introduction

Everyone leads. When I began using this phrase in presentations about Public Allies and chose it as the title of this book, it provoked many questions and debates from people outside the organization.

Some asked if we really meant *everyone*. "Can everyone really lead?" they asked. "Or are you just talking about a certain group of people? Don't you agree that people have different levels of skills, and that some people just aren't meant to be in charge? Aren't there people who don't want to be in charge?"

Others questioned whether anything can get done if everyone feels that he or she is in charge: "Don't you have a problem with too many people feeling entitled? Do you mean that everyone has a say about everything? How is it possible to get clear direction or consensus if everyone believes that he or she is a leader? Don't you need better followers, too?"

I have found a simple and powerful way to answer these critics by reframing the idea of leadership, moving from an emphasis on the noun *leader* to an emphasis on the verb *to lead.* At Public Allies, we talk about leadership in terms of an action one takes, not in terms of a position one holds. Leadership is about taking responsibility—both personal and social—for working with others on shared goals. Everyone has some circle of influence where it is possible to take responsibility for leading. It is also important *how* one leads, and leadership includes the values one uses to bring people together around shared goals. In other words, the means are as important as the ends. Leadership is not about a position that one is entitled to *have*; it is about a process in which one takes responsibility to *engage*. Depending on the goal, group, or task, we may sometimes be leading and sometimes be following.

I've found our lessons on leadership occasionally supported in unlikely places. Not long ago, for example, my children and I watched the Pixar animated film *Ratatouille*, and I was surprised to see that it captured our philosophy of leadership well. In the film, a rat named Rémy dreams of being a chef. He journeys to the Paris restaurant owned by his greatest inspiration, Auguste Gusteau, an author and the TV host of *Everyone Can Cook*. Rémy allies himself with a hapless errand boy, Alfredo Linguini, hiding in Alfredo's *toque blanche* and guiding him to become a master chef. Drama and comedy ensue, and the film ends with a cynical and vicious critic, Anton Ego, declaring Rémy the greatest chef in all of France. Having long disdained Gusteau's claim that everyone can cook, Ego now says, "Not everyone can become a great artist, but a great artist can come from anywhere." In the same way, Public Allies during the past two decades has seen at first hand how great leadership can emerge from uncommon places.

This does not mean that everyone can lead any effort, organization, or institution, or that one who is a good leader in one context is a good leader in other contexts. It does mean that a great leader can come from anywhere, and that unless more people believe in themselves, take responsibility, and work with others to make a difference, we all lose out from the lost potential. At Public Allies, we have developed the leadership qualities of more than 3,800 diverse young adults, from ex-felons and teen parents to graduates of top colleges. There is an incredible amount of idealism, energy, passion, and intelligence in our communities that is overlooked and unharnessed. We need more of these talented community members to step up and lead.

But leadership is often defined as something out of reach for ordinary people. Too often, leadership stories focus on the heroic journeys of famous leaders. And too many people associate leadership with those in positions of power, ignoring the power that diverse individuals have to make a difference. This incomplete definition of leadership causes us to overlook the real leadership stories that are woven through our history. No one who saw Ben Franklin arrive in Philadelphia with nothing more than a loaf of bread to his name would have imagined who this poor printer's apprentice would become. E. D. Nixon and other residents of Montgomery, Alabama, also did not know what to expect of Dr. Martin Luther King Jr., the twenty-six-year-old preacher they chose to be the public leader of their bus boycott. Leadership emerging from humble beginnings is a common narrative throughout our nation's history, whether in social movements, politics, or business. But stories of social change that focus only on the role of heroic leaders are incomplete. Social change has always been the result of ordinary people doing extraordinary things—the courageous acts of many, not just the heroic acts of a few. In this book, I provide examples from the American Revolution and the civil rights movement of how the leadership of many unsung citizens contributed to some of our most important social changes. We need to identify and build more such leaders. When we fail to engage the talent indigenous to our communities, we can't create sustainable change.

Most leadership books today are about how leaders build effective organizations. This one is about how to build effective communities. The lessons here can also apply to organizational effectiveness and management, but our focus at Public Allies has been on how leaders can work in any community to bring diverse individuals and groups together to achieve common goals. There's a good reason for this focus: we see many well-run organizations that demonstrate measurable results in addressing educational, health, or economic needs, but we don't see change in the community's overall results. For example, we see a large after-school program claim that it has helped thousands of young people improve their academic performance, but citywide test scores and graduation rates don't rise. We believe that this is so because such isolated efforts fail to inclusively engage the assets of diverse community members and groups. They fail to enlist collaboration across the many systems that influence the desired outcomes. The evidence is clear: to solve persistent community challenges, it is not enough to build more effective organizations. We need to build more effective *communities*, and our five core values—recognizing and mobilizing community assets, connecting across cultures, facilitating collaborative action, continuously learning and improving, and being accountable to those one works with and those one serves—help leaders do just that. In this book, you will read inspiring stories about leaders from a wide array of backgrounds who are practicing these five core values to build stronger communities.

Everyone Leads describes how Public Allies sees leadership, and it grounds our theory not just in stories but also in practical examples that will help any leader or emerging leader step up and be effective. Our definition of leadership has three parts:

1. Leadership is an action many can take, not a position that only a few can hold.
2. Leadership is about taking personal and social responsibility to work with others for common goals.
3. Leadership is about the practice of values that engage diverse community members and groups in working together effectively.

Overview of the Chapters

Chapter One begins with background information about Public Allies and how we came to the conviction that everyone leads. The chapter describes our program, tells the story of Public Allies' founding and growth, and explains how we developed our definition of leadership. The chapter also makes the case for why our leadership values are so important in solving some of the most pressing problems in our communities, and it includes stories of some inspiring Public Allies graduates who represent the potential in our communities.

Chapter Two is my own story, the story of how I as a leader came to my passion for Public Allies and to our leadership approach. My journey demonstrates why I believe that we must look for leadership potential everywhere, and why I believe that the core values of Public Allies are so important. I hope my personal journey can serve as an inspiration because, as I often say to the Allies, "If someone like me can do this, you can, too."

Chapter Three is the theoretical heart of the book. It connects our definition of leadership to America's democratic history, to our country's movement history (especially the civil rights movement), and to emerging trends. The chapter also includes a survey of some of the most influential leadership books of the past four decades, showing that scholarship in the field has consistently made the case for leadership as a process in which many people can engage, as an assumption of responsibility for working with others around common goals, and as the practicing of values that engage people in working together effectively.

Chapter Four is about the responsibility of a leader. In fact, the first step in leadership is to take responsibility for acting with others to make a difference. Leadership is often a calling, and it often requires us to take risks, push beyond our own capacity, and make bold promises. But we must also be responsible for how we lead because another requirement of leadership is that we inspire, influence, and engage others.

Each of the remaining five chapters covers one of Public Allies' leadership values.

Chapter Five is about recognizing and mobilizing assets. It begins with the idea that, like the proverbial glass, each one of us is both half full and half empty, and so is each of our communities. Yet many leaders in communities are working from a belief that leaders are full, that communities are empty, and that leaders must fill communities' emptiness. This approach has many negative consequences for communities, and it does not lead to sustainable solutions. We all have strengths and shortcomings, and when we understand ourselves to be half-full, half-empty people working with other half-full, half-empty people, we create the opportunity for transformative relationships and work.

Chapter Six tackles diversity and inclusion. The chapter begins with a powerful insight that I gained from another Ally: that diversity embodies an *action*, not an ideal. Diversity is not just something you believe in. It is something you act to bring about, and your results matter. The chapter then moves on to an explanation of how our program works to build inclusive leadership among our very diverse Allies. The chapter describes how we introduce our Allies to each other, how we build a learning community where they can safely take risks and push each other, how we help Allies analyze issues (such as power, privilege, and oppression and ways of dismantling them), and how we use Allies' increasing awareness and confidence to help them become inclusive leaders. This work can be difficult, but inclusive leadership can also be inspiring and joyful and can lead to more effective results.

Chapter Seven describes our approach to facilitating teamwork and collaboration. Leadership is an inherently collaborative act. Self-awareness and emotional intelligence regarding others are the foundations of effective teamwork and collaboration. It is important for teams to use intentional processes that allow people to acknowledge and explore differences in work styles, leadership styles, and communication styles and build more authentic relationships. Collaboration is also the key to solving community problems. No one leader or organization can change a community. Change requires individuals and groups to be brought together across boundaries.

Continuous learning and improvement is the topic of Chapter Eight. Leaders, in order to grow their practice of leadership and inspire others to grow theirs, must take responsibility for their own learning and improvement. This chapter describes what Public

Allies has learned about creating effective learning environments, curricula, and communities. It describes some of our processes for helping leaders give and receive feedback, acquire coaching, reflect on their practice, and take responsibility for their growth.

Chapter Nine discusses integrity and accountability. As leaders, we must be accountable to ourselves and others. We must be true to our own stories, purposes, values, and moral and ethical standards. Accountability to others begins with our responsibility for our promises and relationships, and it includes accountability to the people we serve—their interests must come first. We are also accountable to those who have inspired, influenced, taught, and mentored us.

In addition, as the Afterword describes, integrity is about putting all the pieces together—about how our five core values work together in one system for leading effectively. I hope that by the time you are reading the Afterword you share our conviction and are more aware of your own purpose, values, and potential.

The practices described in this book will help you better engage diverse people and groups to work effectively together because that is really the essence of what leaders do. We face an abundance of challenges—poverty, inadequate or failing schools and social services, limited access to healthy environments and lifestyles, and limited access to health care, to name just a few—that continue to cause suffering for too many of our fellow citizens. No one leader or group can solve these problems. We need many more leaders in all parts of our communities to step up and address injustice, working together across social and ideological differences and across professions and sectors. We really are the ones we have been waiting for. Everyone leads!

Everyone Leads

Part One

ABOUT PUBLIC ALLIES AND THE CONCEPT THAT EVERYONE LEADS

1

COMING TO THE CONVICTION THAT EVERYONE LEADS

Peter Hoeffel

Peter Hoeffel was working at a downtown Milwaukee deli, putting his philosophy degree from the University of Wisconsin-Milwaukee to work making sandwiches. One day, an energetic and friendly young African American woman walked into the shop and asked if she could hang a poster in the window to recruit young adults for Milwaukee's Public Allies program. Peter struck up a conversation and learned that she was looking for young people who were passionate about making a difference and who wanted to turn that passion into a career.

Peter, who was twenty-seven years old at the time, heard his calling. "I wanted to make the world a better place," he says. "I didn't feel like too many places were looking to hire someone with a philosophy degree and a minor in Africology. I wanted to stop just talking about the social change that my friends and I would discuss, and Public Allies seemed like a great place for me to learn how to do just that."[1]

He applied to Public Allies, was accepted, and participated in weekly leadership training at Public Allies while serving full-time at Legal Action Wisconsin. He discovered that he had a passion for people with disabilities, and over the next decade he grew his impact, helping lead a coalition of disability rights groups and eventually leading the Milwaukee chapter of the National Alliance on Mental Illness. There he turned around a financially struggling agency and, through collaborations, expanded its services to the underserved African American and Latino communities that had previously been neglected.

Bizunesh Talbot-Scott

When Bizunesh Talbot-Scott applied to Public Allies, she was an eighteen-year-old single mom with a two-year-old son and was studying at Milwaukee Area Technical College. As an Ally, she worked for the Youth Leadership Academy, providing academic support and life skills to young African American boys.

Biz was young and immature, but she was also vivacious, ambitious, and smart. She gained focus through the program: "I was a smart girl who had no idea of my potential before Public Allies."[2]

After her term was finished, she enrolled at Marquette University, where she excelled, and then at the University of Michigan Law School, where she was elected to the law review. After graduating, Biz moved to Washington, D.C., where she clerked for a federal judge and worked at the prestigious Skadden Arps and Patton Boggs law firms.

One day, a representative from Skadden Arps called Public Allies to make a donation on behalf of one of its associates. That associate was Biz, who was being honored because of her volunteer work in her community, especially at the Legal Aid Society in D.C. Later, during the transition to the Obama administration, Biz was appointed by the National Bar Association to chair the initiative to increase the number of African American attorneys serving in government, and she led a similar project for the National Congress of Black Women. She is now one of the staff leading presidential personnel at the White House.

Frank Alvarez

Frank Alvarez is busy. He directs a YouthBuild Program in Los Angeles that creates opportunities for youth who have left school without a diploma, have been incarcerated, or are otherwise disconnected from education and work. YouthBuild participants learn job and leadership skills while building affordable housing in their communities. Frank has also maintained a 3.7 grade-point average at Los Angeles Trade and Technical College, majoring in community planning and economic development while raising his daughter.

Frank describes his own path to this place: "In my family, education was never emphasized. My male relatives graduated from juvenile hall to county jail and then on to state prison. I was following the same path."[3]

Frank had been involved in a gang and had served time in county jail. But he took a positive turn after getting out. He participated in YouthBuild, where he earned his GED, and then moved on to Public Allies, where he served at LA Works, a community-development organization, while further developing his leadership and a career path.

"I was able to attend classes at LA Trade Tech through Public Allies, which sparked my interest in education," he says. "Here I was, a twenty-three-year old without a high school diploma, and I had fellow Allies with degrees from UCLA, USC, and other schools. I learned from them and gained confidence that I could do this, too. I am proud to be creating opportunities for young people like me to get on the path to leadership and success in our community. I'm able to make amends for damages I caused as a gang member."

Most people don't look at the guy behind the sandwich counter, the single mom attending community college, or the former gang member and see future leaders. We do. Public Allies has developed more than 3,800 leaders like Peter, Bizunesh, and Frank over the past nineteen years. To us, it is tragic that communities and the organizations that serve them miss so much needed talent. Yet this is where most of the talent we need to solve problems resides.

When we look at many great American leaders, entrepreneurs, and organizers of social movements, we often find young people, women, and people from humble or unpromising origins. But many today who are concerned about social problems don't look in communities for leaders. Instead they look outside for heroic leaders who offer impressive, silver-bullet solutions. The press often features fawning articles about celebrities, young Ivy League graduates, or prominent business leaders who have exciting new ideas or projects that will solve our problems. For example, pundits like David Gergen and David Brooks have written glowingly about the number of young Ivy League graduates with "résumé bling" who want to start organizations to address such social challenges as education, health, poverty, and the environment.[4] Such people are admirable and needed, but the media's emphasis on elite and celebrity leaders ignores the vast number of social entrepreneurs who for years have been building innovative nonprofit organizations and community solutions all across the country. A few leaders are celebrated because of their résumés, their media savvy, or their access to wealthy and politically powerful networks, and the many who have been innovating in communities for years are ignored. This kind of attention to celebrities and other elite leaders can actually discourage grassroots leaders, who don't have "résumé bling," from stepping up.

The irony of focusing on young people from elite backgrounds is that when we study the history of social movements, or even the history of *Fortune* 500 companies, we rarely see founders and leaders who came from elite backgrounds. In fact, Northwestern Mutual Life researched five thousand entrepreneurs and created a questionnaire to determine a respondent's EQ, or entrepreneurship quotient. A respondent's EQ was significantly discounted if he or she had been an academic achiever, participated in group activities at school, or followed the opinions of authority figures. The questionnaire found that those who excelled more as entrepreneurs and leaders had developed street smarts, persuasiveness, humor, and creativity.[5]

Public Allies believes that everyone can lead. In saying this, we mean that everyone can step up and take responsibility for influencing and working with others for common goals that benefit our communities or the larger society. Leadership is not exclusively the domain of CEOs, elected officials, charismatic organizers, or celebrities. It is the domain of *citizens*. Our democracy is predicated on all of us stepping up to lead where we see public problems or needs.

By the term *citizen* I mean a member of a community, not a legal status. My use of the term *citizen* throughout the book is inclusive. It refers to any person who is committed to participating in making our communities better, regardless of that person's legal status—and there are many people who are not citizens in the legal sense but who do fit this picture of civic participation. One of my favorite definitions of the term *citizen* comes from Peter Block, who writes that a citizen is "one who is willing to be accountable to the well-being of the whole."[6]

At Public Allies, we see the development of leaders as intertwined with the development of communities. If we want to strengthen our communities and solve problems, we need more leaders to come from our communities and be partners with our communities. In our increasingly diverse society, leaders must also look more like America and be connected to the communities they serve. To create lasting solutions to our most pressing problems, leaders can't just create isolated services. They must build community capacity, think systemically, and collaborate with others. We define the term *community capacity* as a combination of three elements:

1. The leadership and engagement of residents
2. The services and support that neighbors provide to neighbors
3. Coordination and collaboration toward common goals among the citizens, associations, nonprofits, schools, houses of worship, and businesses in a neighborhood

Leaders who can build community capacity often enact the five core practices that form the heart of this book. They recognize and mobilize all of a community's assets, they connect across cultures, they facilitate collaborative action, they continuously learn and improve, and they are accountable to those they work with and those they serve. These are the values that animate Public Allies' definition of leadership and influence how we carry out our mission. They are values that everyone can put into practice.

Our Mission: Changing the Face and Practice of Leadership

The mission of Public Allies is to advance new leadership to strengthen communities, nonprofits, and civic participation. We aim to change both the face and the practice of leadership by bringing new people to the proverbial tables of influence, and by changing the tables themselves. When we change who is sitting at the table, we also change the conversation, the process, and the results. This is how inclusion and collaboration work—it is about all of us working together as co-creators, not inviting others to help us do our work. We believe that, as a key element of solving community problems, leaders in today's communities need the ability to build community capacity. That is why we work on two fronts: we develop a new generation of diverse leaders (that is, we change the face of leadership), and we help them develop the practices they need to build community capacity and solve public problems effectively and sustainably (that is, we change the practice of leadership).

Changing the Face of Leadership

There is tremendous untapped potential for change in our communities. But most policy makers, nonprofit leaders, and community leaders fail to harness the energy, talents, and ideas of our diverse communities, especially among the people who live closest to the challenges.

Although many nonprofit organizations exist to engage citizens in solving problems, such organizations often aren't great at engaging new leadership in communities or within the organizations themselves. Research shows that nonprofit organizations do a poor job of recruiting and retaining diverse talent and often have very limited resources to invest in their people. Moreover, research at New York University and elsewhere has found a corresponding challenge in that very few young people know about careers in nonprofit and public service.[7] It is stunning that organizations that exist to bring Americans together to solve public problems struggle with diversity at the leadership level. Several studies have found that between 80 percent and 90 percent of nonprofit organizations are led by Caucasians, and one study reported that younger CEOs are no more diverse than their older colleagues.[8] And there is a glass ceiling in the nonprofit sector—women, who dominate the sector's workforce, are rare among CEOs of the largest nonprofit organizations and are paid less at all levels than their male colleagues.[9] The groups that should be ameliorating these widespread disparities and engaging citizens of all backgrounds are instead exacerbating them! If nonprofits did a better job of building leadership in our increasingly diverse society, they could address the diversity gap in their own ranks.

In the so-called Millennials, we have a new generation whose members have a strong interest in community service (research shows that they have volunteered more than previous generations), embrace diversity (this is the most diverse generation to date), and prefer to work in teams.[10] Those who seek to engage this generation by looking only at people with the best educational credentials miss a huge number of potential leaders. For example, the fact that only about 30 percent of adults are college graduates means that the practice of looking for new leaders on college campuses excludes a great number of young people.[11] (And, naturally, the practice of looking for young leaders only on the campuses of elite schools excludes an even greater number of potential leaders and leaves us with a pool made up of less than 5 percent of young people, limiting the kinds of talent, creativity, experience, and skills that leaders have.) In our urban communities, only about half of the young people complete high school. Other challenges, such as teen pregnancy, criminal records, foster care, and substance abuse, create daunting barriers to potential leaders. A recent report estimated that approximately 10 percent of youth, or about four million young adults, are disconnected from education and work.[12] Many community groups fail to see the potential leadership in these populations, yet many of these young people know their communities well and can be huge assets to them. Groups like YouthBuild, the Corps Network, Year Up, and our own Public Allies demonstrate the overlooked leadership potential in these populations.

Changing the Practice of Leadership

To solve community problems in a sustainable way requires community capacity. Communities can raise a child, provide security, sustain our health, secure our income, and care for vulnerable people.[13] Nonprofit and public institutions play an important role in all these activities, but they can't create sustainable solutions that really move the needle on these issues without community building and systemic collaboration as core elements of their solutions. Most services focus on linear causality—the idea that one can isolate and treat one need of a person, and that one intervention will "fix" him or her. The reality is much more complex, however, and sustained change requires a variety of interventions and opportunities reinforced by a supportive community. Effective services and outcomes are important, but effective community engagement is also important to sustained success.

For example, public health research finds that the five greatest variables in producing health are personal behavior, social relations, the environment, economic well-being, and access to health care services. In that regard, the Centers for Disease Control and Prevention have come to emphasize community-building strategies as a far richer and more promising way of knowing and acting for long-term health than mobilizing service delivery alone. Better health care services or outcomes won't produce health; healthier communities produce health.[14] Our alumnus Peter Hoeffel echoed this idea in an op-ed about the failures of a local county-funded mental health institution, saying that one in every four individuals will experience a mental illness at least once in his or her lifetime, and that supporting people with mental illness is everyone's responsibility.[15] I've heard a similar case made for recent drops in crime being attributable both to more statistically driven policing efforts and to community policing efforts. This is what Robert Putnam popularized as "social capital" more than a decade ago.[16] Putnam's research showed that the more relationships and group memberships people have in their communities, the more likely they are to have beneficial health, safety, educational, and economic outcomes. Nevertheless, nonprofit and public agencies and programs continue to see community building and the development of social capital as a luxury rather than as a solution.

Over the past decade in Cincinnati, Ohio, there has been a dramatic increase in the high school graduation rate, from 50 percent to 80 percent. One promising phenomenon that groups inside and outside the city point to for this success is the Strive Partnership. As Jeff Edmondson, president of Strive, explains, "The Cincinnati schools were making progress, and we brought together a wide range of leaders to help coordinate existing assets and sustain and improve those results. Rather than launching new programs, we focused on coordination and collaboration. We set the table with a mix of leaders that led to many conflicts, but we set a common goal so our conflicts were constructive toward achieving better results for all the children in our schools. The success here has been because of community building and collaboration, and I don't think you can achieve sustained results without that."[17]

Efforts to build community capacity as a way of solving problems rest on the following elements, which coincide in many respects with Public Allies' five core principles:

- Recognizing individual and community assets
- Building relationships and social capital among community residents and leaders
- Connecting residents with local groups where they can be actively engaged as participants and leaders
- Collaborating across boundaries to unite local businesses, organizations, agencies, schools, and houses of worship in coordinating and collaborating toward common goals
- Engaging those on the margins of the community who are labeled for their conditions and choices (people who are homeless or have mental illness as well as those who are ex-felons, high school dropouts, recipients of public assistance, and so on)
- Making sure that the efforts are accountable to the people who have to live with the results—the needs and interests of the community, as community members understand them, supersede what funders and others outside the community define as the community's needs and interests

Leaders must see that community residents are the most important element of any proposed solution. Building more effective programs, services, and institutions is necessary to but not sufficient for solving problems; community engagement is a critical part of any sustainable solution. Leaders must build community at least to the same extent that they build services, programs, and organizations.

To summarize, new leadership pipelines and new leadership approaches are needed to solve our most pressing problems. Public Allies builds leaders from all backgrounds who practice the values that will make them the effective community builders we so badly need. It is our goal to change both the face and the practice of leadership, thus unleashing the energy of thousands of leaders who have the skills not just to build programs or organizations but also to build community capacity and sustainable solutions. These new leaders can increase the civic participation of people from all backgrounds, building bridges between diverse sets of people and organizations so that work can go forward on achieving common goals and on creating more effective and more responsive nonprofits. That is our mission, and we believe that this approach to leadership will make existing efforts to address community problems far more likely to succeed and to be sustainable.

Our Definition of Leadership

The Public Allies' definition of leadership has evolved from our beliefs and experience. It is also grounded in history, relevant to current trends, and informed by the latest theory (see Chapter Three). Our definition has three components:

1. *Leadership is an action many can take, not a position few can hold.* U.S. history, from the Revolutionary War through social movements, has demonstrated that change always comes from the courageous and extraordinary acts of many ordinary people, not just the inspiration or direction of a few.

2. *Leadership is about taking responsibility—personal and social—to work with others for common goals.* Leaders step up, assume personal responsibility, and accept social responsibility to work on common goals that make positive changes for themselves and others.

3. *Leadership is about the practice of values that engage community members and groups to work effectively together toward common goals.* The five values that we at Public Allies believe are needed to lead our communities toward lasting and effective change in the twenty-first century are recognizing and mobilizing community assets, connecting across cultures, facilitating collaborative action, continuously learning and improving, and being accountable to those we work with and those we serve.

The Story of Public Allies

Our mission and our definition of leadership have evolved from practice, through the development of our leadership program and the many lessons we've learned partnering with organizations to develop leaders in twenty-one cities over nineteen years. There were no guarantees that Public Allies would succeed when it was started by a resourceful community of diverse, idealistic young people. There were challenges and disappointments—and moments when failure seemed more imminent than success. But a set of values and strong beliefs formed and held by the group took the vision of two young women and turned it into a diverse community of thousands, a community that has continued for almost two decades, with the president of the United States and the first lady among those who helped shape it. Here is the story of how Public Allies came to be, and of how we implement our vision, our mission, and our definition of leadership.

In the Beginning

While Vanessa Kirsch was growing up, she struggled with school because of dyslexia. From an early age, she was often pulled out of classes for tutoring. When she applied to Tufts University, she made the case that she should be given a chance at admission despite her low SAT scores. Tufts agreed, and Vanessa's hard work and tenacity indeed made her a great success. In 1991, at the age of twenty-six, she was working for the pollster Peter Hart and had demonstrated her entrepreneurial skills by founding the Women's Information Network, a group supporting young women leaders in Washington, D.C. Vanessa had also recently completed a survey of young people, titled *Democracy's Next Generation,* for the organization People for the American Way. One of her primary findings was that young people wanted to get involved in working for change but did not know how. With Peter Hart's full support, Vanessa decided to leave her job and start an organization to mobilize young people.*

* Peter Hart was a founding board member of Public Allies.

Another young woman who had discovered that organizations were struggling to identify, support, and develop young leaders was Katrina Browne. Katrina, a twenty-three-year-old Princeton graduate from the Philadelphia area, had been working at the Advocacy Institute through Princeton Project 55, a program sponsored by Princeton's graduating class of 1955 that sponsored other Princeton graduates who wanted to pursue public service for a summer or a year. Katrina worked on a study of how nonprofit and public interest organizations were recruiting and developing their next generation of leaders. She discovered that these organizations were having an especially difficult time finding young leaders of color and young leaders from disadvantaged communities in general (the communities that these organizations served).* Katrina's understanding of and passion for history gave the organization not only grounding in past social movements but also inspiration that changing this dynamic in communities would take a new kind of movement led by young people themselves.

Vanessa Kirsch and Katrina Browne met at one of Vanessa's Women's Information Network gatherings. They compared notes and came up with the idea of creating a vehicle to connect young leaders, especially those who were underrepresented in the leadership ranks, with local nonprofit organizations that could make good use of their energy, idealism, and skills in these organizations' mission to make a greater difference. As Katrina explains, "I realized that, because of my background and the school I attended, I had access to my internship, mentors, and other support, and I thought that everybody who wanted to make a difference, especially those coming from the communities served, should have that opportunity."[18] Vanessa and Katrina exemplified a kind of servant leadership that has been core to Public Allies ever since. They understood their privilege and used it cleverly for the benefit of a larger, more inclusive community.

* For more about Katrina Browne's story, see Chapter Six.

In the early 1990s, when the first Public Allies program was launched, young people—known as Generation X—were primarily viewed in a negative way and were often seen as slackers and gangsters. The crack epidemic and gang violence were at their height. Ecstasy-fueled raves were the rage, AIDS was still on the rise (NBA star Magic Johnson had just announced his diagnosis), and "safe sex" was a new mantra. Music was defined by the grunge of Pearl Jam and Nirvana, the pop-country of Garth Brooks and Billy Ray Cyrus, and hip-hop that ranged from the violent rap of NWA, the dance pop of MC Hammer, the positive rap of Arrested Development, and the political rap of Public Enemy. *Slacker*, *Malcolm X*, *Reservoir Dogs*, *Boyz in the Hood*, and *Thelma and Louise* were the films capturing young people's attention. Vice President Dan Quayle and conservative pundits were scandalized by the title character of the TV series *Murphy Brown* because of her choice to have a child out of wedlock. *The Cosby Show* came to a close. MTV still mostly showed music videos. *Seinfeld*, the "show about nothing," was on the rise, and *In Living Color* launched the careers of the Wayans brothers, Jim Carrey, and Jamie Foxx.

On the political scene, a presidential election pitted the later-named Greatest Generation (represented by President George H. W. Bush) against the baby-boom generation (represented by Bill Clinton, then governor of Arkansas), and Rock the Vote was launched to mobilize Generation X. Gays and lesbians were still mostly absent from popular and political culture but were a rising force because of the fight for AIDS-related legislation (such as the Ryan White Care Act) and the battle over whether gays and lesbians could serve openly in the military (a battle that resulted in the "don't ask, don't tell" policy). Other milestones at or around this time were the first Persian Gulf War, an economic recession, and the riots that took place in Los Angeles and led to Rodney King's famous question "Can we all get along?" In this milieu, there was a need to bring Generation X to a new place. According to Vanessa, "There were so many negative stereotypes of our generation as apathetic, uncaring, cynical, selfish, and even violent. We wanted nothing less than to redefine a generation in all its diversity as a positive force for change—as allies for our communities."[19]

Through Princeton Project 55, Katrina Browne met Charlie Bray, president of the Johnson Foundation in Racine, Wisconsin. Katrina and Vanessa, during a fundraising tour, had stopped there in hopes of approaching him for funding, but they discovered that the foundation, instead of giving traditional grants, sponsored small conferences at its large, beautiful Frank Lloyd Wright–designed prairie home, called Wingspread. The Wingspread Conferences, as they were known, were designed to help leaders develop big ideas. (National Public Radio and the National Endowment for the Arts are two examples of organizations whose leaders have participated in the conferences.) Vanessa and Katrina asked Charlie if they could organize a conference to explore their ideas about new leadership, and he agreed. Among the intergenerational group of forty leaders who came to that Wingspread Conference were John "Jody" Kretzmann of the Asset-Based Community Development Institute; Barack Obama, who was then an organizer with Project Vote in Chicago; Jackie Kendall, executive director of the Midwest Academy; and David Cohen, co-director of the Advocacy Institute. One of Vanessa's and Katrina's great strengths as organizers was engaging accomplished mentors while also seeking out younger, diverse talent and entrusting them with positions of leadership. The Wingspread meeting was a chance for these young leaders to engage with well-known academics, organizers, and civic leaders as peers and to brainstorm and debate with them about how to bring Public Allies into reality. Their brainstorming created the initial concept for what today is Public Allies. They also built into the DNA of our leadership model a blend of community organizing, community building, civic engagement, and inclusion, a blend that has remained at our core.*

* At first our organization was named the National Center for Careers in Public Life, but a conversation about stereotypes of young people as "public enemies," which took place in a van among people leaving the conference, led to the new name—Public Allies.

The formation of Public Allies was influenced by two other service groups, Teach for America and VISTA. Wendy Kopp had recently founded Teach for America, recruiting graduates of top colleges to teach in schools in low-income communities. Public Allies liked the Teach for America model but believed that a more diverse, indigenous approach to recruitment was needed to support community organizations. At Wingspread, many of the older leaders attending the conference had been shocked that the younger leaders did not know about VISTA, the Great Society program to create a domestic Peace Corps. VISTA had been gutted by both the Reagan and Bush administrations, and the VISTA stipend was so low that it mostly enrolled poor people (who could maintain public benefits while receiving a VISTA stipend) and those with means. VISTA also provided minimal training and support and was not focused on long-term leadership and service. Public Allies wondered whether it should help promote VISTA and provide added training for its participants. But the older leaders, some of whom were VISTA alumni, thought Public Allies should exist on its own to bring more creativity, nimbleness, focus, and generational energy to the problem of how to identify and engage a new generation of leaders to support organizations in disadvantaged communities. Most important, the experienced leaders pushed the Public Allies founders to make sure they were not replicating the existing models but creating something new that would be impactful, transformative, and true to their belief in inclusive, collaborative leadership.

Vanessa, Katrina, and their growing roster of volunteers, many of whom had met Vanessa while working on the 1988 presidential campaign of Michael Dukakis, began doing outreach by walking through urban neighborhoods to identify and talk to young people. This group of young volunteers, which increased by the week, met every Tuesday night for months to debate both the philosophy and the practicalities (such as budgets and the mission) of building an organization from scratch to engage their peers in transforming communities. They worked out of the office of a mentor, Karen Mulhauser, who became Public Allies' first board chair. This grassroots approach led to many meetings on basketball courts, in housing projects, at youth centers, and on campuses. The volunteers found that many young people were indeed passionate about social issues in their community but felt powerless in addressing them. This experience led Vanessa and Katrina to an even firmer conviction that if a pipeline to public service could be built, there would be many talented and diverse young people ready to work for change.

Vanessa's natural fundraising abilities, along with her unique ability to convey this inspiring vision, led to major grants from the Echoing Green Foundation,* the MacArthur Foundation, Atlantic Philanthropies (which was anonymous at the time), the W.K. Kellogg Foundation, the Surdna Foundation, and others. Her connections from the political world also got her idea into the hands of both the Bush administration and the Clinton for President campaign. These resources helped Vanessa and Katrina hire a dynamic and diverse group of half a dozen young people, who then quickly set out to build a program from their vision. They were a ragtag bunch in many ways, and they reflected courage on the part of the founders to expand their circle to include other strong leaders with different skills, experience, and views. Vanessa took on the role of CEO and, with it, responsibility for shaping this unruly and passionate bunch into an effective team.

The first Public Allies program was launched in September 1992 in Washington, D.C., with a bold vision for transforming communities through the idealism and energy of diverse young leaders. The diverse young staff who built the program believed that if young leaders had the skills to recognize assets, bridge

* The Echoing Green Foundation helps social entrepreneurs with transformative ideas start new nonprofits for social change in America and around the world. Thousands apply each year for grants and support that ultimately go to twenty-four groups.

differences, and facilitate community members and groups, they could be a catalyst for reviving communities from the bottom up. Public Allies believed that a full-time work experience in the community—integrated with intensive training, the building of community with a diverse cohort, team service projects for young leaders to set and accomplish goals together, and coaching—could develop leaders who would succeed at this work. Fundamental to everything was the vision that most of the Allies would come from the same communities and neighborhoods they served, and that they would be people who had a passion for changing their communities over the long term, not just doing a year or two of giving back.

Vanessa attracted an extraordinary group of young leaders to help her and Katrina build the program during the first few years: Marketa Bartel, Richard Blount, Craig Bowman, Paul Caccamo, Michael Canul, Liz Cutler, Julius Davis, Magda Escobar, Ian Fisk, Erin Flannery, David Gaffin, Mark Gillman, Chris Hero, Jay Kim, Kaushik Mukurjee, Monica Palacio, Julian Posada, Allessandra Puvak, Jason Scott, Trabian Shorters, Alma Soonghi-Beck, and Tim Webb. They were African American, Asian American, Latino, Latina, gay, lesbian, straight, and from all parts of the country. Each person brought unique skills and contributed to the new definition of leadership that Public Allies was constructing. Their diverse backgrounds led to struggles over philosophy, roles, hierarchies, and outcomes, and these struggles laid the groundwork for our model. Most of the original participants have gone on to successful public service careers. Their exhaustive conversations and debates, steep learning curves, rookie mistakes, and transformational discoveries, often fueled by caffeine and late-night pizzas, turned an inspiring idea into a real program and a rapidly growing organization. It was a battle to balance their idealism and principles with the practical demands of raising money and executing a program that was trying to redefine the nature of community leadership. Doing all this with a team of young people who had limited experience, an aversion to hierarchy, and a passion for change created challenges. Survival was never certain, much less success. But Vanessa and Katrina balanced their extraordinary skills and passion with those of others to take risks, find great mentors, and shape a common vision and an innovative program model.

The Public Allies Program

The core of the original program model that was built then remains today. We select the program's participants, or Allies, from diverse backgrounds in our communities. They are young people who have a passion for making a difference.

Allies are placed in paid, full-time apprenticeships with nonprofit organizations, where they create, improve, or expand services to meet local needs. They run after-school programs, help ex-felons reenter society and obtain jobs, help people become more culturally competent and collaborative, educate young mothers about child nutrition and health, form neighborhood watches, assist foster children with their transition to independence, clean up rivers, establish community gardens, and much more.

Placements for Allies are selected according to the outcomes of our partner organizations' projects and the commitment the partner organizations have to the apprenticeship experience. Allies are not sent randomly to their placements. We use a two-way matching process in which Ally and partner "finalists" interview and rank each other. We then select the best matches so that there is full buy-in for all the apprenticeships.

One day a week, Allies leave their apprenticeships for intensive leadership-development workshops and for team projects where they learn and practice leadership skills and values. Our comprehensive leadership-development curriculum is based on current adult education theory that blends highly interactive training and workshops, individual coaching, critical reflection, critical feedback, team-building activities, and team projects. Our curriculum helps Allies clarify who they are as leaders—their purposes, values, and practices—along with the skills they need for their jobs and careers.

Through our training and work with the Allies, individually and in teams, we create an environment that challenges them to take greater responsibility for their learning and growth and that supports them in dealing with the inevitable conflicts, mistakes, and obstacles that come with this level of responsibility. Our curriculum is both challenging and nurturing. On the one hand, we push Allies to confront personal difficulties, growth needs, and conflicts within the group. On the other hand, we coach Allies to clarify their purposes and values while building practices for working with others more effectively. In our program, if you talk a lot, you'll learn to listen. If you are too quiet, you'll build your confidence as a speaker. If you are always late, you'll learn to be on time. If you always think you know best, you'll learn to invite and consider others' opinions.

We use a variety of assessment tools and processes to help Allies identify where they want to grow as leaders and how they are progressing:

- *Individual Development Plans*, which establish educational, career, and community goals and the steps needed to achieve them
- *Personal Impact and Service Documentation*, which tracks Allies' progress on service goals and outcomes
- *360-Degree Reviews*, which assess how well Allies are practicing the five core Public Allies values
- *Feedback Circles*, where Allies review their practice of the core values with their teams and supervisors
- *Presentations of Learning*, where Allies defend how they have met our learning outcomes (this process is described in Chapter Eight)

A typical training day, held on Friday, begins in the morning, with Allies checking in about their lives, their work, and community issues. Then local leaders and Public Allies staff facilitate interactive workshops on topics related to our core values or to skills (such as public speaking, facilitation, conflict resolution, and fundraising) that will help the Allies be effective in their placements. In the afternoon, Allies meet in teams of eight to ten for work on team projects that they plan and execute over the course of the year. Finally, they evaluate their training day and close out together.

Many Allies report that one of the things that really drew them to the program was the prospect of being surrounded by peers who shared their passion for service and community change, and they often find that their most powerful learning comes from each other. A married young mother of two, a recent high school graduate, an Ivy League graduate, and a thirty-year-old gay activist, all working on different issues in different neighborhoods, will find themselves working together and sharing their different perspectives, experiences, and lessons with each other. Together, these experiences are creating a new generation of leaders who know both how to build community and how to work for effective solutions.

The Big Breaks: From Pilot Program to National Model

Early in the development of Public Allies, the organization's vision of diverse young people as a positive force gained a lot of attention from the media and even from the White House. Several events that occurred almost simultaneously established Public Allies with three presidential administrations, one concurrent with the founding of our first program and two still in the future.

President George H. W. Bush had already created the Commission on National and Community Service, which famously launched the Points of Light Foundation. Through Vanessa's passion and leadership and the promise represented by the first class of D.C. Allies, the commission identified the fledgling Public Allies as one of fourteen demonstration projects for a national service program and funded our second site, which opened in Chicago in 1993.

The Chicago site had been organized in much the same way as the Public Allies site in Washington, D.C. There was a committee of diverse young people meeting on Tuesday nights and engaging mentors. It was decided that with the federal funding, we needed a more professional leader. One of our board members, Barack Obama, recommended his wife, Michelle, who then worked for Mayor Richard Daley and had previously been an attorney at the prestigious Sidley Austin firm. Vanessa Kirsch and Jason Scott, the director of site development for Public Allies, met with Mrs. Obama and initially faced some resistance. "It sounded risky and just out there," Mrs. Obama recounts, "but for some reason it just spoke to me. This was the first time I said 'This is what I say I care about. Right here. And I will have to run it.'"[20] She called a week later to accept the job, and to this day she claims it is the best job she has ever had.[21] Hiring Michelle Obama was a coup, not because of who she later became but because of who she was then—at twenty-eight, the oldest, most experienced, most accomplished, most coolheaded, and most professional member of our youthful staff. In an entrepreneurial start-up with an average staff age of twenty-four, she was our model professional and a leader inside the organization, and she helped strengthen the organization in many ways.*

The spring of 1993 was also significant to us for another reason. In early 1992, Public Allies had invited two people to be keynote speakers at the launch event that would be held later that year for Public Allies D.C. The first was Senator Harris Wofford, a Democrat from Pennsylvania, who had been

---

* In a speech delivered on October 16, 2009, at the twentieth anniversary of the Points of Light Foundation, celebrated at the Presidential Forum on Community Service, George H. W. Bush Presidential Library, Texas A&M University, College Station, President Barack Obama thanked former President Bush for creating a national service program that launched his wife's career in public service: "It's a vision that's changed lives across this country, including that of a young woman who went to work for an organization called Public Allies to prepare young people for public service careers—an organization initially funded by the Bush administration. And her experience there inspired her to devote her own life to serving others, and that young woman happens to be my wife, Michelle Obama."

promoting national service for thirty years and was crafting the legislation that eventually created AmeriCorps. The second was Marian Wright Edelman, a famous civil rights activist and founder of the Children's Defense Fund. As luck would have it, on the day of the event Senator Wofford's staff called and asked if he could bring the first lady of Arkansas, who was also a friend of Mrs. Edelman. Hillary Clinton was so inspired by the diverse group of young leaders that she offered to host an event for Public Allies in the Rose Garden of the White House if her husband were to be elected president that November. Thanks to the organization's nascent success and Vanessa's diligent follow-up, First Lady Hilary Clinton fulfilled her promise the following April. Also in 1993, as President Bill Clinton was working on the creation of AmeriCorps, he often spoke of Public Allies as a model for national service, once referring to us as a "gang for good."* The national service bill signed by President Clinton in 1993 created the Corporation for National and Community Service, an independent government agency that supports service across the country through Senior Corps (older Americans), Learn and Serve America (K–12 schools), VISTA, the National Civilian Conservation Corps (which helps with disaster relief and public lands), and AmeriCorps.

Public Allies, like national service itself, has appealed across political party lines because we are nonpartisan in our approach to solving community problems. We have strong beliefs about social justice and inclusion that are attractive to those on the Left. And our concerns about the effectiveness of large institutions and services have attracted conservatives who share our belief that local communities, including grassroots, faith-based, and private

---

* A decade later, Senator Hillary Rodham Clinton of New York had this to say at a Save AmeriCorps event held in Washington, D.C., on September 3, 2003: "I was very honored to speak at the first-ever Public Allies event back in 1992, and the next one we held in the Rose Garden. It was a really great commitment for me to be able to fulfill, to bring these wonderful young people to the White House."

organizations, often are better at solving problems and achieving results. Our values, especially diversity and inclusion, lead us to see engaging diverse perspectives as important to leadership. As this book illustrates, our approach challenges established leaders, regardless of ideology, to think differently about how to engage communities and new leadership in solving problems.

Public Allies and AmeriCorps

We competed successfully to be one of the first AmeriCorps grantees in 1994, and all that attention and support helped Public Allies grow in our first three years from serving one city to serving six.The AmeriCorps program provides grants directly to national organizations and to bipartisan commissions in all fifty states so they can support local programs that employ service participants (AmeriCorps members) to meet community needs.

In 2011, there are approximately 87,000 AmeriCorps members serving across the country, addressing such issues as education, health, poverty, veterans, disaster relief, and the environment through local nonprofit organizations. Public Allies receives AmeriCorps funds nationally, and also from states, to support our Allies. Along with matching dollars that we raise in our communities, these funds enable us to pay Allies a full-time stipend, provide health care and child care for those who need it, and offer Allies a $5,500 education award that they can use to pay their existing student loans or their future education costs.

Public Allies has grown along with AmeriCorps, supporting more than 3,800 Allies in twenty-one communities through four presidential administrations. According to David Eisner, who led national service efforts under President George W. Bush and now serves on our board, "Public Allies has always played a unique and important role in national service by bringing a new, more diverse population to service. Public Allies then brings that service to local community-based organizations who need the help most. It is a bottom-up community effort that works."[22]

A Distinct Leadership-Development Model

The program model we've built is distinct from other AmeriCorps programs and other leadership programs in several key ways:

- *We build homegrown leadership.* More than 80 percent of Allies come from the communities and often the very neighborhoods they serve. Most national AmeriCorps programs recruit nationally and export talent to communities. We do accept Allies from outside our communities, but they generally come from communities without a Public Allies program, and they bring assets from their backgrounds, beliefs, or experiences that will be unique additions to our group.

- *We are both diverse and selective.* Public Allies receives, on average, six applicants per slot, and this surplus of applicants allows us to find the best potential leaders, whether they have GEDs or Ivy League degrees. On average, Allies have been 67 percent people of color, 60 percent women, 50 percent college graduates, and 15 percent self-identified as lesbian, gay, bisexual, or transgender. We work to be inclusive of leadership potential from all parts of our communities.

- *We seek young people who are committed to a lifetime of working for community and social change.* We seek young adults with fire in their bellies and a passion to make a difference over the long term rather than those who want to take a year off to do something altruistic or charitable. Of our 3,800 graduates, 87 percent are currently pursuing careers in nonprofit and public service.

- *We place Allies in a wide variety of nonprofits to help them create, improve, and expand services.* We believe it is important that communities and groups on the front lines define how we can help them build capacity, innovate, and serve. Over 90 percent of our partner organizations (the groups that host our Allies) report every year that Allies met or exceeded their expectations, and 74 percent report that Allies built capacity by helping them collaborate with other organizations, practice diversity and inclusion, improve their supervision of young talent, recruit and support volunteers, engage community members, and evaluate impact. In addition, Allies benefit by learning from each other because they are working on different issues—education, health, poverty, and the environment—in different neighborhoods. Every Ally who completes the program comes to know a city's various neighborhoods, issues, organizations, and resources as well as a diverse network of peers working in other organizations.

- *Our rigorous and comprehensive leadership curriculum is values-based.* Unlike leadership programs that focus on the management side of leadership, we focus on building the community side of leadership, which brings citizens and groups together to work on common goals. Therefore, we emphasize our five core leadership values.

- *We do service* with *communities, not* to *communities.* This is perhaps our most important principle. We believe in building solutions from the inside out. That means seeing *citizens* where others see clients, seeing *resources* where others see problems, and seeing *partners* where others see competition. We reject the notion that the best ideas or the expertise needed to solve problems can be found only outside communities. We see community residents (even those who are often labeled for their challenges) and local associations and organizations as partners we can work with to create change. In 2010, our Allies recruited 21,905 volunteers to join them in service; over half of those volunteers were from the neighborhoods or client bases served by the organizations they helped, and 74 percent of the volunteers served more than once. Our partners also reported that Allies had helped them form 4,307 new collaborations with groups these organizations had not worked with before in their communities.

Five Leadership Stories

To date, as mentioned earlier, more than 3,800 diverse young leaders have completed our leadership program in twenty-one cities, and their stories, passions, innovation, and initiative continually demonstrate our conviction that everyone leads. They are social entrepreneurs, youth workers, public officials, teachers, community organizers, police officers, and activists. They also demonstrate how their community-building approach to leadership builds better solutions. Here are some of their stories.

José Rico

José Rico was born in the small town of Jeruco, Mexico. When he was seven years old, José and his family immigrated to the United States, where his father became a railroad worker. José attended and graduated from the Chicago public school system, where his achievements earned him a full-ride scholarship to study engineering at the University of Illinois-Urbana. After a six-month internship at Amoco during his senior year, José realized he'd lost interest in engineering and took a job as a science teacher at Chicago's Latino Youth Alternative High School. In 1994, he joined Public Allies Chicago, and after completing the program he was hired as a staff member. While on staff, he earned his B.A. degree at Northeastern Illinois University and was encouraged by his boss, Michelle Obama, to pursue his dream of opening a school. José followed that path and became an education organizer for the Illinois Coalition for Immigrant Rights, working for programs that supported small schools. He also earned graduate degrees in curriculum instruction from the University of Illinois-Chicago and in educational administration from National Louis University. In 2001 he worked with a group of other Public Allies alumni to mobilize residents of Chicago's Little Village neighborhood, a mostly poor immigrant community, to fight for new, quality high schools for their kids. The mobilization effort culminated in a nineteen-day hunger strike that brought national attention and then funding to create four schools with neighborhood participation. José Rico became the first principal of Chicago's Multicultural Arts High School in 2005. U.S. Secretary of

Education Arne Duncan, formerly superintendent of Chicago's public schools, brought José Rico and his family to Washington, D.C., where he is now deputy director at the White House Initiative on Educational Excellence for Hispanics.[23]

Tanisha Brown

Tanisha Brown can't recall exactly how she found out about Public Allies, but she remembers feeling desperate for the change in her life that Public Allies represented. At the time, she was an unemployed single mom with a two-year-old and a four-year-old. Her own mother had given birth to her at the age of fourteen, and for years she was unable to care for Tanisha because of drug addiction. When Tanisha came to Public Allies, she had a high school degree, she was bright, and she was determined. But she possessed few of the practical and professional skills she needed for a good job, and she had no clue about how to get those skills. She was, in her own words, "a complete angry mess. I was angry at my mom, the world, all the people who said no, at myself for being a young mom."[24] At Public Allies, she was challenged to understand where the anger came from, and she was humbled to find that she wasn't the only one with a sad story. Her fellow Allies gave her some tough feedback that helped her shift her attitude. She also learned computer and networking skills. She soaked up the Friday trainings like a sponge. Today, Tanisha is close to earning a bachelor's degree in behavioral science, and she has a job where she counsels emancipated foster children. She's also preparing to apply to law school. Her dream is to create a haven of support, mentoring, and skill building for young parents so that they don't lose sight of their futures the way she almost did. "Public Allies really, really saved and changed my life," she says, "so I can only give back."

Nigel Okunubi

While Nigel Okunubi was growing up, he spent a lot of time at a youth center near his public housing project in the Adams Morgan neighborhood of Washington, D.C. When the center closed, in 2007, he knew he couldn't let the kids in his old neighborhood down. He led an effort to create the Adams Morgan Youth Leadership Academy, which aims to cultivate the next generation of classroom, community, and workforce leaders among local teenagers in the nation's capital. No one would have pegged Nigel as a leader when he was a kid. He barely took any interest in school: "I graduated high school with a 1.2 grade point average—1.2!"[25]

At the academy, he wants to target kids like himself who are disconnected but have potential. "There's a whole different level of credibility and accountability," he says. "I'm serving the children of some of the folks who raised me." He built the organization on a shoestring while also raising his own ten-year-old son, and he engages the whole community in supporting the kids, approaching everyone from community residents to the owners of local businesses that offer internships and financial support, inviting everyone to get involved in all aspects of the program. "Public Allies is a godsend," he says, and he wonders where he'd be if he hadn't found Public Allies when he did. "The Public Allies thumbprint is all over the services I provide today."

Milo Neild

Milo Neild was home-schooled and then attended a small Christian high school on the East Coast before moving to Arizona and attending public high school. Stereotyped, misunderstood, and misdiagnosed with mental illness, Milo dropped out midway through his senior year.

Recovering from a few years of social isolation and various therapies, he felt comfortable and supported enough to transition from female to male. His confidence grew enough that he began taking classes at a community college while delivering pizza to earn his way. He had also become active with a local LGBT organization, 1n10, that referred him to Public Allies Arizona.

He was nervous about being accepted into the program because he was transgendered but learned that his concerns were unfounded.

"I started out assuming that people wouldn't support me," he says, "and Public Allies taught me the opposite. I had never worked in a professional job and didn't even know what to wear, and some Allies took me shopping."[26]

Along with a supportive community, Public Allies gave Milo new confidence and direction.

"I realized I had a voice." he says. "I was so nervous about public speaking that I just couldn't do it, and now I speak at classrooms and on panels all the time."

Today, Milo is completing a degree in business and applied computing at Arizona State University. After graduation, he will pursue a career in nonprofit technology. He continues to be a leader in the local LGBT community.

Giselle John

Giselle John grew up in the foster care system and was aging out in August 1999. On a path to homelessness, she discovered Public Allies New York and was selected to begin the program in September. "Public Allies was the bridge between the foster care experience and a professional path that kept me from being out on the streets," she says.[27] Giselle put her life experience and leadership to work by serving as a program director with Youth Communication, where she worked to empower youth in the foster care system by helping them find their voices and share their experiences and skills with the community through a youth magazine and other media. More important, she found her calling: "I decided that I wanted to devote my career to working with other kids in the foster care system." After graduating from Public Allies, Giselle continued to work with youth in the foster care and juvenile justice systems while completing her B.A. degree at John Jay College. Now she is serving as a consultant with the Annie E. Casey Foundation's Family to Family Initiative, where she provides technical assistance to reform foster care systems in Kentucky, North Carolina, and Ohio and empower the young people who are in the system. Her inspiring story has also been featured in a book with a foreword by President Jimmy Carter.[28] "Because of Public Allies, I do work that makes me excited to wake up every morning," Giselle says. "I'm making a huge difference for young people who are just like me."

These are only five among nearly four thousand amazing young leaders who have reinforced our conviction that everyone leads. You will meet several others elsewhere in this book. Some will be CEOs, social entrepreneurs, or elected officials. Others will make contributions to social change as volunteers, activists, and frontline workers in their communities. Change has always been the outcome of many leaders making contributions across a spectrum. We've already developed several thousand contributors, and soon we'll be developing more than a thousand leaders every year. We train and support them to multiply their own leadership so that the number of citizens working for solutions continually expands. And it's a start—but our communities and our society need more.

Every year, our program ends with participants doing Presentations of Learning, in which Allies describe how they met the learning outcomes of our program (practice of the five core values) and how they will apply those lessons while working for change in the future. It is a great way for them to document their transformation. I attend a number of the presentations each year and walk away inspired by the transformation that is possible when individuals with passion and potential acquire the self-confidence, leadership practices, and support network to begin their leadership journeys.

I also feel a tinge of sadness when I think about how this potential might have gone unrealized if we had not selected these young leaders for our program, and I am reminded of how much untapped potential there still is in our communities—people who have a passion and a desire to make a positive difference but don't know how to start or how to advance their leadership to the next level. Solving our biggest problems will require the engagement of many more leaders. Imagine if Peter Hoeffel were still working in a deli, or if Bizunesh Talbot-Scott had not gone to college, or if Frank Alvarez were unemployed. Imagine losing the positive impact that José Rico, Tanisha Brown, Nigel Okunubi, Milo Neild, and Giselle John are having on their communities. More of us need to stand up and work with others to make a difference. How will *you* lead?

Key Ideas and Lessons

At Public Allies, we define leadership as follows:

1. Leadership is a process in which many can engage, not a position that only a few can hold.

2. Leadership is about taking personal and social responsibility for working with others to achieve common goals.
3. Leadership is about practicing the five core values that engage diverse community members and groups in working together effectively.

Here are the five core leadership values that we at Public Allies believe are critical today:

1. Recognizing and mobilizing community assets
2. Connecting across cultures
3. Facilitating collaborative action
4. Continuously learning and improving
5. Being accountable to those one works with and those one serves

Reflections

- Consider Public Allies' three-part definition of leadership. What in this definition is new to you?
- What are the values that you seek to practice when you work with others?
- Who are the leaders who have had the most direct influence on you?
- What is it about those leaders' approaches that was most effective in getting you engaged? Why did you accept those leaders' influence?
- What is it about leaders' approaches that has most turned you off?

2

MY LEADERSHIP JOURNEY

Our Allies begin the program by sharing their life stories—the journeys that brought them to their purposes, values, and commitments. The conviction that everyone leads is at the core of my leadership practice because my own story parallels those of many of our Allies. So here is my story—an account of the journey that led me to Public Allies, to my conviction that everyone leads, and to the values that guide my own and Public Allies' work.

Starting Out

I never saw myself as a future leader—far from it. I grew up as one of six children in a conservative Catholic middle-class family in the city of Glendale, Wisconsin, just north of Milwaukee. My five siblings were older by a range of five to thirteen years; my oldest sister entered college the year I started kindergarten.

My father was an engineer and a sales executive for a manufacturer of industrial brake lining for large equipment and oil rigs. My mother was a homemaker. I was born when my parents were nearing their mid forties, which meant that we were two generations apart. Most of my friends' parents had grown up in the era of the Vietnam War and Woodstock, but my parents had grown up in the era of World War II and the Great Depression. To me, while I was growing up, my parents appeared not only immune to but actively resistant to changes in the culture that my friends' families had embraced years before. I felt like I was living in an era very different from theirs, and that gap widened as I got older.

I never felt like I measured up to my five older siblings—in school, sports, or other areas. Ours was a competitive, critical, outspoken family, and so those deficiencies were often amplified, and any sensitivity to the merciless teasing was viewed as a weakness. And I was a very sensitive and emotional child. My deficiencies were amplified outside my home as well. My best friends in the neighborhood were more privileged than I was, attracted to physical danger, and hot-tempered. They were stronger than I was, too, so I lost numerous dares and fights. I never really understood what I was good at, which added to my sense of never feeling like I fit in well at home, in my neighborhood, or at school. To compensate for my low self-esteem and depression, I developed a potent mix of rebelliousness and humor. I could be alternately sharp-tongued and silly, gaining attention by performing as much as playing, and relishing people's reactions when they experienced me as crazy or weird. I also took the teasing directed at me and often turned it on others whom I perceived as physically or emotionally weaker.

In a family of engineers, I was a dreamer, and play often involved imaginative acting. For example, I reenacted scenes from the movie *Star Wars*, or I pretended to be one of the Beatles, playing a tennis racquet "guitar" in front of the mirror. I also watched a ton of television and sought solace in my greatest passion—spinning the record collection that had grown from my income as a paperboy. A huge Beatles fan, I was most affected by John Lennon's songs; his sadness, his vulnerability, and his rebelliousness spoke to me (and his political activism slowly awakened me). I also loved The Who at that time, especially their album *Quadrophenia*, which encapsulated the conflicting ups and downs I was feeling at the time.

At school, I was a mischievous class clown at best and a defiant rebel at worst. Even in first grade, my teacher dismissed me as a poor student who detracted from the learning environment.

I had intimate knowledge of the principal's office, and I finished sixth grade in the hallway because my teacher had kicked me out of the classroom for the final six weeks. By then, I had earned comments on my report card like "Paul always seems tired, listless, and bored" and "He puts nothing into the class situation" and "He is on track to fail" and "He seems so pessimistic." Even though my family did not live close to Saint Monica's, the school I attended, I somehow convinced my parents to give their permission for me to get a pass that allowed me to leave school for lunch when I was in grades seven and eight. I parlayed that freedom into becoming the candy purveyor at school and racking up record scores on the video game *Zaxxon* at Mike's Arcade. Every year, I started school with the intention of being good and earning better grades, but at some point I would become discouraged, slide back, and give up.

In eighth grade, before filing in with my classmates to the graduation mass and ceremony that marked the end of our school days at Saint Monica's, I had the foresight to hide a little bag behind a toilet in the men's restroom. The bag contained a bottle of Liquid Paper, an eraser, and pens with ink in a variety of colors. After walking up to the front of the church to receive my diploma and my final report card with its handwritten grades, I excused myself and returned to the restroom, where I went to work on my report card, changing F's and D's to B's, and minuses to pluses. At the end of the ceremony, my family approached me and my brother David snatched my report card and held it up so that my sister Judy could snap a photo of it. They joked that they wanted to preserve the evidence before I could alter it. Too late! Whatever my shortcomings, I certainly had two assets—initiative and a knack for creative and comprehensive problem solving. (And I still have the photo of that doctored report card.)

I did occasionally put these assets to good use. In seventh grade, Saint Monica's had given us cartons to collect money for the mission of Sister María Rosa in Tegucigalpa, Honduras.

My family had always recycled aluminum cans, and I had often gone to the local garbage dump to get more so I could earn the twenty-five cents per pound they fetched (and buy more records). So I suggested that we organize a can drive at my school instead of going door to door for pennies, and that we turn a large closet in the school basement into a can-crushing and can-storage space. As a result, our school raised hundreds of dollars instead of buckets of change. I also participated in a Toastmasters International program through the archdiocese, mainly to get out of the house with friends one night a week. I prepared a speech at the last minute for a tournament and was yelled at by my parents for my lack of preparation—but I won. For some reason, though, I never saw myself as being a good communicator, as being interested in service, or as having leadership qualities, and I received no encouragement for these things at home or at school. My accomplishments in these areas were merely treated as exceptions in the life of an otherwise mischievous boy.

I had begun drinking alcohol in elementary school. My older brothers' and sisters' drinking parties had offered an introduction, but I also drank on my own. I savored the feeling of pleasure and escape that drinking offered. Unfortunately, I never knew my limits—blackouts and vomiting were common. In seventh grade, for example, I had a little too much wine before the Easter Vigil Mass where I was to serve as an altar boy. Standing in the center of the church, holding the Easter candle during the annual blessing of the holy water, I passed out and dropped the candle, which went rolling down the aisle. Fortunately for me, the heat of the candle took the blame for my blackout, and after we got home, one of my brothers showed up with a black eye, which took the attention off me.

Alcohol also lubricated my entry into the big public suburban high school I attended, where I didn't know many of the other students, and where most of them were more privileged than I was. It accelerated my friendships, and before long I was using drugs, too—whatever was available. Soon I was dealing as well. I also created a Ponzi scheme, borrowing money from other students, promising to give them a 25 percent return the following week, and using the money to buy drugs that I would sell. To be clear, this was not *Scarface*. It was weekend-party dealing, with occasional leaps into more dangerous territory. But, beyond the highs and the money, which helped me upgrade my stereo and my record collection, dealing made me feel like I was the center of something. I had lots of offers to hang out at school and on weekends.

Not long after my sixteenth birthday, I hit a wall. I was in trouble at home, at school, with friends, and with dealers because I was using more than I was selling, and I was insufficiently covering the gap with money from my dishwashing job in a small Catholic college's cafeteria. During the spring, my brother finally busted me, and I tried to quit and get myself together for my last two months of school that year. But I slipped several times, each time finding ways to justify to myself the fact that I was continuing to use. The summer after my sophomore year was a combination of close calls with busts, angry dealers, and customers I increasingly tried to avoid, and escalating conflicts at home.

My parents took a short vacation in northern Wisconsin, and I knew that when they returned they would confront me about my problems at school and at home. To make matters worse—much worse—one of my sisters found my stash of cocaine and flushed it down the toilet. I was out of control and badly in need of help. It seemed that my only options were to run away, commit suicide, or enter treatment. All three were on the table, but I thought that if I could go to a treatment center and get away from my family and everyone else for a while, I could cool off and figure out how to solve my problems.

I had to get away. Shortly after my parents returned from their trip, I went to a nearby Catholic church—not the one we belonged to, so I could be semianonymous—and approached the priest after Mass, knowing he was obliged to keep whatever I told him confidential. My heart was racing, and I almost hyperventilated as I revealed that I had a drug problem and needed help.

I was lucky that Father Gordon was a compassionate man. He talked to me without judgment. My parents met us at the rectory, and with Father Gordon's help I came clean with them about my problem and my desire to get help. It turned out that Father Gordon's brother Don was the chaplain at DePaul Rehabilitation Hospital, and he guided me into treatment. And although I entered DePaul with no intention of permanently quitting drugs and alcohol, the experience—thank God—changed my life.*

A New Beginning

In treatment, I was confronted with a new world, both inside me and around me. For the first time, I unraveled my past, my feelings, and who I was, and I owned up to the damage I had done to my family and friends. I sorted this out and shared many intimate details about my life while surrounded by people of different ages, races, and backgrounds, including gang members, kids from juvenile corrections, and individuals with mental illnesses. I began going to twelve-step group meetings, where I continued sharing about myself, hearing others' stories, and building relationships with people I never would have imagined encountering before. I had never before experienced any real diversity, and I held prejudices, especially regarding race and sexual orientation. For the first time, I began questioning these beliefs. I learned about things I had in common with these people. They became members of my support network as I realized that a messed-up addict like me was in no position to judge others.

One part of recovery proved enormously influential in my life. I had to ask someone to be my sponsor, someone to help

* Father Gordon transferred from the parish not long after that. I saw him again twelve years later, at the baptism of a friend's child. I was proud to share with him what had become of my life. He remembered our meeting and was elated to see me.

guide and coach my recovery and be the person who would take my call at any hour of the day or night when I needed help. My sponsor, Wayne, was a cattle buyer for a meat-packing company. He had a cool wife and two young kids. He had volunteered to drive people one night each week from DePaul Hospital to a twelve-step meeting close to where I lived, and I was lucky to get into his car. We hit it off right on our first drive, and after the meetings, we would often go out for pie and talk. I loved Wayne's insight, warmth, authenticity, and sense of humor. He nurtured me when I needed nurturing and held me accountable when I deserved to be held accountable.

One of the first things I did with Wayne was the twelve-step program's fourth step—taking a personal inventory of my shortcomings and of all the wrongs I could remember having done to others. With Wayne's guidance, I added to that step a list of my strengths and of good things I had done. It was the first time in my life I had considered or owned any strengths. After writing down my inventory, I had to share it verbally with Wayne. Naturally, I was ashamed of the bad and was even embarrassed by the good. And after I finished, there was a terrifying pause, when I expected Wayne to judge me, criticize me, and maybe even reject me. Instead, he shared his own, similar stories, and he told me that I was OK and worthy of love despite my wrongs and shortcomings. It was a powerful experience, and it set the stage for a number of lessons about leadership and community—for example, that we all have strengths and shortcomings, that our shortcomings are human, and that we gain from sharing our shortcomings and challenges with others.

Another part of sobriety involved service. I've often joked that I came to social justice and service from the three R's—religion (lessons on service and social justice at Catholic school), rock and roll (John Lennon, Bob Dylan, Bono, and others who sang about issues that awakened my social conscience), and recovery (one of the twelve steps of recovery is taking responsibility for continually giving back to other addicts and alcoholics). My first act of service was to speak each year about my addiction to the freshman class at my high school, and I continued to do so for a decade after I graduated. The first time, I was only a few months into my junior year, and that was quite humbling, to say the least. I also volunteered for a hotline, helped clean up after recovery meetings, was secretary for a young people's meeting, and eventually even sponsored others (and that's where I learned, the hard way, about how much we can help others before we hit the boundary of their own responsibility for taking action to improve their own lives). I learned that everyone was to be welcomed into these recovery groups—after all, who were we, as addicts ourselves, to judge others' faults? Through meetings with such diverse and different people, I began overcoming my own prejudices.

I stayed sober through the last two years of high school—and that was a daily, often nail-biting struggle when everyone else was experimenting with drugs and alcohol. My grades improved, but only marginally, because I was so focused on wrestling with the emotions and depression I had always medicated and buried. At home, I could not identify with my parents. With friends, I was trying to have fun without the painful temptation to relapse.

I turned my entrepreneurial skills to making tie-dye and silk-screened T-shirts that I sold at Grateful Dead concerts. As one of the first members of the Wharf Rats, a group of sober Deadheads who met, hung out, and camped together at Grateful Dead concerts, I'm probably one of the only people who can say that touring with the Grateful Dead was a key part of my sobriety. Unfortunately, however, this activity led to one misadventure—I was busted by U.S. marshals at concerts in Wisconsin and Pennsylvania for having copyrighted images of the Dead on my T-shirts. The marshals confiscated my shirts, but, thankfully, no other harmful consequences arose from the case of *The Grateful Dead* v. *Paul Schmitz* (U.S. Federal Court, Wisconsin Eastern District).

As I was finishing high school, I was paralyzed with fear and uncertainty about what to do next, and so I skipped applying to college. In a high school where over 90 percent of graduates went on to college, I graduated without a plan. Using income from my T-shirt sales and a dishwashing job, I moved into a small, shabby studio apartment and answered an ad for my first full-time job, as a canvasser for a local environmental organization, Citizens for a Better Environment (CBE)—my fortuitous entrée into the nonprofit sector.

Walking door to door on urban, suburban, and rural roads, and asking people for money to protect the environment, I learned a lot about rejection, persistence, and adapting to different people and cultures. That experience also taught me that in all parts of our region, even those I had prejudged as right-wing, redneck, or poor, I would find kind, interesting, welcoming, generous people who would open their doors and occasionally their wallets to a long-haired, skinny kid with a clipboard. Six months later, Susan Mudd, executive director of CBE, sponsored me on a lobbying trip to Washington, D.C., and that was the beginning of my interest in politics and policy. (My only previous experience had been attending a reelection rally for President Ronald Reagan in 1984 with a friend and his mom.) I studied my talking points, and I greatly enjoyed visiting with members of Congress and their staffs on Capitol Hill. I also received acknowledgment from others in the group that I was good at this. For the first time in my life, I began to study outside the confines of school, burying myself in history, current events, and classic fiction, and reading authors from Dostoyevsky to Kerouac on the county buses to and from work and at Brewster's Café, where I spent hours downing coffee.

But I was still on the edge—with my emotions, with finances, and with sobriety. My depression deepened, and I was often lonely because my friends had all left for college. I was disconnected from my family and too ashamed to reach out for help. I was still lost.

After the New Year, I followed a girlfriend to Boston, where a few other friends were studying, and spent eight months living out of a backpack. I crashed in her dorm, in other friends' dorm rooms, and on various couches, all the while trying to figure out what to do with my life. And I hit another wall. My journals from that time are bleak. Suicide was a distressingly common theme.

The following summer I was back in Milwaukee, where two events proved pivotal. I had struck out finding someone to stay with one night and was hanging out at a late-night diner, with the intention of crashing outside closer to morning. An old friend from recovery came into the diner shortly before midnight, and after hearing my story he offered me a place to stay for two months, in the basement of a townhouse he was rehabbing (it had no plumbing, but I could ride my bike to a gas station a few blocks away and go to friends' homes to shower). And the night after that, a chance introduction led to a full-time job gardening and doing house chores at a mansion for $180 a week in cash. Ironically, the man I gardened for was a drug kingpin, as I discovered a few years later, when he was arrested by the FBI.* By the end of that summer, I had enough money to move into an apartment with friends I had met in recovery. In September, I started classes at the University of Wisconsin–Milwaukee. My life was getting back on track.

My out-of-school reading, my environmental fundraising, and my taste for public policy had all helped motivate me to go to college. My four roommates and I lived in an apartment near campus and created a sober lifestyle filled with fun and adventure. Mostly we went to see live bands, and usually we were the rowdiest guys in the place. I started doing well in school, was invited into the honors program, and scored a regular job as a telemarketer for an insurance agency. Over the next two years, a combination of support from friends and family, recovery meetings, therapy,

* After he served his time, which had been reduced for good behavior and risky cooperation, we became friends. He lived a life of service to others who struggled with drug and alcohol addiction, until he died of a heart attack, in 2010.

intellectual growth, steady income, exercise, and reconciliation with my parents helped me feel healthy, centered, and self-confident for the first time. I had an incredible network of friends who supported me.

I remember the day I realized I had overcome my depression. I had taken a second summer job as a gardener and learned one morning before work about a friend who had gotten back in trouble with drugs. All day, while digging in the dirt, I thought about my life, and for the first time I was grateful for who I was, for the friends I had, and for the life opportunities that were still ahead of me. This was my first real experience of faith. I came to believe that if I could get past the depression that had shadowed me for so long, a depression I had thought would never end, I could persevere through any other challenges. That faith and the resilience it brought have been tested many times by tragedy, but they have held fast for twenty years and have been invaluable assets in my life.

As I came to feel more confident, I felt ready for a change. I received a scholarship to study abroad in Japan as the only foreign student at a small college outside Tokyo. Being a minority of one under a microscope was tough. Add to that my rebellious nature in a conformist culture with the motto "The nail that sticks out gets pounded down," and the romance of the adventure was matched by struggle. I had to wrestle with my identity and beliefs in new ways. But without the baggage of my past, I opened myself up to this amazing opportunity to learn about a new culture and about myself. To take care of myself, I looked for twelve-step meetings in Tokyo. I found one I really liked, where I befriended two older men. Bill was a smart, disheveled English professor, and Jerry was a charming, handsome real estate investor and part-time model whom I would occasionally see in television commercials. Both had been sober for many years, and they shared a lot of wisdom with the group. Thinking it would be good to have more than one sponsor while I was so far from home, one night at an Indian restaurant, after our meeting, I asked both of them to sponsor me.

Bill gave me a confused look. “Paul, are you gay?”

“No,” I quickly replied. “Why?”

Bill smirked. “You do realize you’ve been going to a gay meeting?”

In my naïveté, I had not realized this. “Well, I like the meeting, and I like you. I still want you to sponsor me if you’ll have me.”

They agreed. I stuck with that meeting, and my main expatriate friends, whom I saw twice a week for the remainder of my stay, were all gay. This situation further broadened my boundaries and perspective.

Along with taking classes in Japanese and experiencing new cultures in Japan, I continued educating myself through novels, classic films, and biographies. A woman named Lee, whom I had met through recovery, encouraged me to read Gloria Steinem (“If Men Could Menstruate” was my start), Susan Faludi, and others for what would become a crash course in women’s studies. During a period bookended by the first Persian Gulf War and the 1992 riots in Los Angeles, I followed the daily news from America on CNN, and in magazines at the library, with a new lens. Living in a country and a culture that were so foreign to me, I felt American for the first time and valued my own culture. I learned more about myself as I navigated Japanese culture, built relationships, and established myself. When I returned to America, eighteen months later, I was clearer than ever before about my identity, my beliefs, and my purpose. I was also clear that living in America gave me the opportunity to be myself, not conform to others’ beliefs or rules, and have second chances when I failed. I was devoted to making a difference, and I felt a greater desire to learn about and work on injustices in my community and in my country.

Upon my return to the University of Wisconsin, I joined the College Democrats. My passion to make a difference led to my election as president of the group at my second meeting. We worked on three exciting campaigns, including Bill Clinton’s first presidential campaign. When the campaign season was over, and we had won all the races we had worked on, I felt two conflicting emotions. It was exhilarating to have played a part in a victorious, forward-looking campaign, but witnessing the egotism and the selfishness behind the political process increased my cynicism about the people and the process I had just seen at first hand. I was more committed to policy and problem solving than I was to political posturing and to attacks that didn't seem to solve anything. I decided that politics wasn't the best route for me to make change, and I began searching for another way. President Clinton's call for national service and his belief in diverse people working together inspired me, but I didn't know how to connect to his call.

Serendipity Strikes

Then serendipity struck. I received a fellowship from the Johnson Foundation, which brings groups of leaders together at Wingspread (see Chapter One). After finishing my last exam for the fall semester, I drove down to my first Wingspread conference to be a student observer of a group of ideologically and otherwise diverse leaders. They had gathered to hammer out ways that the new Clinton administration could support communities and our nation's sense of community, a topic I had become fascinated with after studying and writing about the book *Habits of the Heart.*[1] I arrived a little late, so I sat down to dinner in the last seat available, and that seat at Charlie Bray's table changed my life.

Charlie, president of the foundation, had a regal and refined presence that belied his warmth, curiosity, and inclusive spirit. He led our table in a discussion that made me feel comfortable and valued even though I was only supposed to be a student observer. Sitting next to him was Lisa Sullivan, the intelligent, passionate, generous leader of the Children's Defense Fund's Black Student

Leadership Network. Next to her was John McKnight, an older, bearded, provocative, gracious Northwestern University professor and storyteller who was then in the process of coauthoring a book on community building.[2] Also at the table was Vanessa Kirsch, the charismatic, charming, smart young CEO of Public Allies, whom we met in Chapter One.

As an organization, Public Allies seemed to combine all the ideas I was hearing from Charlie, Lisa, and John. Vanessa announced that Public Allies was becoming an element of President Clinton's national service program, something I had been quite interested in. Vanessa inspired me by describing Public Allies as a program that was finding young people who were passionate about making a difference but did not know how to put that passion to work. This was exactly what I had been looking for. Then she issued a fateful invitation: "Why don't you start a Public Allies in Milwaukee?"

I drove home from Wingspread at NASCAR speed, having found my calling—I was going to start a Public Allies chapter in Milwaukee. I asked Charlie Bray to mentor me, and we began having monthly lunches. As president of the College Democrats on my campus, I traveled to Washington to attend President Clinton's inaugural and was able to meet the folks at Public Allies in Washington, D.C., who only lifted my inspiration higher. I visited once again with Lisa Sullivan, who encouraged me to build a truly diverse coalition to start Public Allies Milwaukee, and with John McKnight, who advised me on how to apply his community-building concepts to my effort. I was going to do this right!

I shifted from full-time to part-time study, and the insurance agency where I still telemarketed allowed me to use its office, phone, and fax to start up Public Allies. My ex-girlfriend's parents, Jim and Joanne Murphy, allowed me to move into their home, loaned me a car, and set me up with a small furnished office in Milwaukee's Brewer's Hill neighborhood, which served as Public Allies Milwaukee's office for our first few years.

Public Allies had not considered a Milwaukee site in its initial plan for strategic growth, and Vanessa Kirsch wanted to ensure that I could back up my idealistic aspirations. Others on the D.C. staff were just hoping I would go away; they issued increasingly complex requests for me to demonstrate that there really was support for this new site. They wanted letters from the governor of Wisconsin, the mayor of Milwaukee, our state's senators and congressional representatives, philanthropists, and dozens of nonprofit and community leaders. I was too enthusiastic, idealistic, and naïve to give up or realize that I had no experience or skills in doing what they wanted me to do. I just kept going.

I pulled together a diverse group of young people working in nonprofits, a group formed through friends and flyers, and we began organizing. One of them was Josh Zepnick (now a Wisconsin state representative). Josh was an intern at the Greater Milwaukee Committee, a coalition of the CEOs of the largest businesses, foundations, universities, nonprofits, and unions in our area. He helped me understand the power dynamics of the city. He identified the key governmental, nonprofit, and business leaders who could make my dream happen. He also introduced me to Kimberly Tuck, a young African American woman who worked at a job placement organization. She was an active volunteer and eventually became my first hire and my partner in starting the program.

My first donations, totaling $3,500, came from Charlie Bray, my parents, my sister Janet, the Murphys, and another high school friend's parents, and these contributions boosted my morale.* With Charlie's and Josh's help, many doors opened, and I began requesting larger grants. It was Jim Marks, vice president of the Greater Milwaukee Foundation, who took the biggest risk.

---

* Janet died in a plane crash in 1996 along with her husband, Jack, and their daughter, Caitlin. Two days after that tragic accident, I received a letter from Janet, telling me how proud she was of my work at Public Allies.

He saw my potential and was attracted to the idea of Public Allies Milwaukee, and so he invited me to submit a start-up proposal. At a lunch hosted by Charlie at the University Club, I met Jim Forbes, CEO of the Badger Meter Corporation, and Linda Stephenson, CEO of Zigman Joseph Stephenson, a prominent public relations firm in Wisconsin. These two business leaders took me under their wings and taught me how to work with the business community and much more. They were both exemplary civic leaders and role models. In six months, my team pulled together all the support that Public Allies in D.C. had requested. We sent in a report, and then we waited anxiously.

Public Allies did not know what to do with me or with Suzanne Sysko, who had also approached Public Allies with a proposal for a Public Allies site in Wilmington, Delaware. In the eyes of the Public Allies board, ours were not strategic sites for a new national organization. The Public Allies executive team finally invited us to a board meeting to present our cases directly. The reception was chilly. One board member—also one of Public Allies' largest donors—thought that the organization should take a chance only on the "best and brightest" from America's top colleges ("everyone leads" was not yet a universal belief at Public Allies, and my résumé was admittedly weak). But, with Vanessa's backing, Public Allies ultimately allowed Suzanne and me to start Public Allies sites in Delaware and Milwaukee, although the organization was apparently more committed to Jason Scott, the Duke graduate who had left the D.C. office to start Public Allies North Carolina, and to Michelle Obama, the Princeton and Harvard Law graduate who had been hired to lead Public Allies Chicago. Thankfully, however, Jason and Michelle were both great colleagues and supporters of Suzanne and me. They were also great examples of inclusive leadership. For example, I vividly remember Michelle saying, "For every young leader we find at Northwestern or DePaul or the University of Chicago, we will find one in Cabrini Green, Little Village, and the Robert Taylor Homes."*

Instead of deterring me, my experience with the Public Allies board motivated me to build the best Public Allies site in the country. I spent a year continuing to organize and build support in the community, regularly visiting Chicago to learn from Michelle Obama's program, which was already under way. An old Milwaukee community organizer, Ace Backus, recruited me to join the board of the Mid-Town Neighborhood Association, led by a great young leader, Joe Cayen, in one of Milwaukee's poorest neighborhoods, and that became my first board experience. Joe and I were peers. We learned a lot together and partnered on many projects.

Ace also linked me to the Milwaukee Violence Prevention Coalition, one of whose projects was to create a directory of all the programs and services in Milwaukee. I volunteered to create that directory. It was grunt work that no one else wanted to do, and it earned Public Allies and me not only the coalition's appreciation but also a phone list of potential partner organizations for our Allies.

In addition to Kimberly Tuck, I hired Michelle Dobbs and Ed Minter, young leaders connected to our advisory group. The four of us were almost a perfect team in how we balanced and complemented one another in terms of our skills and perspectives. The interviews with prospective Allies humbled me—many of the candidates had more experience and greater qualifications than I did, even though I was the leader of the organization. And we had so many great candidates among our 150 or so applicants!

* After Suzanne successfully built Public Allies Delaware with her colleague Tony Allen, she became a physician and founded WellDoc, a medical technology company. Tony, now a vice president at the Bank of America, also serves on several prominent boards in Delaware. Jason leads a fund that invests in environmental sustainability. Everyone leads!

In September 1994, we selected twenty-four diverse young men and women and began our Public Allies Milwaukee program with a team-building retreat at a camp an hour outside Milwaukee. Several of our new Allies were older and more experienced than I was. It was an incredible group.

The first night, we told our life stories, recounting the events in our lives that had shaped our purposes, our values, and our commitment to work for change. People in the group told about their experiences with gangs, with graduating from college into dead-end jobs, with child abuse, with coming out of the closet and identifying as gay, and more. Hearing about all the obstacles that our Allies had overcome and the hopes and dreams they had for themselves and Public Allies, I could only cry when it was my turn, overwhelmed by the beauty of what I had helped to build and the potential of these incredible people.

But what I had helped to build was a mess—perhaps a beautiful mess, but still a mess. Public Allies as a whole had many of the advantages and shortcomings of a start-up. The organization had energy and innovation, but it had no clear curriculum, and it even lacked a single mission statement common to all its sites. As mentioned in Chapter One, the average age of the staff was twenty-four, and none of us except Michelle Obama had ever managed anyone or anything. The diversity of the organization was its great strength, but it also led to conflicts. For example, the first national staff retreat that I attended was centered on a very difficult conversation about racism in the service field and on conflicts over people's different leadership styles. I felt intimidated by much of the conversation, but I walked away resolved that Public Allies would be an organization that would dive into the deep and difficult conversations (and it has continued to do so).

Back in Milwaukee, I was so afraid of mistakes and failure that I was a reactive, micromanaging, perfectionist executive director. My team experienced more conflict than collaboration. Fortunately, we all had the humility to understand our lack of experience, and we constantly sought out mentoring and support from experienced leaders. Dr. David Henderson, a counselor and team-building consultant who had trained the Allies, noticed our discord and offered to meet with our team every week for what turned out to be six months. He helped us become a high-functioning team that began leading other sites in collaborating to define the program model. I had gained experience with sponsors during my recovery, and so I continued to build relationships with mentors to guide my growth as a leader, meeting regularly with Charlie Bray, Linda Stephenson, and Dr. Howard Fuller, a well-known education reformer and civil rights activist who had recently stepped down as superintendent of the Milwaukee Public Schools.

In 1996, Vanessa Kirsch left Public Allies to travel and study social entrepreneurship and civic engagement around the world. She remained on the board and founded New Profit, a venture philanthropy group that has been a pioneer in applying private investment models to helping nonprofit organizations grow. (At Public Allies, Vanessa had learned the hard way about the difficulty of expanding a new program after the initial start-up money dries up.)

Katrina Browne also left to attend divinity school, and then she made a documentary film, *Traces of the Trade*, about her ancestors' ties to the slave trade and its role in her family's generations of privilege.

Our second national CEO, Chuck Supple, arrived in Washington, D.C., with his Superman good looks, friendly smile, and extensive experience of leading the California Campus Compact, a coalition of colleges promoting service and civic engagement among students, and his work helping launch AmeriCorps during the Clinton administration. He asked Michelle Dobbs and me to serve on the team crafting Public Allies' first real strategic growth plan. Upon completion of the plan, he invited us both to become national vice presidents of Public Allies. My position was vice president and chief strategist, with responsibilities that included research and development, external relations, fundraising, leading national initiatives, and starting new sites in New York, Los Angeles, and Cincinnati. I also spent six months as the interim executive director of Public Allies Chicago, not long after Michelle Obama, soon to be a mother, left for a job as associate dean of student services at the University of Chicago.

My leadership was also being recognized and developed outside Public Allies. Emboldened by my successful entrepreneurship at Public Allies, I co-founded two other groups in Milwaukee. One established youth-run credit unions at local Boys and Girls Clubs, and the other mobilized students and parents to be effective advocates for education reform. My role at Public Allies also led me to attend more conferences and build relationships in other communities, and that expanded my knowledge and networks.

In 1997, John McKnight and his colleague and coauthor John "Jody" Kretzmann asked Michelle Obama and me to join the faculty of the Asset-Based Community Development Institute at Northwestern University, where I would meet with other community builders to develop the practice of recognizing and mobilizing community assets and then disseminate what we had learned through writing and speaking. In the same year, Lisa Sullivan moved to the Rockefeller Foundation, where she nominated me to be a Next Generation Leadership Fellow. I was interviewed by an all-star team of Lisa, Jacqueline Novogratz (founder and now CEO of the Acumen Fund), and Angela Glover Blackwell (founder and now CEO of PolicyLink) and was thankful to make it through, despite being one of the youngest and least-experienced candidates. My experience as a Next Generation Leadership Fellow challenged me in new ways, expanded my networks even more, and helped me clarify my personal vision for and commitment to social change.

Becoming CEO

In December 1999, Chuck Supple, our CEO, stunned me by calling to say that he and his partner, Daniel Zingale, had been offered top jobs in the new administration of Governor Gray

Davis of California. He told me that he would support my candidacy for CEO of the national organization if I wanted the job.

Chuck had codified the Public Allies mission, values, and program. He had helped us professionalize our organization and build our brand. He is a leader and a mentor whom I continue to admire greatly. But, despite Chuck's best efforts, Public Allies was in rough shape.

When the start-up funds are gone and an organization has limited results and limited scale but still needs to build core capacity, the second round of funding is very hard to raise. (Wendy Kopp had this experience at Teach for America and later wrote about it.)[3] We were increasing our debt, living payroll to payroll, and the funders who had launched us had moved on to other, newer things. The national office had shrunk down to just a handful of people, and all our other sites were struggling to secure a second wave of community funding. In this precarious financial situation, the challenge of becoming CEO was compounded by the expected arrival of my wife's and my first daughter and by my enrollment at the University of Wisconsin–Milwaukee to earn a master's degree in urban studies. After nights of stressful deliberation, and with the support of my wife, I decided to go for it, but only on the condition that Public Allies' headquarters would be moved from Washington to Milwaukee. Michelle Dobbs and I had both been working out of our homes in Milwaukee, and Merilou Gonzales, one of the few D.C. staff left, wanted to move back to the Midwest. The board approved, and I took the job.

My first decade as CEO included leading a lot of change. We refined our mission more than once, and we established our five core values as our leadership outcomes. We created new program standards and curricula. We developed and executed two five-year strategic growth plans. We worked through a major reorganization, moving from being a national organization with local branches to being a quasi-franchise, with universities and nonprofit organizations operating Public Allies chapters in each community. We rebranded ourselves and defined our purpose and our message more clearly. Our private funding roller-coastered. At one point, our AmeriCorps funding—our core support—was almost eliminated. I was tested and retested as a leader, and I discovered new strengths and new learning through many unfortunate mistakes.

Through it all, we grew from 201 Allies in nine communities, with a $4 million budget and 794 alumni, to 656 Allies in twenty-one communities, with a $20 million budget and more than 3,800 alumni. The reports that came in each year from our Allies, partners, and alumni across the country continued to inspire me with the belief that everyone can lead. And, despite our organizational growth and challenges over the years, our program continues to deliver high-quality results for our Allies, partners, and communities. The success of our program in developing a new and diverse generation of leaders and in strengthening our communities has also increased our influence in the fields of leadership, service, nonprofit capacity building, and civic engagement.

My influence as leader of Public Allies has also grown over time. I've been selected for and elected to other leadership roles in my community and at the national level, where I've continued to lead and advocate on the basis of Public Allies' values. My growth as a leader, like Public Allies' growth in programs and influence, is the result of the work of many people at Public Allies. I have benefited from working with talented and diverse staff and board members who have worked and struggled together to support the organization's success. Despite differences and conflicts, we have kept our hands on the wheel and moved forward together. My colleagues have also supported my leadership, and we have often applied the principles of Public Allies, and even the tools and exercises we use with our Allies, to ourselves. We continue to have deep and difficult conversations. We don't use these tools and exercises perfectly—they are not easy—but we do strive. I participate in a 360-degree review of my performance and leadership each year and have done my own Presentations of Learning. For example, after a very difficult two-year change process, the biggest challenge I had ever faced, I created a Presentation of Learning titled "The Worst Practices of Social Entrepreneurship," cataloging the worst mistakes that Public Allies and I had made and learned from over the years. I shared this presentation publicly and wrote about it for the *Stanford Social Innovation Review*.

My leadership journey took a new turn in 2007, when I volunteered, in my private life and on my own time, for the Obama presidential campaign. Along with the creation of Public Allies Milwaukee and the birth of my three children, the campaign was one of the most exciting experiences of my life. Knowing the Obamas and their beliefs about community, leadership, citizen engagement, and social change, I was honored to support the campaign in Wisconsin as a fundraiser and organizer. I also participated in the Urban Policy Group and co-chaired the campaign's Civic Engagement Policy Group, where I worked with the well-known civic engagement theorist Harry Boyte; Bob Weissbourd, chair of the Urban Policy Committee; Carlos Monje, deputy policy director of Obama for America; and several other thought leaders and practitioners to think about civic engagement, social innovation, national service, and strengthening nonprofits—issues I had worked on for years at Public Allies. Our group thought about how to translate the "Yes, we can," bottom-up ethos of the campaign into policy and governance. These were ideas of personal importance to the Obamas, and that made the work even more fulfilling.

After the election, I was invited to join the Presidential Transition Team and worked on social innovation and national service, helping develop and pass the bipartisan Edward M. Kennedy Serve America Act. It was the thrill of a lifetime. As much as I loved the work, I loved our team even more. This group of genuine, kind, smart, caring people made this important opportunity more impactful and more fun. Our team included Sonal Shah, who worked on global development at

Google; Michele Jolin, a policy expert from the Center for American Progress; Marta Urquilla, an organizer and community builder with the Praxis Project; Howard Buffett, a recent Columbia graduate who had worked for the campaign; Cheryl Dorsey, the CEO of Echoing Green; Jonathan Greenblatt, the founder of Ethos Water, who taught social enterprise at UCLA; John McKnaught, an amazing student from Indiana University who also came from the campaign; and, once again, Carlos Monje. My cynicism about politics had led me to believe that after Barack Obama won the presidency, the "mean people" would take over, but I was wrong. The transition team was diverse, smart, humble, hardworking, and truly interested in gathering a wide range of ideas and input. And the values, beliefs, and networks that I'd gained from Public Allies fit well into the team's agenda. At our bittersweet closing dinner, I shared a photo of myself at eighteen years old—gaunt, angry, long-haired, and wearing a tie-dye T-shirt—and shared a bit of my story. With a few tears, I thanked everyone for the experience of serving on the team and said that the boy in that photo could never have imagined having the opportunity to work with them and advise the president of the United States. Everyone leads!

If I Can, So Can You

I believe that if someone from my background can grow up to be CEO of Public Allies and an advisor to the president of the United States, then that kind of leadership is also possible for many others. That is why I am so passionate about the idea that everyone leads.

When it comes to leadership, I'm not an exception to the rule. Rather, my experience indicates that there is a whole group of people who are missing from public participation. A great deal of potential that our communities and our country need is being neglected.

Many of our Allies never saw themselves as being leaders and never saw their potential to make a difference. That is tragic. I'm so glad I did not miss the connections, opportunities, and relationships that built my leadership. If I had not sought treatment for my addiction, if I had missed that early Wingspread Conference, if I had not met the many mentors and colleagues who have developed me—who knows what I would be doing? Stories like mine can become the norm, and when we look back honestly at the many great public leaders and even the private entrepreneurs in our history, stories like mine are much more common than many acknowledge. But the ranks of the privileged have grown over time, and leadership programs too often reinforce privilege in how they identify and develop future leaders. Many potential leaders lack the social networks and opportunities to advance, and our organizations and institutions don't know how to find them or recognize their assets, beyond credentials that don't speak to a person's vision, intelligence, creativity, or life experience.

My experiences also inculcated in me the values that Public Allies has found to be so effective in building communities. From my time in treatment and recovery among a diverse group of people, I gained the value of recognizing and mobilizing assets. That experience, furthered by my time in Japan, where I experienced another culture and hung out with gay expatriates, helped me improve how I connect across cultures and see the benefits of inclusion. Early on in my time at Public Allies, I was tested and failed to collaborate well, and that forced me to change the way I was building and participating in teams. Through it all, I've climbed many steep learning curves, and because of my early lessons in recovery, I seek out mentors and constructive feedback and try continuously to improve as a leader. Grounded in my own experience, purpose, and values, I've tried to be true to myself and take responsibility for my leadership and my work. I am grateful to Public Allies for building my leadership and that of more than 3,800 other Allies so far.

Key Ideas and Lessons

I believe that understanding and sharing our personal stories—how we have formed our beliefs, values, and experiences—is important to leading. When I look back, I think that four common threads running through my story have furthered my leadership more than anything else:

1. My understanding of and acceptance of myself as having strengths as well as faults, mistakes, and shortcomings, and my attempts to understand others as having both strengths and weaknesses
2. My willingness to be vulnerable and share my story, asking for feedback, support, and help, as well as opening a door for others to share their stories with me
3. The boldness to step up when I saw an opportunity to make a difference, and my willingness to accept the risk, mistakes, and lessons that came with that commitment
4. The ability to be mentored—finding people to be role models for my work, leadership, and personal life, and building mutually supportive relationships with them

I always share these things with Allies because so many young people think that leadership means never being vulnerable and that showing weakness is bad. None of us can do it alone or have all that we need to lead. We need others.

Leadership is something everyone can take part in, and these leadership practices must be learned and developed—*they are not natural to most of us.* I had to overcome a lot of obstacles and baggage to become a leader. Hopefully, your path will be less tortuous. If I can do this, so can you. We need many more leaders in our society. Everyone leads.

Exercise and Reflection

Life Maps

The Allies begin our program year by using words and images to convey their life maps—the major events and circumstances in their lives that have brought them to their purposes, values, and commitments. Then they share their life maps in a circle with each other. Everyone presents his or her life map. It takes time, but everyone finds unique ways to connect with everyone else in the room and understand others at a deeper, more personal level. This practice establishes a foundation for people to understand each other and not make assumptions about others' backgrounds, beliefs, motivations, or perspectives.

- What are the events and circumstances that have most shaped your purpose, values, and commitments?
- Who has influenced you the most?
- What lessons from those experiences guide you most today?

3

THE TRADITION AND FUTURE OF THE CONCEPT THAT EVERYONE LEADS

As mentioned and reinforced in previous chapters, our conviction that everyone leads is about the idea that leadership represents actions that many people can take, not positions that only a few people can hold. Leadership is about taking personal and social responsibility for working with others on common goals, and about practicing the values that engage those you lead to work effectively with you and others. Public Allies evolved both this definition of leadership and our leadership-development model from our own organic practice, which has included many lessons learned the hard way over the past nineteen years. Nevertheless, our definition is not necessarily new. My own studies indicate that this definition of leadership is rooted in the democratic tradition of the United States. It is relevant to changes taking hold in the twenty-first century, and it is consistent with the past four decades of leadership theory. A survey of our history and current trends, together with a survey of recent leadership theory, will demonstrate why building leadership and community from the bottom up is so powerful and necessary today.

Leadership from the Community Up: History and Current Trends

Rooted in the American Democratic Tradition

The history of social change in America, as President Obama reminded us during his 2008 campaign, shows that ordinary people can do extraordinary things, and that lasting social change most often comes from the bottom up. From the American Revolution through the civil rights movement and other movements for social change, it has been the courageous actions of many, not just the inspiration and direction of a few, that has created change. Although bottom-up efforts have often coalesced with the actions of people in leadership positions to create change, top-down efforts without any bottom-up engagement have rarely succeeded or been sustained over the long term.

The idea of citizen-led, bottom-up collaborative change was baked into our nation's very founding. Yes, we rightly honor the esteemed gentlemen geniuses who gathered in Philadelphia to courageously declare independence and conceive a great democracy. But their words mattered only because of the actions of often unheralded citizen leaders back in the colonies. The revolution that brought the Founding Fathers' ideas to bear on conditions in the thirteen original colonies was sparked in Lexington and Concord, Massachusetts, when a farmer, John Parker, organized about sixty shopkeepers, dairy farmers, and free African Americans into a ragtag militia to stand up to hundreds of British soldiers—the best-trained and most successful army in the world. These people's actions were echoed across the colonies as citizens and others courageously stepped up to act with their families and neighbors to fight a powerful empire, risking their lives, their families, and their property to enact the Founding Fathers' vision that in the United States of America, citizens would lead. Indeed, the American Revolution was won with the leadership of the Founding Fathers as well as with the leadership of thousands of unsung Founding Mothers, Brothers, and Sisters, without whom the idea of democracy would never have triumphed.

Their vision of citizen leadership was tragically incomplete, however, because of the odious stain of slavery and the patriarchy and classism that defined the term *citizen*. But even though the Founding Fathers failed to include so many Americans in the new republic's official public life, the excluded Americans and their allies were able to use the very system and

American democratic ideals that the founders had constructed to struggle for and eventually win their rights as citizens.

The spirit of citizen leadership that animated the American Revolution took root and branched out during the nation's first few decades. The French writer Alexis de Tocqueville traveled from France in the 1830s to study America's new democratic system and culture. In his book *Democracy in America,* Tocqueville highlighted the importance of citizen leadership at every level while also critically acknowledging the evils of slavery and of our nation's treatment of Native Americans. Despite these injustices, he saw that citizen leadership was more than an ideal of American democracy. He wrote that "Americans of all ages, all stations of life, and all types of disposition" were "forever forming associations" to solve public problems and build hospitals, schools, libraries, and other public goods. "In every case," he continued, "at the head of any new undertaking, where in France you will find the government or in England some territorial magnate, in the United States you are sure to find an association. . . . I have often admired the extreme skills [Americans] show in proposing a common object for the exertions of very many and in inducing them to voluntarily pursue it."[1]

Collaborative leadership among citizens had indeed taken root in our country and in our culture. Democracy was not just about voting for a representative government but about citizens solving problems, by themselves and with their government.

Manifested in the Struggle for Civil Rights

The spirit of citizen leadership and association probably had its greatest modern manifestation in the civil rights movement. Often, however, civil rights history focuses on the big moments and big leaders but fails to amplify the broader struggle and the leadership of the many who built and sustained the movement.

The historian David Garrow expands the landscape of movement leadership: "What the carefully scrutinized historical record shows is that the actual human catalysts of the movement, the people who really gave direction to the movement's organizing work, the individuals whose records reflect the greatest substantive accomplishments, were not administrators or spokespersons, and were not those whom most scholarship on the movement identifies as the 'leaders.'"[2] And according to Harry Boyte, a civic theorist, "While mobilization efforts like marches and sit-ins are best known, community-level organizing was the movement's foundation."[3] For example, Charles Payne's history of the struggle in Mississippi shows that it was decades of organizing that built the leadership of many ordinary people who were ready to act courageously to catapult the movement when the time was right.[4] If we dig deeper into two iconic moments—Rosa Parks's courageous refusal to sit in the "colored" section of a bus in Montgomery, Alabama, and Dr. Martin Luther King Jr.'s delivery of his inspirational "I Have a Dream" speech at the Lincoln Memorial during the 1963 March on Washington for Jobs and Freedom—we can see how many other leaders contributed to these two leaders' successes.

On December 1, 1955, when Rosa Parks refused an order to give up her seat on the bus to make room for a white passenger, she was more than just a tired seamstress, as legend and even her *New York Times* obituary have mischaracterized her. She was a volunteer leader with the local chapter of the National Association for the Advancement of Colored People (NAACP) and had been trained in civil disobedience at the Highlander School in Tennessee by the great organizer Ella Baker. Parks's boss at the NAACP, E. D. Nixon, was also a member of the Brotherhood of Sleeping Car Porters (BSCP) and had been mentored by a fellow BSCP member, the civil rights pioneer A. Philip Randolph. When Rosa Parks was arrested, Nixon realized that the arrest represented an opportunity to mobilize the black community in Montgomery. He worked with the Women's Political Council, led by Jo Ann Robinson, who had the idea for the boycott, and with Parks's permission he stayed up all night copying thirty-five thousand handbills to promote the boycott. As the boycott grew from a one-day action to a movement, Nixon and others chose Dr. King to lead the effort because of his eloquence and his youth (King was then only twenty-six years old), believing that if the effort failed, King could simply pack up and leave town.

By this time, Nixon had the help not just of Ella Baker but also of two other master organizers, Bayard Rustin and Stanley Levinson, who created a group called In Trust to support the Montgomery effort and link it to other Southern organizing efforts, and Baker took Parks on a fundraising tour of the Northeast. These organizers, recognizing Dr. King's immense talents, built the Southern Christian Leadership Council (SCLC) to create a base for his leadership. The courage of Parks, the strategy of Nixon, the passion of Robinson, and the eloquence of King were all critical, but just as critical were daily acts of courage and sacrifice by thousands of citizens who spread the word and led by example and influence. In fact, when some of the movement leaders considered ending the boycott, it was the black citizens of Montgomery who led their leaders, refusing to compromise until they won. Rosa Parks's heroic act was an essential spark, but that spark led to change because of the leadership of citizens at many levels.

We often read about Dr. King's transformative "I Have a Dream" speech but fail to reflect on how the March on Washington for Jobs and Freedom came about. Who organized the event at the Lincoln Memorial and the two hundred thousand marchers who attended? The answer begins with A. Philip Randolph of the BSCP. Randolph proposed the march, and to organize it he selected Rustin, who had co-founded the Congress for Racial Equality (CORE) and mentored the creation of both the Student Nonviolent Coordinating Committee (SNCC) and the SCLC. Rustin pulled together, for the first time, an alphabet-soup coalition—the BSCP, the NAACP, CORE, SNCC, and the SCLC along with the National Urban League. The United Auto Workers as well as Jewish, Catholic, and Protestant civil rights groups soon stepped up as well. This coalescing effort was not easy—Dr. King, ironically, was the last holdout. And Rustin was not the obvious leader of this coalition; the NAACP's leadership was concerned that a man known to be gay and a pacifist, a man who had been a conscientious objector to World War II, could harm the effort. But the rest of the coalition demanded Rustin, knowing of his unique organizational brilliance and of the trusting relationships that he had with each organization.

They set a goal of one hundred thousand marchers and had only seven weeks to arrange all the logistics—mobilizing leaders throughout the South and the North to organize marchers, arrange transportation, and coordinate food, water, sanitation, nurses, and housing during Washington's punishing August heat—and they pulled it off without modern communications technology. (Imagine what that took!) At the time, reports in *The New York Times*, *Life* magazine, and other media outlets marveled at how this voluntary network could do so much with so little capacity and so few resources.[5] But Rustin's decades of building grassroots leaders paid off. The event, including Dr. King's nationally televised speech, was a huge success and greatly influenced the passage of civil rights legislation. The speech was witnessed not only by the two hundred thousand people gathered on the National Mall in Washington but also by millions more watching at home, thanks to the facilitative leadership of Rustin and his team, supported by thousands of leaders across the country who influenced and mobilized their neighbors, friends, and associates to step up and participate. In fact, it was Bayard Rustin and A. Philip Randolph, not Dr. King, who graced the cover of *Life* the week after the march.

Dr. Charles McKinney, a former Public Allies North Carolina colleague who is now a civil rights historian at Rhodes College, sums it up this way:

> When we elevate leaders of particular movements to the mythic status of great man or woman, we do a disservice to everyone. By placing people on a historical pedestal, we forget that they grew,

> learned, made mistakes, and struggled throughout the tenure of their leadership, and we forget that these leaders were mentored, collaborated with other leaders, and had to get their followers to believe in their own capacity to step up and lead. Hero worship relegates the work, thought, and effort of "ordinary people" to something akin to pleasant background music. Local agents for change and progress lose their voice and are mercilessly converted into mindless, thoughtless followers of the great man or woman who "leads" them. In this frequently zero-sum game, all parties are diminished. In order for us to understand and build on this history, we must honor the true leadership paradigm, where leaders at all levels—those few who get recognized and the countless others who contribute silently—are necessary for change.[6]

Applying the same analysis to the labor movement, the women's movement, and other social change efforts throughout our history, we can see how the leadership of many—that of the visible few and that of the unsung many, operating at different levels—has always been necessary for change. Unfortunately, however, our nation's focus on stories of heroic individuals often obscures stories of true leadership among many others who have contributed to change. Nevertheless, this bottom-up leadership tradition is gaining more relevance in our fast-changing times.

Leadership in the Twenty-First Century

This historic approach to bottom-up change has been reinvented for the twenty-first century. Technology, the rise of a new generation, and growing diversity have necessitated new ways to organize, develop leadership, and create change in communities.

Communications technologies, access to information, and social networks have fundamentally changed the way in which individuals can empower themselves to act. We can gather information from a plethora of sources in an instant. We can communicate with and organize ever-expanding networks of people faster than ever to work on public opportunities and problems. And there is no contradiction between forming communities online and yearning for community where we live. Technology does not have to replace face-to-face interaction, as some fear or criticize, but in fact often accelerates and enhances it. We can form new relationships and deepen existing ones—keeping in greater touch, learning more about each other, and joining with each other in more groups and activities. Using social media, I have donated to new groups, learned about issues, attended public meetings, met new friends, and deepened relationships.

Robin Dunbar, an author and an evolutionary anthropologist at Oxford University, argues that most people can maintain about 150 meaningful relationships, but that in the faster, more mobile modern world, maintaining relationships is harder for people. But, Dunbar says, "Facebook and other social networking sites allow us to keep up with friendships that would otherwise rapidly wither away. And they do something else that's probably more important, if much less obvious: they allow us to reintegrate our networks so that, rather than having several disconnected subsets of friends, we can rebuild, albeit virtually, the kind of old rural communities where everyone knew everyone else."[7]

In terms of organizing for change—from our neighborhoods to global issues like the environment, poverty, and genocide—technology is a crucial tool for leadership and mobilization. Critics have argued that technology offers weak ties with others (on Facebook, for example, the bar for "friend" is pretty low) and can produce only weak action (clicking "like" instead of writing letters, attending meetings, volunteering, or protesting). They are only half right. Technology and social networks certainly have their limits, and although technology is useful, it should not be the only tool you use. It really depends on how you use the tool and what else is in your box. My best friend owns a construction company. He and I each have a hammer. In my hands, a hammer is good for hanging pictures, and I'm inept at much else. In his hands, a hammer can fix almost anything and produce beautiful woodwork. Social networking tools are similar. For some, they are a means of sharing photos or occasionally checking to see what others are doing, whereas if you're adept at organizing, and if you're networked with people you know personally who are active volunteers and activists, on the ground as well as online, then social networking tools can accelerate your work. Building a broader network of weak ties and light commitments can often surface more individuals with strong ties and strong commitments to action. I can see many ways in which social networks would have accelerated and eased much of the work I had to do in organizing people to start Public Allies Milwaukee. Social networks would not have replaced the interpersonal, on-the-ground work, but they would have accelerated and broadened it.

Technology has also bred new beliefs among the younger generation about hierarchy, empowerment, authenticity, transparency, and collaboration. The Millennial generation consists of those born roughly between 1982 and 2000, who comprise the largest and most diverse generation in American history.[8] They are a generation of team players and joiners, more tolerant of diversity, and much less cynical than past generations about institutions and their ability to create change. They participate in volunteer service more than any previous generation, and technology has fundamentally altered their expectations of participation at work, in their communities, and in our democracy. According to one account of this generation, published in 2008,

> their arrival was heralded by "Baby on Board" signs in minivans twenty-five years ago. Now Millennials are entering young adulthood with a sense of confidence and commitment that reflects their sheltered and yet, at the same time, pressured childhood. Millennials are also the first American generation to be raised with access to the Internet and the incredibly greater communication opportunities the Web offers. . . . Their team orientation

> and desire to constantly share information are just two of the Millennial behaviors that are impacting American culture and politics. . . . [Each generation as it comes to power] demands that the nation's institutions change to accommodate its beliefs and values. The Millennials are about to make those demands on America.[9]

The advance of technology and of a new generation is taking place in the context of an increasingly diverse America. By 2050, Caucasian Americans will for the first time be a minority, and in many communities they already are. In fact, in 2011, for the first time, the majority of children born in America are expected to be nonwhite.[10] Leaders who wish to engage communities in working for change must be inclusive. Many public problems, such as those related to education, health, and economic security, still have a disproportionate impact on people and communities of color. Creating more lasting, equitable solutions will require the effective engagement of diverse leaders, organizations, and communities.

Such engagement will not come about automatically or through good intentions. Research from many communities shows that those leading nonprofit organizations—the organizations often bringing citizens together to solve problems—are overwhelmingly white. And community residents don't know how to work together effectively. In fact, Robert Putnam, former dean of Harvard's Kennedy School of Government and author of *Bowling Alone*, conducted research on civic engagement in dozens of communities across the country. After controlling for every variable he could, he found an inverse relationship between diversity and civic engagement. He describes a "turtle effect," whereby the more diverse a community becomes, the less its residents leave their homes to build relationships with or collaborate with others, even with people like themselves.[11] New leadership must reverse the "turtle effect "and engage diverse communities to work together on common goals. The demographic trend line is moving in only one direction on diversity, and so building inclusive, collaborative leadership from the community up is more important than ever.

Regardless of one's politics, the presidential campaign waged in 2008 by then-Senator Barack Obama offers lessons on how to lead in this new environment. Obama and his team harnessed these twenty-first-century forces masterfully. They turned César Chávez's *Sí, se puede* ("Yes, we can") and June Jordan's "We are the ones we have been waiting for" into an organizing ethos.[12] Imbuing the campaign's communications with authenticity, transparency, and opportunities to participate and engage, they inspired a new generation. They brought diverse Americans together with common, often measurable goals, and they engaged and recognized donors, making them feel like they belonged to the team, regardless of the amounts they gave. They recognized how people form communities online and yearn for community where they live, and they facilitated both kinds of community. They offered people the tools, whether through technology and social networking or retail offices and face-to-face organizing, that empowered them to lead efforts from the bottom up to participate in their own communities and spheres of influence. In fact, at one point during the primary campaign, Obama's supporters used these tools against him. They created online groups and petitions and clogged his message boards to criticize a vote that Obama had cast in the Senate in support of the Foreign Intelligence Surveillance Act. But the candidate did not shut down his Web site or his online organizing effort. Instead, he responded with a video acknowledging this difference with his supporters and encouraging them to continue promoting their views and holding him accountable.

These efforts encompass important lessons about using technology along with on-the-ground organizing, about authentic and transparent communication, about respecting the leadership that resides within communities and constituencies, about facilitating the leadership of many to influence their networks, about bridging diverse communities and networks, and about mobilizing around achievable, measurable, common goals. All these factors are important to leading in the twenty-first century. In fact, President Obama's opponents in the so-called Tea Party are now using many of these methods themselves to create a populist, multileader organizing effort.

Everyone Leads: A Survey of Recent Leadership Theory

We built our Public Allies model of bottom-up, values-based leadership organically from our own experience, but it shares elements with the major leadership theories that have emerged over the past forty years, all of which differ markedly from earlier views of leadership. A survey of the past four decades of leadership theory and research confirms that the idea and the practice of bottom-up leadership, which resonate both with our history and with current trends, are also backed up by recent literature on leadership.

For most of the twentieth century, the focus in leadership studies was on "great men" and their attributes. In management studies, the focus was on how leaders of institutions could induce their subordinates and followers to accomplish the leaders' goals. In recent decades, however, theory and research in the field of leadership—whether we mean community leadership, leadership of causes, or institutional leadership—have focused increasingly on a populist, values-based model of how everyone can lead, and on the values that allow one to lead others most effectively. Over the last several years, leadership articles in the *Harvard Business Review* have increasingly echoed ideas, which grassroots organizers have taught for decades, about collaborative, distributive leadership models. What follows is a survey of seven seminal theories or books on leadership, from diverse perspectives, that have influenced or reinforced our approach.[13]

Marshall Ganz, "Organizing"

Public Allies was influenced early by many community organizers who helped shape our leadership-development model with the practices of community organizing. In many ways over the past eighteen years, we have seen much of the rest of the world catch up with community organizing–based theories about developing and supporting leadership. From the work of Saul Alinsky to the civil rights movement and other organizing efforts, the role of organizers as people who enlist, empower, and launch other leaders has always been crucial.[14] So is the belief that leadership, in order to succeed, must be built at all levels. Often organizing work is confused with mobilizing, but mobilizing efforts seek to compel large groups of people to take an action defined by a leader, such as a protest. The people who participate aren't co-creators but are simply actors. True organizing is about building relationships, an activity in which an organizer gets to know the stories, motivations, and interests of people and helps *them* step up to lead.[15]

Marshall Ganz, an author and former United Farm Workers organizer who is now a professor at Harvard's Kennedy School of Government, was the architect of the Obama campaign's community organizing strategy.[16] In an online course on community organizing, Ganz outlines his key leadership approach.[17] His teaching echoes all three elements of Public Allies' bottom-up, responsibility- and values-based approach to leadership.

Ganz begins by asking, "Who is a leader?" He observes that for many this question calls to mind Dr. Martin Luther King Jr., Nelson Mandela, Jane Addams, Robert Kennedy, or Ronald Reagan. But, "in reality, we find leaders everywhere—linking together networks through which we work to achieve common purposes. In every community, church, classroom, and organization hundreds of people are doing the work of leadership without which these efforts would not survive." He then discusses what makes these people leaders: "Leaders accept responsibility for enabling others to achieve their purposes." They accept responsibility for engaging others, enabling them to work together to define and achieve desired goals. Leadership or individual empowerment always begins with accepting responsibility.

The field of community organizing, in Ganz's view, is all about building leadership. He describes organizers as those who "identify, recruit, and develop leadership; build community around leadership; and build power out of community." Organizers develop new relationships out of old ones, sometimes by linking one person to another and sometimes by linking whole networks of people together. Organizers motivate action by building relationships with people and helping "deepen people's understanding of who they are, what they want, and why they want it: their values." Organizers then challenge them to act with others on behalf of shared values and interests. In sum, organizers build community by building leaders and leadership and enhancing those leaders' skills, values, and commitments.

This definition draws a straight line to Public Allies' definition of leadership. Public Allies, in essence, acts as an organizer—recruiting, developing, and linking leaders on the basis of the commitments they make to their communities, their constituencies, and their values. The traditional work of organizing, based on models of distributed leadership (that is, leadership among many people) and of shared values and purposes, has become more and more relevant to definitions of leadership in other fields.

Robert Greenleaf, *Servant Leadership*

Robert Greenleaf, born in 1904, worked for decades building leaders at AT&T and learning from and mentoring leaders in business, philanthropy, higher education, and other fields. His pioneering *Servant Leadership* was published in 1977 and begins with the core conviction that leaders are servants first, and that when people feel that their leaders are genuinely interested in serving them, they will dedicate themselves to a common cause.

Greenleaf was one of the first to challenge notions of leadership based on power and authority and to posit a more populist vision for leadership development, one based on leaders' legitimacy in the eyes of followers.

Greenleaf's thesis echoes Alexis de Tocqueville and even community organizers with respect to the role of citizens and associations: "Caring for persons, the more able and the less able serving each other, is the rock upon which the good society is built."[18] Because so many urgent problems are the results of individual failures and leadership failures, the only way to change society, he believed, is to "produce enough people who will change it."[19] He believed that the essence of leadership is "going out ahead and showing the way: *I will go, come with me*."[20] He focused more on the qualities of leadership than on its values, but he recognized that leadership qualities are undergirded by values. Leaders must be attuned to their environment, must listen first, and must practice empathy and acceptance.

Greenleaf himself was attuned to signals coming from an increasingly diverse population, and to the need for leadership to emerge from communities. He predicted in 1977 that racially and economically diverse leaders would emerge on their own over the next thirty years, without the help of the privileged elite. He added that "today's privileged, who will live into the twenty-first century, will find it interesting if they can abandon their present notions of how they can best serve their less-favored neighbor and wait and listen until the less favored find their own enlightenment, then define their needs in their own way and, finally, state clearly how they want to be served."[21] Quoting Paulo Freire's *Pedagogy of the Oppressed*, he warned of leaders who believe that their job is to define the needs of others and fill them rather than to engage and work together with others as fellow community members—an observation still very relevant today.

Greenleaf was truly a pioneer in pivoting leadership development from being about the exercise of power and privilege to being about serving others and practicing values that engage others. He was the first to propose that one could build influence by serving and supporting others, not just by holding a hierarchical position over them. Leaders serve others instead of directing them. He also recognized the need for community building to solve problems and, just as important, he paved the way for the belief that leadership is something in which many people can and must participate at all levels of society. Greenleaf's work inspired us at Public Allies to believe that service is a great vehicle for developing leaders, and that values are essential to developing leaders with an orientation to service.

James Kouzes and Barry Posner, *The Leadership Challenge*

In 1995, when Public Allies opened our site in Silicon Valley, we were incredibly lucky to have Barry Posner, dean of the business school at Santa Clara University, chair our local advisory board. Posner had just coauthored, with management consultant Jim Kouzes, one of the most influential and best-selling books of all time on leadership, *The Leadership Challenge*. Kouzes and Posner surveyed more than fifty thousand leaders and followers about the best moments of leadership they had experienced. This research proved that leadership "isn't the private reserve of a few charismatic men and women, but a process ordinary people use when they're bringing forth the best from themselves and others."[22] Leadership is not about a position, but about having the courage and spirit to move from whatever place you are in to make a difference, learning along the way from overcoming obstacles and mistakes. Good leadership is a universal and learnable process.

Kouzes and Posner define leadership as "the art of mobilizing others to want to struggle for shared aspirations," and they emphasize that great leadership is not mobilizing people to struggle but mobilizing them to *want* to struggle *with you as their leader*.[23] That desire comes from the values a leader exemplifies in practice. Leaders must know their constituents—their dreams, hopes, aspirations, visions, and values—breathing life into the hopes and desires of others and helping them become leaders, too. A leader builds relationships: "Without constituents, a prospective leader is all alone, taking no one anywhere. Without leaders, constituents have no energizer to ignite their passions, no example to follow, no compass by which to be guided."[24]

The model they offer for being a leader people want to follow is a learnable set of ten commitments organized into five core practices that will inspire others to want to struggle, with you as their leader:[25]

- Challenge the process
  1. Search out challenging opportunities to change, grow, innovate, and improve.
  2. Experiment, take risks, and learn from the accompanying mistakes.
- Inspire a shared vision
  3. Envision an uplifting and ennobling future.
  4. Enlist others in a common vision by appealing to their values, interests, hopes, and dreams.
- Enable others to act
  5. Foster collaboration by promoting cooperative goals and building trust.
  6. Strengthen people by giving power away, providing choice, developing competence, assigning critical tasks, and offering visible support.
- Model the way
  7. Set the example by behaving in ways that are consistent with shared values.
  8. Achieve small wins that promote consistent progress and build commitment.

- Encourage the heart
    9. Recognize individual contributions to the success of every project.
    10. Celebrate team accomplishments regularly.

In many ways, Kouzes and Posner extended and, with rigorous research, proved Greenleaf's assertions that more leaders are needed, that leadership has to come from many places, and that leadership is about who you are and how you lead, not just about what you accomplish. Barry Posner advised us on our leadership approach and curriculum. He helped us clarify our belief in leadership as a shared practice and in values as the outcome of our leadership curriculum. His advice helped us shift our emphasis from developing nonprofit leadership *skills* to developing leadership *values*. Although we do also train people in professional skills, our leadership values are the core outcome of our curriculum.

Frances Hesselbein and Eric Shinseki, *Be Know Do*

Funders and partners have often asked Public Allies why we focus more on leadership values than on leadership skills—specifically, nonprofit management skills. We often used to answer with ideas from our roots in organizing, but when a board member suggested some leadership books to help us make our case, we were surprised to find that the one that best described our model was about the U.S. Army.

In *Be Know Do: Leadership the Army Way*, Frances Hesselbein and General Eric Shinseki (USA Ret.) present the army's unique approach to building leadership.* The reality of the army is that it depends on "the ability of leaders at all levels to inspire and lead,

---

* Frances Hesselbein, the legendary Girl Scouts leader, is CEO of the Leader to Leader Institute (formerly the Peter Drucker Foundation); Eric Shinseki, a retired army general, is currently serving as secretary of veterans affairs in the Obama administration.

often under the most harrowing conditions and unimaginable levels of stress."[26] Everyone must lead. Anyone who influences others, motivating them to action or influencing their thinking or decisions, is a leader, and so everyone in the army is at some point both a leader and a follower. The army can't import leadership from outside, and so it must grow its own.

The authors acknowledge the surprise that civilians like myself must feel when we realize that our stereotype of the army's "command and control" leadership model is not merely outdated but just plain wrong. They define leadership as "influencing people by providing purpose, direction, and motivation while operating to accomplish the mission and inspiring an organization. . . . Leadership transforms, in essence, human potential into effective performance."[27] That does not sound like command and control.

They argue that leadership values must come before skills and action: "Many people naively think that leadership is a matter of a set of skills that the leader uses on other people: how to influence others, how to inspire others, how to rally others to a cause."[28] They criticize most leadership development in the corporate sector as the inculcation of management skills rather than leadership practices, and they argue that the corporate sector wrongly sees attention to the personal development of the leader as "soft." Leadership really starts with a focus on oneself and on building the character that will lead people to want to follow. Leaders of the future will not focus on "how to do it" but on "how to be." No knowledge or skills will make up for a lack of character, and so "be, know, do" is the correct sequence in the process of developing leadership. Hesselbein and Shinseki describe these three components as follows:[29]

- *Be: the character of a leader.* As a leader, you must first make sure your own house is in order, and you must cultivate the key values that will inspire and persuade people to follow you. The authors quote a set of values from Kouzes and Posner's *The*

Leadership Challenge—being honest, competent, forward-looking, and inspiring.

• *Know: the competence of a leader.* The authors outline four sets of skills: interpersonal (coaching, teaching, motivating, team building), conceptual (thinking creatively; reasoning analytically, critically, and ethically), technical (job-related abilities), and tactical (the combination of skills appropriate to a role, responsibility, or mission).

• *Do: character and competence underlie everything a leader does.* Leaders act, they do—they bring together everything they are, everything they believe, and everything they know how to do, and they provide purpose, direction, and motivation to others.

The Public Allies model is firmly rooted in the "be" of leadership. In our leadership-development program, we spend much more time helping leaders explore their personal missions, their life stories, their values, and how they want to *be* as leaders than on what they *do* as nonprofit and community leaders. We also offer the Allies training in many skills, of course, such as fundraising, volunteer coordination, planning, and public speaking, but we believe that those skills must rest on a foundation of values. We believe that too many leadership programs focus on skills and networks, and that too few build the foundation on which skills must rest. To illustrate, consider how one of our site directors, Tonya Mantilla, responded to a visiting donor's concern about the lack of "hard skills" in our curriculum: "Are most of the challenges you've had with colleagues or on boards the result of skills or of values and behaviors?" The donor grasped what Tonya meant right away. The sequence of "be" before "know" and "do" applies to community leadership as much as to leadership in the army.

Bill George, *Authentic Leadership* and *True North*

One night, while catching up on e-mail very late, I turned on *Charlie Rose* and chanced upon Bill George, the former CEO of

Fortune 500 medical device maker Medtronic and now a professor at Harvard Business School. He spoke about how great leaders often emerge from "crucible moments"—difficult and even tragic times that test a leader to his core but result in a transformation of his purpose and an acceleration of his development. He described his own experience overcoming the sudden loss of his mother and of his fiancée shortly before their planned wedding, and he talked about how those tragic experiences opened his heart and led him to think more profoundly about his own purpose and values. He then described similar personal and professional tragedies in the lives of other prominent leaders and talked about how they had gained purpose, values, and insights from their experiences.

Identifying with the theme of "crucible moments" in my own life and in the stories of so many Allies, I picked up George's two books, *Authentic Leadership* and *True North*, and appreciated their lessons about values and leadership. George focuses on the private sector, and, although his lessons are universal, he begins by bemoaning the ego, greed, short-term thinking, and lack of quality leadership that pervade executive suites, and he argues that leaders are needed who have integrity, a deep sense of purpose, clear values, and a commitment to enduring change. Echoing Robert Greenleaf, George believes that authentic leaders desire to serve others first, empowering the people they lead to make a difference. Such leaders are guided by qualities of the heart, by passion and compassion, not by money, power, or prestige. This does not mean that leaders of institutions don't make hard choices, such as choices about layoffs, terminations, budget cuts, or changes in strategic direction, but they come to those choices and decisions with their values as their guide.

George notes the following characteristics of authentic leaders:[30]

1. They understand their purpose and are passionate about it.
2. They practice solid values that underlie their behavior.
3. They lead with the heart by showing compassion for others.

4. They establish connected relationships.
5. They demonstrate self-discipline by being consistent.

George argues that leaders lose their way and become inauthentic when they focus on external gratification rather than internal satisfaction, reject honest critics, fear failure, or feel entitled. The authentic leader accepts her faults as well as her strengths, developing a leadership style consistent with her own personality and character, and adapting her style to the demands of each situation, without losing her center.

George expounds further on this theme in *True North*, which resulted from interviews with 125 leaders about the "crucible moments" that had shaped their purposes, values, and motivations. He shows how leadership emerges from life stories, and how the painful moments and mistakes are often the most powerful teachers. He constructs a "compass" for helping leaders be at their best:[31]

- *Self-awareness (center)*: What is my story? What are my strengths and development needs?
- *Principles and values (north)*: What are my most deeply held values? What principles guide my leadership?
- *Motivations (east)*: What motivates me? How do I balance external and internal motivations?
- *Support team (south)*: Who are the people I can count on (family, friends, mentors) to guide and support me along the way?
- *Integrated life (west)*: How can I integrate all aspects of my life—community and friends, family life, personal life, professional life—so I can be a whole person?

George's thinking on leadership demonstrates that a values-based model of leadership is as important for corporate leaders as it is for community leaders. Like Hesselbein and Shinseki, George begins with who you are as a leader: What is your story, and what are your values?

He also points out that big obstacles often make great leaders, and that great leaders have very often failed many times before succeeding. Our fallibility is a reality. Those who have faced obstacles in becoming leaders, or who have failed major leadership tests along the way, can take heart and use these experiences to strengthen their purpose, values, and skills. At Public Allies, we begin with life stories so we can understand our own and others' backgrounds, motivations, values, and crucible moments. We also help Allies recognize that our values of continuous learning and improvement exist because Allies have to persevere through many challenges and failures on their leadership journeys, and integrity means being authentic and guided by values.

Susan Komives and Wendy Wagner, *Leadership for a Better World*

An "ensemble" of leadership scholars and directors of university-based leadership programs met for two years to create a social change–based model for leadership, answering two questions:

1. What is the intended impact of leadership development for university students?
2. What do students need to know and be able to do to achieve that impact?

Leadership for a Better World was written by that ensemble and edited by Susan Komives and Wendy Wagner of the National Clearinghouse for Leadership Programs at the University of Maryland–College Park. The book is geared to college students and those who teach them. The contributors' and editors' thorough research reinforces many of the core aspects of the Public Allies program.

Like others, Komives and Wagner point to Greenleaf as the pioneer who pivoted the field from "great man" and "command and control" definitions of leadership to more populist, values-based concepts. They argue that current theory emphasizes values that engage people to work together for change, and that it embraces a nonhierarchical approach. This approach "expands the number of potential leaders working to create change, while simultaneously transforming the process by which leadership is exercised."[32] This is essentially what Public Allies means when we talk about changing the face (the "who") and the practice (the "how") of leadership.

The contributors to the volume define leadership as a dynamic, collaborative, values-based process grounded in relationships and intending positive social change. This definition holds several assumptions: that leadership is about effecting positive change on behalf of others, that it is collaborative, that it represents a process rather than formal positions, that it is values-based, that it is inclusive and accessible to anyone, and that community involvement and service are powerful vehicles for developing leadership.[33] The leadership research discussed in the book shows that leadership is something in which everyone can engage. Leadership is not about one's intellect or charisma but about the willingness to step up and act, without waiting for the perfect circumstances, the perfect cause, or perfect knowledge.[34]

The research compiled by Komives and Wagner clearly shows leadership not as a style or a recipe to be mastered but as a practice that can be learned and developed. Their model describes two primary goals of leadership development:[35]

1. Building self-knowledge (understanding one's own talents, values, and interests)
2. Leadership competence (the capacity to mobilize oneself and others to work collaboratively)

They work from the assumption that leadership can be developed by anyone, and they conclude that a values-based model offers a framework for working well with others, which is the core of leadership. They argue that values are critical because change—the result of leadership—is inherently neither good nor bad but is also not neutral. People will be better or worse off as a result of change, and therefore change inevitably involves active or passive resistance. But the values of a leader can create the transformational and sustainable change that people embrace, and to which they adapt.[36]

Along with research, examples, and exercises, Komives and Wagner offer a model that outlines seven values:[37]

1. Citizenship
2. Common purpose
3. Collaboration
4. Controversy with civility
5. Consciousness of self
6. Congruence
7. Commitment

These align well with Public Allies' core values. Komives and Wagner's and their contributors' rigorous research again backs up what we have learned from our own experience: leadership is a process, not a position; it means taking responsibility to work with others on common goals, and it means practicing values.

The Bottom Line: Everyone Can Lead and Practice Leadership Values

The theories and books that we have just discussed are congruent with promoting a view of leadership as a process in which many people can engage, as the act of taking responsibility for working with others on common goals, and as the practice of values. There is agreement from many quarters—community organizers, the academy, the U.S. Army, and business—that everyone can lead, and that effective leaders begin by developing their own purposes, values, and ability to work with and motivate others effectively. But who is developing values among our leaders?

Most leadership programs still focus on "the leader" as a person in charge—a manager or supervisor. They emphasize the "know" and the "do" of the U.S. Army's paradigm, maybe touching briefly on the "be." They prepare people for positional "leadership," emphasizing the knowledge and skills of management, not the purposes and values that ought to underlie a leader's actions. Our culture still emphasizes heroic leadership, whether looking back at history or propping up celebrity leaders today, and it rewards ego, self-promotion, and greed more than purpose, values, and impact. This tendency even infects the social service sector, where nonprofit leaders are often celebrated more in connection with money raised, media attention, and social contacts among powerful people than in connection with impacts achieved or courageously advocated for on behalf of communities. To be clear, I do not intend to disparage charismatic leaders (many consider me charismatic) but rather to emphasize that charisma and management skills are not enough and can backfire when a leader lacks purpose, responsibility, and values—the "north" point on Bill George's compass.

Values are not just "soft" skills. They are the essence of what makes people work well together. Values drive productivity in any endeavor. The army gets that, and the corporate sector increasingly gets it. Jim Collins, author of the business classic *Good to Great*, describes the leaders who have built the best companies as those who possess a paradoxical blend of professional boldness and personal humility, and who are driven by values first.[38] They probably become Collins's "level 5" leaders (those who face brutal facts while maintaining a pragmatic hope that they will prevail) after experiencing the "crucible moments" that Bill

George has written about, times that help leaders produce a new clarity of purpose, possibility, limitations, and values. These values have even been reinforced by Manpower International, the largest employment agency in the world, in a recent report on the talent gap that exists in the workforce.[39] Manpower's report shows that the attributes workers will need most in the future include collaboration, inclusiveness, continuous learning, and integrity. If these attributes are embraced first as values, the relevant skills follow and become consistent in practice.

This is why Public Allies built our leadership-development model on five core values as learning outcomes that Allies must demonstrate in order to graduate from our program. These values can be practiced by anyone. We find that most leadership-development programs continue to reinforce privilege in terms of who attains and maintains leadership, that they facilitate closed social networks among those already in leadership positions, and that they focus on what they are doing or have done, not on their underlying purposes, values, and practice. The 3,800 young leaders who have completed our program have developed their leadership through service. They have clarified their purposes and focused on developing themselves as leaders by practicing clearly articulated values that help them engage with others more productively.

The five values we have identified—recognizing and mobilizing community assets, connecting across cultures, facilitating collaborative action, continuously learning and improving, and being accountable—help leaders build the capacity of communities to solve problems. They allow leaders to build other leaders, connect individuals and groups that haven't yet worked together, ensure that new voices come to the table, identify resources and solutions that others don't yet see, consider new options, ensure effective results, and more. But to lead with these values, Allies know that they have to step up to the plate. Leadership begins with taking responsibility for leading others toward a common goal. That responsibility is the subject of the next chapter.

Key Ideas and Lessons

1. The reality that everyone can lead and that leadership at all levels is needed for change has been demonstrated clearly throughout American history.
2. Because of increasing diversity, new technologies, and the rise of a new generation, more collaborative and more inclusive approaches to leadership are required.
3. Over the past forty years, leadership theory across disciplines has consistently pointed to leadership as being about actions that many people can take, about taking responsibility for working with others toward common goals, and about practicing values that engage people to work together effectively.

Reflections

- What are some leadership books you've read or leadership theories you've learned about? How do they align with or differ from the examples provided in this chapter?
- Consider how you have thought about leadership over time. Did you think leadership was something that could be practiced by anyone, or did you think it was something only people in positions of authority could practice?
- Looking back at your life, can you find examples of leadership—things you've done, participated in, or watched others do that you now see as leadership but did not see as leadership at the time?

4

THE RESPONSIBILITY OF LEADERSHIP

Lisa Sullivan: "We Are the Ones We Have Been Waiting For"

I first heard the phrase "We are the ones we have been waiting for" from my mentor, friend, and former Public Allies board member Lisa Sullivan, who said it often. She got it from June Jordan's "Poem for South African Women."[1] Its origins are often attributed to a Hopi proverb: "It is time to speak your truth. Create your community. And do not look outside yourself for the leader. We are the ones we've been waiting for." As I heard Barack Obama repeat this phrase on the campaign trail in 2008, I wondered if he had learned it from Lisa when they participated in Robert Putnam's two-year seminar on civic engagement, which led to Putnam's book *Bowling Alone*.[2]

Another participant in that seminar, the faith-based social justice leader Reverend Jim Wallis, dedicated the last chapter of his book *God's Politics* to Lisa: "When people would complain, as they often do, that we don't have any leaders today or would ask where the Martin Luther Kings are now, Lisa would get angry. 'We're the ones we have been waiting for,' she would declare. Lisa was a person of faith. And hers was a powerful call to leadership and responsibility and a deep affirmation of hope."[3]

In 2001, when Lisa died of pulmonary hypertension at the tragically young age of forty, she was eulogized by Marian Wright

Edelman and others as a mentor, organizer, institution builder, applied intellectual, and servant leader. She was first and foremost a leadership multiplier—one who called on and supported thousands of others to take responsibility and act on the problems they saw in their communities or in the broader society.

The inflection point in Lisa's leadership journey arrived by serendipity. Lisa grew up in a working-class environment in Washington, D.C., and her parents pushed her hard on education. She practically lived at the Martin Luther King Jr. Public Library at 9th and G streets and was there one summer night after returning from Clark College in Atlanta when she chanced upon a flyer—the civil rights activist Joanne Grant would be screening her new film *Fundi: The Ella Baker Story* that night at the library. Lisa was the youngest person at the screening, and she listened intently as Grant and others shared their memories of Baker. She slipped out with a clear vision and a commitment to follow the example of Ella Baker.[4]

Baker had been committed to grassroots democracy and decentralized leadership. She saw women, poor people, and youth as the leaders who had been the backbone of the civil rights movement. Lisa took Baker's example to heart. She studied political and social movements at Clark College and Yale University while also increasing her activism. In New Haven, while in graduate school, she built a leadership network among young people that registered five thousand youth voters and elected the city's first African American mayor. She then advanced to the national stage as field director at the Children's Defense Fund, creating the Black Student Leadership Network, which trained and supported over seven hundred young leaders of color in political and grassroots organizing. From there she went to the Rockefeller Foundation to help create its Next Generation Leadership Program, a comprehensive educational fellowship program that supported 120 young leaders over five years. Her lessons from these experiences culminated in the creation of the Local Initiative Support, Training, and Education Network (LISTEN). LISTEN trained, supported, and networked with grassroots leaders, especially young leaders of color and those from poor and marginalized communities. LISTEN also convened established leaders from philanthropy, academia, nonprofits, business, and government to better engage and support this new generation of leadership, recognizing that effective leaders have to cross boundaries effectively.

Lisa left behind a legacy of thousands of leaders whom she had cultivated and developed, and she mentored people across boundaries of race, class, and age.*

Lisa believed in me and so many other young leaders, and she had very high expectations of us. She saw leadership as encompassing tremendous responsibility. If you were going to step up, you had to be prepared to make sacrifices, to be criticized—even attacked—and to persevere despite inevitable obstacles. She challenged us to look inside ourselves—to clarify our purposes, our values, and our knowledge of what contributions we could make and where we needed help. She believed that a solid inner core was necessary before anyone could make outward change. She cautioned against being moved by anger—not against feeling anger, but against organizing on the basis of anger. Such anger places accountability on others rather than on ourselves. Instead of pointing fingers, she encouraged leaders to look at their responsibilities first. She believed that leaders had to be able to cross boundaries of race, class, and ideology in the interest of their constituents, even if their peers saw them as traitors or sellouts. She encouraged us to have many mentors, reasoning that leaders need people who can help them reflect on and share experience, who will have their backs, and who will tell them truths that may be hard to hear.

At her funeral, hundreds of diverse people filled the church—middle schoolers, college students, hip-hop activists, and major nonprofit and philanthropic leaders. It was a testament to the breadth of her mentorship. As we acknowledged the load her heart had borne, many of us felt ashamed that we weren't doing more. Just as Lisa believed in us and mentored us, she demanded that we take

* I was fortunate to be one of them. After I met Lisa at the Wingspread Conference, she sent me a personal note: "I really enjoyed meeting you and know that one day soon I'll read in *The New York Times* or *The Washington Post* about the dynamic young leader from Wisconsin. Please stay in touch." I gratefully accepted her invitation, and she became a key mentor of mine for the next eight years. She recruited me into the Rockefeller Foundation's Next Generation Leadership Program as the second youngest person in that program, and probably the least experienced. She had great influence on my career as well as on my notions of leadership, social justice, diversity, and community.

fundamental responsibility for mentoring and supporting others, for multiplying our own leadership, and for using whatever privilege we had gained to help others advance with us. These lessons and her example constitute one of the chief inspirations for my leadership and had a major impact on the development of the Public Allies approach.

In Lisa's story, "We are the ones we have been waiting for" is both an invitation and a challenge. We don't have to wait for someone in a position of leadership to solve a problem. We don't have to wait until we have all the knowledge, answers, resources, or plans in place. When we see an opportunity to make a difference, in our communities or on larger public issues that concern us, we can take responsibility for doing it. That responsibility implies a level of accountability to ourselves and to others that we will do our best to achieve the goal we establish. It means also taking responsibility for the means we use in working with others to achieve a goal. Such responsibility is the basis of our democracy—citizens taking action to work with their neighbors to solve problems. These are the responsibilities Lisa taught and exemplified so well—the responsibility to step up, the responsibility to work with and develop others, and the responsibility we have as citizens.*

Stepping Up

In the tradition of Lisa Sullivan, Public Allies is a leadership multiplier. We believe that everyone can lead. This doesn't mean that we think that everyone should lead in every circumstance, or that there shouldn't be followers. As the U.S. Army teaches, everyone is at times a leader and a follower.[5] Leadership is not an entitlement; it is the result of a making a courageous choice. Leadership is possible for all of us, but only when we choose to take responsibility to mobilize people and resources toward a

* Again, I am using the term *citizen* in its philosophical sense, not to denote a legal status.

common goal and own the consequences of that choice. When we take initiative to seize an opportunity or solve a problem with others, we are leading, whether or not we are in a formal leadership position. It is a combination of personal responsibility (I will step up and be accountable) and social responsibility (I will work with others on common goals that will make positive change for others).

We teach our Allies that with every choice we make, we assume responsibility for the consequences—intended or unintended—of that choice. We walk Allies through ten principles of personal responsibility:

1. You and only you are responsible for your choices.
2. You are responsible for your thoughts and feelings.
3. You are responsible for the direction of your life.
4. No one else is responsible for your choices.
5. Groups and organizations you belong to are responsible for the well-being of the whole, not individual well-being, which is each person's own responsibility.
6. You must stop blaming others for the outcomes of your choices and understand the logic of why you blame them.
7. You must support yourself first.
8. You are ultimately not responsible for others.
9. Responsibility does not appear by itself—you must find structure for what you want to do.
10. Stop being angry with people in the past who let you down; no one is stopping you now from making choices now.

These are some consequences of not accepting responsibility:

- We can become dependent on others for positive reinforcement.
- We can become continually frustrated and unpleasant about how we have been unfairly treated.

- We can become scared to ever take risks.
- We can become continually unsuccessful in our endeavors and relationships.
- We can become physically and emotionally unhealthy.
- We can become responsible for other people.
- We can become distrustful and refuse to be vulnerable.

One way Public Allies encourages such responsibility is through our assessment processes. Allies participate in 360-degree reviews, in which their fellow team members, their supervisors at their placements, and the Public Allies program manager evaluate them. Peers and supervisors comment on Allies' enactment of our five core values: their ability to recognize and mobilize community assets, connect across cultures, facilitate collaborative action, continuously learn and improve, and be accountable to those they work with and those they serve. The Allies are given the results of their 360-degree reviews while sitting in a circle with those who have reviewed them. Each Ally acknowledges the feedback, asks questions, and then makes a commitment to using the feedback in his or her continued development. You can't ignore your shortcomings or challenges in this environment; you must take responsibility for improving.

At the end of the year, Allies also demonstrate how they've met the learning outcomes of our program in a Presentation of Learning before their peers, supervisors, staff, and community leaders. Each Ally begins by preparing a portfolio with samples of his or her work and impact, a portfolio that includes a series of ten *I used to be . . . Now I am . . .* statements that document ways they have grown. After presenting what they have learned and how they will use these lessons in the future, Allies take questions (Chapter Eight describes this process in greater detail).

Making a choice to step up and own the consequences of our choices is a courageous act. It means taking risks and being vulnerable. To take action is to open ourselves to being challenged, questioned, second-guessed, and called out on our mistakes.

When a leadership opportunity arises, it often doesn't feel like a choice. It is a calling, maybe even an adrenaline rush. We feel a passion inside, and the commitment is easy. We don't just want to take action, we *need* to take action. That passion might come from our moral values, from a personal experience we or others we care about have had with an issue, or from a belief that we have the right skills, knowledge, talent, and time to make a difference. Whatever leads us to take that step, we take it, regardless of how ready we are. When I drove home from the Wingspread Conference and decided to start Public Allies Milwaukee, it did not feel like a choice; it was something I felt deep inside that I had to do. It never occurred to me that I had no experience at all. I had never run a nonprofit, had never created or implemented a program, had never managed anyone, had never written a grant proposal, had never read a financial statement, and had never created or worked with a board. But I accepted responsibility for making all that happen and doing whatever it took to deliver. And that meant making mistakes and learning constantly along the way.

When I look back, though, I can see that there were small leadership impulses along the way that hinted at what I could do—the can drive for Sister María Rosa in seventh grade, the creation of a high school Amnesty International club, the leadership of a twelve-step meeting, and my election to lead the College Democrats at the University of Wisconsin–Milwaukee. I can see the same evolution in Lisa Sullivan's journey as she started out leading on campus and among peers, then leading local youth, then building programs to institutionalize the leadership development she had done informally. Public Allies D.C. alumnus Paul Griffin's story echoes this evolution, too.

Paul Griffin

As an Ally in 1993–1994, Paul Griffin was an energetic, bright, fast-talking theater graduate from Indiana University with short red hair and a slight beard. He was placed at the No-Neck Monsters Theater Company, which was doing community arts and theater programming for youth in Washington, D.C. At the time, Washington was considered the murder capital of America, and Paul realized two things—that the youth program had much greater potential and needed a bigger vision to be successful, and that the theater company would not be capable of sustaining that vision.

We've experienced situations like this before, where an Ally's host organization is on shaky ground. Often the Ally gives up or sits back and waits for the staff at Public Allies to find him or her something new. Not Paul. He met with the Public Allies staff, presented his vision for a new organization, and talked about his desire to bring it to life. He was connected with Creative Response, a group that was interested in his vision. As a result, City at Peace (later renamed the Possibility Project) was born.

Paul's vision was to engage young people in service, help them identify issues in their lives and communities, and then create musical theater from their experiences: "I went to the Public Allies staff every day and asked 'What do I do now?' I really didn't know what I was getting into," Paul says. "I just had to do it. I went to Public Allies' board chair and asked her to help me build a board. I used the only resources I knew at the time—Public Allies—to make it happen. The Allies became my volunteers, staff, and board members. There was no chance of me not doing it. Public Allies gave me the awareness I could lead, that I had the capacity to do this."[6]

Paul incorporated the program during his Ally term. Today Paul's program operates in five U.S. cities as well as in Israel and South Africa. The Possibility Project's productions have been performed in front of forty thousand audience members, been seen on ABC and HBO, and improved the cultural competence, civic competence, self-confidence, and academic performance of over two thousand youths. In Paul's programs, 99 percent of the youths, who are selected not for their talent but for their commitment, have gone on to complete high school or a GED, and 92 percent have gone on to college. The Possibility Project is now also specifically working with teens in foster care in New York City.

Each step we take, each leadership call we answer, builds confidence and prepares us to answer bigger and bigger calls. Dr. Charles McKinney's analysis of civil rights leadership (see Chapter Three) is echoed by Susan Komives and Wendy Wagner's *Leadership for a Better World*—that one of the dangers of the heroic leadership stories we see so often is that they make us think we can't act as leaders ourselves.[7] We think we have to start big, and we forget that change requires leadership at all levels. Heroic stories lead us to forget that many famous leaders emerged over time. Peter Block argues that one of our biggest problems as a society is the romanticizing of positional leaders, whereby we see leaders as "cause" and everyone else as "effect."[8] When we see accountability only at the top, we limit our ability to create an alternative future. We place ourselves in the position of being passive, entitled clients and customers. The research is clear and consistent: leadership is something in which all of us can engage. We don't have to lead by being in charge of an organization or a group. We can start by influencing the people around us.

Leadership is not about our credentials or charisma but about our commitment and credibility. Commitment, in the words of Block, is the willingness to make promises with no expectations from others in return. The moment a commitment is contingent on other events or people, it is not an authentic commitment.[9] James Kouzes and Barry Posner have written a great deal on the credibility of leaders, and they believe that leadership comes down to honesty, enthusiasm, and competence: "We want leaders who are credible . . . . We must believe that their word can be trusted, that they'll do what they say, that they're personally excited and enthusiastic about the direction in which we're headed, and that they have the knowledge and skill to lead. We have come to refer to this as the First Law of Leadership: If we don't believe in the messenger, we won't believe the message."[10] We might not always know all that we need to know. But our commitment to learn what we need to learn and mobilize all available resources will tell those we are trying to influence that we are worthy of their own commitment and effort.

All of us have some sphere of influence in which we have credibility that gives us the ability to influence others to join an effort we are committed to. This is where the personal responsibility that we take when we step up and lead is connected to social responsibility, and to our desire to better not just ourselves but also other people, our communities, and even our planet. Here are three places where anyone can get started influencing others:

1. *Home*. We can take our first steps at home, making decisions that influence our family members and close friends. We can make lifestyle and consumer choices that reflect our values and have social impact, such as reducing our energy consumption, supporting neighborhood businesses, researching the social responsibility of products, mentoring neighborhood kids, donating to causes, and walking or bicycling instead of driving. We can also influence those closest to us by educating them about issues, sharing information, and inviting them to attend public meetings and events with us.

2. *Community*. We can work to bring neighbors together to address local issues. We may organize neighbors around a local problem, such as an unsafe intersection, a troublesome tavern, vacant land that could be a community garden or playground, a school that needs tutors and supplies, a health fair that needs to be promoted, or a school board or city council issue that needs citizens' input or influence. We can volunteer and encourage others to join us in serving others and our community. It can feel presumptuous or risky to ask for help, but we usually learn that many people share our concerns, and for some of our friends and neighbors, our own involvement is the only reason they need for getting involved.

3. *Causes*. We can address larger public issues by writing letters to the editor; working on legislation; organizing petitions, protests and boycotts; blogging; raising money; joining membership groups that advocate and lobby for policy changes; and advocating to public officials directly. Online tools and social networks make these efforts easier and their potential impact even greater.

Where you start doesn't matter; what matters is *that* you start. You can accept responsibility within the spheres of influence that are most comfortable for you, and your leadership will grow with each experience. The contributions of many leaders are essential to any change. In the civil rights movement, for example, there were people who courageously stood up for their rights, set a moral example for others, or influenced their families to make sacrifices for the cause. Others mobilized associations or took leadership roles with local groups to mobilize their neighbors. And then there were those who mobilized resources and support by donating money, forming groups, writing letters to the editor, advocating for legislation, and so on. Success was the result of action on the part of many leaders at different levels—all contributions are valuable and move us closer to the goal.

Stepping Up for Youth: Reggie Moore and Sharlen Bowen Moore

I first met Reggie Moore and Sharlen Bowen Moore when they were eighteen, before they were married. The three of us were among the honorees at a banquet honoring volunteers in Milwaukee. They have since become heroes of mine, and their leadership journey illustrates how leaders can emerge from anywhere to make a great difference.

They both got an early start. Sharlen Bowen, an immigrant from Jamaica, had an accent and struggled to fit in at school. Then, one day in fifth grade, she noticed an Asian American girl being teased and defiantly stuck up for her. She took the next step of asking an art teacher if they could do something at school to celebrate ethnic diversity. A cultural fair was created, and from this "crucible moment" Sharlen grew into an advocate for other youth.*

Reggie says that his inspiration started at home. "My Mom ran our house like a community organization. She had strong faith and practiced it by helping other families in the neighborhood, inviting homeless people in to shower and eat, providing food and tutoring to neighborhood kids, and demonstrating generosity in spite of how much or little we had."[11] That example inspired in Reggie a commitment to practice his faith by helping others at a young age. "No one ever told me I couldn't. I was blessed to meet positive people throughout my life who encouraged me even against the odds. Regardless of age, I see confidence and competence as both important, and if you have the confidence behind your purpose, you have to do what is necessary to build the competence to do it right."

Reggie and Sharlen met in high school and participated in the YMCA's Black Achievers Program. They immediately discovered a common commitment to helping other young people. After graduating from high school, they began studying education in college and created the Urban Outreach Association, where they recruited their peers to teach life and leadership skills at middle schools and high schools. Recognizing their talents and tenacity, I helped hire them to work for two different nonprofit organizations where I served as a board member.

After I had left for the national office, Public Allies Milwaukee hired Reggie to manage an initiative in partnership with the Greater Milwaukee Foundation, called the Milwaukee Youth Initiative. This was a community organizing effort that Reggie led, in which five youth organizers, all of whom were older than he was, worked in neighborhoods with youths to identify the opportunities and supports they and their peers needed to influence grant making by the foundation. This ambitious effort faltered when the young people's efforts ran counter to the interests of the larger youth agencies in the city and of the foundation's trustees.

When the youth Initiative was phasing out, I was reading the paper one morning and discovered that a new youth-organizing group was emerging—Urban Underground, founded by Reggie and Sharlen. A month before, there had been a mass arrest of teenagers in Milwaukee's Sherman Park neighborhood. The youths had been

*The term *crucible moment* comes from the work of Bill George; see Chapter Three.

"cruising" in neighborhoods, which meant, effectively, that large groups had been driving around and creating outdoor parties with each other, and one night the police barricaded a large area and arrested all of them. Reggie, upset that teens were misunderstood and had nowhere to go, organized a citywide meeting, bringing together youths, parents, residents, radio disc jockeys, youth workers, police, and others. "I saw what the young people around me needed, and rather than complain about what was missing, I chose to build it," he says, adding, "Too many youth programs simply strive to keep kids off the streets, prevent them from being 'bad.' They don't approach these young people as potential doctors or CEOs or senators or anything like that. Young people experience low expectations from adults in almost every facet of their everyday lives. They are defined by what they are not, and their goal is to be *not*—not a dropout, not a teen mom, not a criminal. At Urban Underground, we don't treat or fix young people. We support their potential, and we raise the bar for them."

Sharlen agrees: "I want young people to have the best opportunities to be successful, regardless of where they started. Recreation and tutoring are good, but I want to see youths use their minds and skills to help the community."

Over five hundred youths completed the year-long Urban Underground leadership program during its first decade, and they have mobilized young people around important local issues, including education, juvenile justice, racial profiling, domestic violence, reproductive health, and more. Each year, over eight hundred teenagers apply to Urban Underground. We've recruited many Allies from their ranks, and they have been some of our finest.

Public Allies served as the fiscal agent for Urban Underground for its first seven years. We know Reggie and Sharlen's tenacity, resourcefulness, and resilience as leaders. Their sense of mission never wavered, not even after they got married and began a family. I've seen them start a program year without enough funding and go without paychecks. I've seen them mobilize quickly when youth issues flared up in the community, regardless of capacity. Reggie even took a job with a foundation in another city, living there part-time, so that he could support his and Sharlen's work with Urban Underground. They've had unbelievable success against the odds and have been recognized by youth organizers nationally and by city leaders in Milwaukee. They have also gained much themselves.

Reggie says, "I've devoted myself to developing the leadership of others, and the collateral benefit has been that my own leadership has grown," and Sharlen adds, "You know what? If there is something to deal with in the community, it is up to me to be part of that solution. Not talking about it, not griping, but working for a solution."

Reggie and Sharlen's level of leadership and responsibility is an inspiration.

Working with Others

Reggie and Sharlen Moore, Paul Griffin, and Lisa Sullivan are all leadership multipliers. Each of them not only stepped up to lead but also expanded opportunities for others to lead, helping more people find the confidence, voice, and initiative to step up themselves. This is the same role that Public Allies plays. Kouzes and Posner argue that empowering others is the essence of leadership—enabling others to be in charge of their own lives, turning constituents into leaders.[12] If the first step of leadership is taking responsibility to mobilize others toward a common goal, then the second step is the actual mobilization and engagement of those people. Kouzes and Posner also observe that "a person with no constituents is not a leader, and people will not follow until they accept a vision as their own. Leaders cannot command commitment, only inspire it."[13]

Leadership is an inherently collaborative process, and our ability to collaborate effectively with others is essential to accomplishing our goals. If, like Robert Greenleaf, we believe that leadership is in service to those who follow us, then we have to be intentional about how we engage the people or constituencies we mobilize.[14] As leaders, we must be conscious not only of our progress toward goals but also of how we are achieving those goals—how we engage others' commitment, voices, and efforts. It is our commitment and credibility that make this possible, and it is our values and how we practice them that define our commitment and credibility. That is why values are so essential to leadership, and especially to leadership that is transformative. According to Komives and Wagner, commenting on the work of the historian James MacGregor Burns, "Burns's concept of transforming leadership espouses a relationship between leaders and followers in which each transforms the other. . . . the aim of leadership is not just to reach a goal, but also to transform leaders and followers into better, more self-actualized people."[15] This is how leadership multiplies. It is also essentially what Reggie Moore meant when he said, "I've devoted myself to developing the leadership of others, and the collateral benefit has been that my own leadership has grown."

This kind of leadership means that leaders must successfully recognize assets, collaborate, include, learn, and be accountable. It also means that visions and goals are not fixed in concrete but are really hypotheses that a leader will test and refine with followers. Leaders need input from people whose different strengths and perspectives will help achieve mutual goals. Kouzes and Posner argue that leadership is the art of mobilizing others to *want* to struggle for shared aspirations—leaders have to inspire shared visions that make people want to struggle with them.[16] Great leadership today is less about Moses coming down from Mount Sinai with commandments and more about Lao-Tzu, who said:

> *With the best of leaders,*
> *When the work is done,*
> *The project completed,*
> *The people all say*
> *"We did it ourselves."*[17]

We have an exercise at Public Allies for selecting our Allies each year. It's called the Fishbowl. After panel interviews, in which some combination of three staff members, alumni, and community leaders interview Ally candidates directly, the candidates are brought back in groups of eight or so and given a team exercise to do. (It is called the Fishbowl because the Public Allies staff introduces the exercise to the group and then sits on the outside of the group to observe, without offering coaching or help.) This process helps us identify whether leaders who might demonstrate competence in a panel interview are actually facilitative, collaborative, and inclusive or are perhaps instead dominating, arrogant, and so on. We always learn a great deal about people in this process. For example, I once had a candidate call me afterward to complain about not getting into Public Allies. "I don't get it," he said. "The panel really liked me—I could tell. And in the group exercise, I got the group to solve the puzzle." *He* got the group to solve the puzzle—that is not the kind of leadership we are looking for at Public Allies.

Such directive or heroic leadership is one of the pitfalls leaders often encounter, especially early on. Leaders may believe that they have to do it all, and that success rests only on their shoulders. They often become both heroes and martyrs for their causes. I struggled with this when I started Public Allies Milwaukee and was a very directive leader, driven by fear of failure and by the belief that I had to prove that I was worthy to lead by making everything appear perfect and by making no mistakes. I believed that I had to and could do it all. It was a horrible experience for everyone, myself included. Fortunately, I had colleagues and mentors who helped me out of the heroic leadership trap.

Heroic leaders believe that leadership means being in charge, having all the answers. Komives and Wagner list some of the pitfalls that new leaders often struggle with when working for social change:[18]

- Paternalism (thinking that I, the helper, know better than those I am helping)
- Assimilation (assuming that my community or my culture is better and that others just need to do things my way)
- Taking a deficit-based perspective (defining others and their communities only by their needs, and not seeing their assets)
- Seeking a magic bullet (believing in simple solutions to problems that are often complex and interrelated)

- Ignoring cultural differences (being ignorant of or devaluing other cultures)

When we are leading efforts, we must "replace notions of 'helping others' or 'fixing others' with a sense of being in *community* with others."[19] That is the approach that is needed today for effective leadership.

The Responsibility Virus

Perhaps the best analysis of the heroic leadership trap is the model that Roger Martin, dean of the Joseph L. Rotman School of Management at the University of Toronto, calls "the responsibility virus." Responsibility is the core of leadership, but it must be shared as we begin working with others for change. When one person takes on too much responsibility and others take on too little, a vicious cycle begins, and it constitutes another potential pitfall in leadership. According to Martin, "Take-charge leadership misapplied not only fails to inspire and engage, it produces passivity and alienation."[20] When leaders "assume 'heroic' responsibility for making critical choices, when their reaction to problems is to go it alone, work harder, and do more—with no collaboration and sharing of leadership—their 'heroism' is often their undoing."[21] We've all seen this before. I've been on both sides of it, especially the heroic side, and have learned to be more intentional about calibrating how much responsibility I take. Leaders can possibly win a few victories with such leadership, but they can't sustain anything because such victories rest on one person alone.

The Responsibility Virus is often set in motion when a leader sees a subordinate "flinch under pressure and responds by taking a disproportionate share of responsibility, prompting the subordinate to hesitate and become passive. The heroic leader reacts by leaping to fill the void. The passive employee retreats further, abdicating more responsibility, becoming distant, cynical, and lethargic. The leader, unable to cope with an impossible workload, becomes contemptuous and angry. A once-promising project becomes rudderless and spirals toward failure."[22]

I have seen this work the other way, too, when a subordinate does not ask for help, assumes responsibility beyond his or her capacity, fails to delegate, and begins a cycle that leaves peers and supervisors with few options—duplication of effort, micromanagement, or avoidance or termination of the person. These people set themselves up to fail and fail again, and then they often blame others for not supporting them. I have also seen people take on responsibility for others' issues as a personal cause, becoming self-designated advocates instead of encouraging others to take responsibility for addressing their own issues. It is a chicken-or-egg situation: Did the overbearing leader or the unresponsive follower initiate the virus? Either way, the vicious cycle harms both.

Martin contends that modern psychology would place the origin of the Responsibility Virus on the dread that we all have of doing the wrong thing and on the great lengths to which we will go to avoid making choices or even viewing ourselves as choosers. It is human nature to claim credit when things go well and to avoid blame when they go badly. He references the research of Chris Argyris, the Harvard Business School professor emeritus who has described the "governing values behind most human interactions"—we want to win, maintain control, avoid embarrassment, and stay rational.[23] Confronted by failure or the anticipation of failure, we often choose fight (seizing total responsibility) or flight (assuming no responsibility so that if we lose, it's not our fault). Martin offers useful tools to exit this vicious cycle and to clarify responsibilities, choices, and commitments.

The idea of the Responsibility Virus calls on leaders to pay attention to how much control we take, and also to how much responsibility followers take. Taking responsibility as a leader does not mean hoarding responsibility. We have to be thoughtful about how we create opportunities for others to lead as well. When we seize too much control and don't encourage and distribute some of the responsibility, we set ourselves up to fail. The goal is for leadership not to be a zero-sum proposition (with one person taking more and someone else consequently taking less) but a non-zero-sum proposition (with one person taking more but someone else also taking more) as both leaders and followers take on greater responsibility.

Making the Solution Bigger

Taking responsibility is tricky. It is proactive and solution-focused, and it makes us accountable. Taking responsibility is an act of courage; we don't wait for others, we take a risk and make the first move. We don't "social-work" a problem, trying to determine the chain of blame for what happened and how we feel about that; we make the choice to solve it. It is not cynical, accusatory, dismissive, or ambivalent to take responsibility. Often, when confronted by challenges or decisions we don't like, we complain, blame, or withdraw, but these are not leadership values or practices. Negativity can attract attention and sympathizers (cases in point: the news, and our nation's political discourse). Of course, we all get angry and oppose others' ideas, perspectives, or decisions. But we have a choice about what we *do* with those feelings. We always have choices. Another way of thinking about responsibility, in any conflict or challenge, is to realize that we are either making the problem bigger or making the solution bigger.

If we resign ourselves to an unsatisfactory status quo or wait for the other person (or a leader or a situation) to change, we are failing to take appropriate responsibility. This does not mean that others don't also have responsibility or may in fact be wrong. It just means that we must make sure we are doing what we are responsible for in every interaction or activity—keeping our side of the fence clean. If we talk behind someone's back, withholding feedback rather than sharing it, we make the problem bigger. If we disagree with a decision but remain silent and resentful, we make the problem bigger. If we complain that our city government doesn't care about schools but never go to school board meetings or advocate at city hall, we make the problem bigger. If we point fingers at a manager for his or her decisions but we've not offered direct feedback or viable alternatives, we make the problem bigger. If we don't like our elected officials but don't vote, we make the problem bigger. As Rita Dove, former U.S. poet laureate, once said, "There are times in life, when, instead of complaining, you do something about your complaints."[24]

Peter Block writes about accountability as the willingness to acknowledge that we have participated in creating, by commission or omission, the conditions we wish to see changed. He thinks every leader should begin by asking, "How have I contributed to creating the current reality?" He suggests that leaders think of themselves as the "cause" rather than the "effect" of decisions, circumstances, conflicts, and so on.[25] Block also dives deeper into this idea, alluding to the concepts of the philosopher Peter Koestenbaum in describing freedom as "the choice to be creator of our own experience and accept the unbearable responsibility that goes with that. Out of this insight grows the idea that perhaps the real task of leadership is to confront people with their freedom. This may be the ultimate act of love that is called for from those who hold power over others. Choosing our freedom is also the source of our willingness to choose to be accountable."[26] Holding ourselves and others accountable is critical to leadership, and it is what allows others to assume the responsibility of leadership. Leaders don't point a finger of blame at others unless we recognize that in so doing we point three fingers back at ourselves.

This lesson about making choices was learned in an unfortunate way by my colleague David McKinney, our vice president of programs, when he was an Ally in Milwaukee in 1997. David's placement was at a Boys and Girls Club, and after work one day, in the park adjoining the club, he was playing soccer tennis, which uses a soccer ball instead of a tennis ball and feet instead of racquets. Suddenly David heard what sounded like loud firecrackers near the street, and then he painfully realized that he had been hit by a bullet—which, fortunately, only grazed him. Regardless, it was a terrifying experience, and David, with some justification as the shooting victim, looked for others to take care of him and fix his problem. In David's words, "I wanted someone—some authority—to come in and fix everything. I had experiences with racial profiling and harassment by police, so I didn't think they were going to do anything for me. It was outside the Boys and Girls Club that I was shot, so I didn't think they were going to take care of me. I went to the Public Allies office and expected the staff to take care of me and, among other things, transfer me to a new placement where I would be safe. Instead, the staff asked, 'What are you going to do?' *What am I going to do?* I was shot! I wanted to be transferred. The staff argued that transferring me wouldn't solve the problem—it would just ignore the situation and transfer another resource away from the kids. I had an *Aha!* moment right then. I had a responsibility to make choices—a choice to stay and a choice to do something with the experience. I realized I could use this moment to connect with the youth around how they were experiencing violence in their neighborhood. The young people were dealing with it more than I had."[27]

Karla Radka's experience offers another useful example of this lesson. Family Services of Metro Orlando had partnered with Public Allies to open a site serving central Florida. Karla was hired as the executive director and got the program off to a beautiful start. Then, two months into the program, Family Services lost its state funding, which had contributed 90 percent of the organization's budget. It appeared that the organization was going to fold. Karla could have blamed the national office for picking a poor partner. She could have blamed the agency for losing its other funding. She could have approached the agency's

CEO and Public Allies' national office and demanded that we fix the problem. Instead, she assumed responsibility and set an amazing example for her Allies. She raised a grant to move the organization through the transition, received an offer of free rent, and secured interest from five potential partners—all in the course of a month. Public Allies Orlando found a new partner, Community Based Care of Central Florida, and continued its programs. Karla made the solution bigger.

David and Karla both realized their responsibility, and that allowed them to become involved in solutions rather than just being victims. It is this kind of responsibility that shifts us from the status of client to that of citizen—the status of someone committed to being responsible for making our communities better.

The Responsibility of Citizens

The Responsibility Virus writ large happens in our communities every day. When we wait for others to solve problems, when we criticize and blame others, or when we give up on making change, we feed the virus. As citizens step back, institutions—businesses and government as well as nonprofits and the professionals, experts, and positional leaders who populate them—step forward. We rely on outsiders to fix our problems, and we abnegate our role as producers of change. We relegate ourselves to being victims, clients, consumers, or spectators, not citizens.

John McKnight has devoted his career to challenging the way institutions and systems have replaced the role of citizens in communities and in our democracy. John is a community organizer who became the Midwest director of the U.S. Commission on Civil Rights in the 1960s before becoming the first and only tenured professor ever at Northwestern with no academic credential beyond a bachelor's degree. With his bushy beard, a twinkle in his eye, and a gift for storytelling, he exemplifies the capacities he believes are essential to community—kindness, hospitality, generosity, and cooperation. He has been an organizer and a teacher who has helped leaders and citizens around the world reconsider their own roles and responsibilities and the roles and responsibilities of institutions and systems.

Throughout his career, John has been a harsh critic of the role of institutions and systems in our communities and of how they have pushed citizens to the margins. His book *The Careless Society* includes an essay titled "Professionalized Service and Disabling Help," in which he shows how citizens have been turned into clients.[28] He argues that clients are defined by their needs, not recognized as people who are needed, and he claims that institutions and systems offer management, not care.

According to McKnight, the professionalization of service has had three disabling effects:

1. The service industry translates a need, which may be related to a condition, a want, or a right, into an unfortunate instance of personal emptiness or deficiency.
2. Professionals must then place this need *into* a client, isolating the need from its community context, thus distorting the individual's need and the professional's ability to meet it.
3. The professional definition of the concept of need leads to professional specialization, and rational systems are built to address isolated individual needs. The service systems say to people, "You are deficient. You are the problem. You have a collection of problems."

And systems respond to this dynamic ("you are the problem, we are the experts") in four ways:[29]

1. *I, the professional, am the answer*. "As you are the problem, the assumption is that I, the professional servicer, am the answer. You are not the answer. Your peers are not the answer. The political, social, and economic environment is not the answer. Nor is

it possible that there is no answer."[30] The relationship is within a system; it is managed for efficiency, not care, and the relationship is one-way.

2. *I know what you need.* Where there is a remedy, a need must be defined, and the professional is best at diagnosing need. There is an assumption that the client doesn't understand what he or she needs: "There is no greater power than the right to define the question. From that right flows a set of necessary answers. If the servicer can effectively assert the right to define the appropriate question, he has the power to determine the need rather than to meet the need."[31] In many ways, the professional develops a tool or technology and then must translate people's complex lives into a simple need that this tool or technology can meet.

3. *You can't understand what you need.* Professionals then code the problem and the solution into language that is incomprehensible to citizens: "While it is clearly disabling to be told you can't decide whether you have a problem and how it can be dealt with, the professional imperative compounds the dilemma by demonstrating that you couldn't understand the problem or solution anyway. The only people competent enough to decide whether the servicing process has any merit are the professional peers, each affirming the basic assumption of the other. The critical disabling effect of professional coding is its impact upon citizen capacities to deal with cause and effect. If I cannot understand the question or the answer—the need or remedy—I exist at the sufferance of expert systems. My world is not a place where I do or act with others. Rather, it is a mysterious place, a strange land beyond my comprehension or control. It is understood only by professionals who understand how it works, what I need, and how my need is met. I am the object rather than the actor. My life and our society are technical problems (the realm of experts) rather than political problems (the realm of citizens)."[32]

4. *We'll tell you if the solution is successful.* Servicers define the output of their service in accordance with their own satisfaction with the results. Professionals, not citizens or the people who receive service, have the power to decide whether the "help" offered is effective. The client is viewed as a deficient person, unable to know whether he or she has been helped. Citizens learn that their satisfaction comes from being effective clients rather than from being problem solvers.

These responses create, in effect, clienthood, which, along with the service ideology that produces it, is consummated when citizens learn to believe that they cannot know whether they have a need, cannot know what the remedy is, cannot understand the process that purports to meet or remedy the need, and cannot even know whether the need is met unless professionals express their own satisfaction. This process of learned paralysis, of going from active citizen to silent spectator, is all too common, and it is why nonprofit organizations and community service agencies are not always assets in a community—their very structure can undermine their intentions by creating neighborhoods of clients rather than of citizens. Leadership comes to be about the CEOs of nonprofits and businesses, about philanthropists, and about government officials, not about community members themselves.

McKnight's critique is echoed in a Case Foundation–commissioned report written by former Public Allies board member Cindy Gibson, who argues that although volunteering has been on the rise, there is compelling research showing that civic engagement and membership in associations have continued to decline:

> Americans feel more isolated than ever and powerless to do anything about the problems facing their communities and the nation. As a result, they are turning away from civic and public life to engage in activities—including volunteering and charitable

> giving—that may be less an impetus for deeper civic engagement than attempts to assuage the inchoate yet palpable sense among increasing numbers of Americans that things are spiraling out of control, that there is little connection between people and their public institutions and leaders, and that the country has drifted away from its core democratic values to those emphasizing materialism, celebrity, and *me* rather than *we*.[33]

Gibson argues that community service, philanthropy, and other forms of help are not enough when they are organized by groups, not citizens, and when they relegate people to the role of occasional participants. More powerful solutions arise from "creating opportunities for ordinary citizens to come together, deliberate, and take action collectively to address public problems or issues that *citizens themselves* define as important and in ways that *citizens themselves* decide are appropriate and/or needed—whether it is political action, community service, volunteering, or organizing."[34]

Harry Boyte, director of the Center for Democracy and Citizenship at Augsburg College (Minneapolis) and a senior fellow at the University of Minnesota's Humphrey School of Public Affairs, has been a prolific promoter of citizens' efforts to solve problems rather than rely on experts and professionals. In a recent study, he quotes Josiah Ober's work contrasting modern practices with practices in ancient Athens, where expert and amateur knowledge were aggregated:

> Contemporary practice often treats free citizens as passive subjects by discounting the value of what they know. Willful ignorance is practiced by the right and left alike.... The cult of the expert has many effects. Professionals have narrowed [the scope of their professional] identities from [the] "civic" to [the] "disciplinary" [realm]—no longer are most teachers or clergy or businessmen and women schooled to think of themselves as building the civic life of a place through their work. Dominant models of knowledge-making undercut the moral and civic authority

> of forms of knowledge that are not academic—wisdom passed down by cultural elders, spiritual insight, local and craft knowledge, the common sense of a community about raising children. As they do, they undermine the confidence, standing, and authority of everyday citizens without degrees or formally credentialed expertise.[35]

Public Allies strongly believes in citizen-centered and community-centered leadership. We believe that responsibility for solving public problems is something that resides with all of us in communities. We also believe that the solutions to problems involving education, health, poverty, crime, and the environment are often resident within communities themselves, but that the assets and leadership often aren't developed and connected. That is why we see responsibility for stepping up as matched with responsibility for how we engage others—only efforts that multiply and share leadership in a community have a chance to solve our most vexing problems.

This is what Lisa Sullivan, Reggie and Sharlen Moore, Paul Griffin, John McKnight, and others have taught us so well. In fact, Lisa and I once coauthored an article to which she added a line that sums it up beautifully. She wrote that today's leaders "build bridges, establish free spaces where citizens can be supported as community change agents and problem solvers, and continuously foster the emergence of new leaders."[36] That is, *responsibility belongs to all of us*.

The Five Core Values

Now that we have delved into the "what" of leadership, in Part Two of the book we will turn to the "how." The next five chapters explore the five core values of Public Allies. These values combine to transform leaders into community builders who engage citizens, associations, and institutions to build leadership, community capacity, and solutions. Our five core values—asset-based community development, diversity and inclusion, collaboration, continuous learning, and integrity—include the practices that leaders need today to do that work. We begin in Chapter Five with asset-based community development, which is the foundation of our approach and strengthens all the other values.

Key Ideas and Lessons

1. Leadership is ultimately about taking responsibility–personal responsibility and social responsibility–for working with others toward a common goal.
2. We can't wait to step up until we have all the information, data, tools, or relationships we might need. We must often take risks, make mistakes, learn, and improve on our leadership journeys. Each goal we achieve or fail to achieve prepares us for our next leadership opportunity.
3. We must also be responsible for how we lead–for the approach and the values we use in working with others, and for how we receive feedback.
4. Leadership is an inherently collaborative process. When we believe that everything rests entirely on our own shoulders, or if we fail to step up when others are relying on us, we create an unhealthy dynamic for ourselves and others.
5. When we face a challenge, we can either make the problem bigger and become victims or take responsibility by creating a bigger solution.
6. The institutions and professionals serving our communities have replaced the responsibility that neighbors used to have for each other and their community. We must rebuild that sense of responsibility and calibrate the relationship between institutions and citizens in solving local problems.

Exercises and Reflections

- Describe a situation in which you took responsibility in a way that involved taking a risk or making yourself vulnerable. What happened? Were you glad that you stepped up? Did the effort increase your confidence?

- Describe a situation in which you did not take responsibility, expecting and waiting for someone else to take responsibility. What happened? Did you blame someone? If so, what happened to the relationship between you and that person? What happened to the group? What do you think would have happened if you had stepped up instead of waiting for another to do so?
- Has there ever been a time when you took on too much responsibility for a project? Do you think the project could have succeeded if you had taken less responsibility or shared more responsibility? What are the signals that you have taken on too much and need to seek help?

Part Two

THE FIVE CORE PUBLIC ALLIES LEADERSHIP VALUES

5

RECOGNIZING AND MOBILIZING ALL OF A COMMUNITY'S ASSETS

Steve Ramos: It Takes Children to Raise a Whole Village

The work of Esteban "Steve" Ramos at Fresh Youth Initiatives, in the Washington Heights neighborhood of New York City, turns a famous proverb on its head: Fresh Youth Initiatives believes it takes children to raise a whole village.

Steve grew up in Washington Heights, was kicked out of two high schools, completed his GED at seventeen, and enrolled in an associate's degree program at LaGuardia Community College. As he finished his degree, he landed an internship with a youth program in Queens, where he learned about Public Allies.

"I was at a crossroads in life," he says, "nineteen years old, with no idea what I wanted to do other than possibly becoming a cop. I saw the program was about leadership. I didn't know what a leader was. I never looked at myself as one."[1]

When he joined Public Allies New York, in 1999, Steve served at Fresh Youth Initiatives. There he helped lead a satellite after-school program for youths between the ages of ten and eighteen at Holy Trinity Church, in his mostly African American and Latino neighborhood of Washington Heights. A few months into his placement, he learned that the food pantry that had operated for years out of Holy Trinity Church was closing. Steve asked if he could pick up the reins, and his supervisor at Fresh Youth Initiatives agreed. In time, Steve cultivated a group of local youths to keep the food bank going. The youths, most from low-income households themselves, have since collected and distributed over 550,000 pounds of food for families in the neighborhood through the Helping Hands Food Bank.

Steve continued on at Fresh Youth Initiatives after he graduated from Public Allies, in July 2000, while also furthering his education. Eventually he earned a youth-development certificate at CUNY, a B.A. with honors at Lehman College, and a master's degree in social work at Yeshiva University. He also completed a program in executive nonprofit leadership at Columbia University, started a family, raised three daughters, and took on increasing responsibility at Fresh Youth Initiatives. In 2009, Steve became CEO of Fresh Youth Initiatives, where he advances the belief that youth in the community are part of the solution to many local problems.

According to the organization's Web site, Fresh Youth Initiatives

> views young people as assets to be developed (not problems who need fixing), who have the time, ideas, creativity, connections in the community, and willingness to work hard in order to help themselves and others. Providing them with support and encouragement, experience, and skills, Fresh Youth Initiatives endeavors to demonstrate that young people, given the chance, can be strong and positive change agents, playing a meaningful role in meeting community needs.

No description of "at-risk youth" here—Steve sees them as "at-promise youth." The youth engaged with Fresh Youth Initiatives stay with the program an average of five years and show improvements in self-esteem and self-efficacy, a sense of belonging in their community, and academic progress—80 percent of them graduate from high school on time and go on to college. And the program continues to seek out ways to engage more young people, especially those on the margins of the community. Fresh Youth Initiatives recently began a program to match immigrant youth with peer mentors and service opportunities to help them become full members of their new home communities.

All the work at Fresh Youth Initiatives is done through neighborhood collaborations, which try to knit together the people and groups who work with the youth and build relationships that help them succeed. That collaborative spirit was built into the DNA of Fresh Youth Initiatives, which began in 1993 as a collaborative effort aided by local community builders and groups, especially three youth organizations (a Scout troop, a girls' program, and a dropout-prevention program). Fresh Youth Initiatives states:

> The bonds and trust formed in the years of very close collaboration are at the heart of making today's work as effective as possible. We are all trying to work with young people, providing them support and working towards their growth, safety, and positive development. It would be self-defeating to look at other groups as "turf" or "competition," especially when there is a burgeoning youth population in the neighborhood. We have found that maintaining this network of relationships has contributed to a stronger sense of community in Washington Heights.

Steve's personal story and Fresh Youth Initiative's work highlight the cornerstone of Public Allies' leadership approach and curriculum—recognizing and mobilizing community assets. This practice is also known as *asset-based community development* (ABCD). The ABCD approach, first presented by John "Jody" Kretzmann and John McKnight in their groundbreaking book *Building Communities from the Inside Out*, has influenced hundreds of thousands of community builders around the world.[2] ABCD is not a program or set of steps but an approach that puts citizens at the center of building community. Inherent in the ABCD approach is the belief that at this center lies a rich and often untapped array of assets that can be mobilized to build strong communities. In every community, these assets—the skills and talents of individuals, the power of associations and social capital, the resources of local institutions, and the land and physical structures in the community along with the local economy and the community's culture, tradition, and stories—represent building blocks. The primary community-building strategy of ABCD is to help local residents, especially in low-income or otherwise marginalized communities, identify, contribute, and connect their assets with each other to create citizen power that strengthens communities, democracy, and social justice.

At Public Allies, we have found that this practice is essential for leaders who want to be effective at creating lasting solutions. If a leader puts community members in charge of change initiatives, those changes are more likely to be sustained. The asset-based approach also strengthens the ability to practice all of Public Allies' values. That is why it is the cornerstone of our approach. If you get this right, you will be more effective at diversity and inclusion, collaboration, continuous learning, and integrity.

The Proverbial Glass: Half Empty and Half Full

At the heart of the ABCD approach is the answer to a proverbial question: Is the glass half empty or half full? Traditionally, the pessimist answers that it is half empty and the optimist answers that it is half full, but the asset-based organizer simply answers, "Yes."

The ABCD approach sees our communities, our families, our friends, our neighbors, and ourselves as both half full and half empty. Each of us has assets—the gifts, talents, and skills that make us good workers, neighbors, friends, and family members. We also all have deficits—things we don't do so well, things that get in the way of our relationships, and mistakes we have made. In fact, sometimes our shortcomings are related to our strengths. For example, I am an organizer and strategist but not a great detail or process person, and so my ability to see the big picture and go after big goals can lead me to see short-term steps as unimportant or distracting.

So the philosophy behind the asset-based approach sees us all as great in many ways, despite our many shortcomings. Unfortunately, some of us are recognized primarily for our fullness, and others among us are recognized and labeled only for our emptiness. That difference is the most pernicious barrier to building strong relationships and communities. It is the half-full part—the assets—where the ingredients for building strong relationships and communities reside.

If we reflect for a moment on the idea that we are all both half full and half empty, we begin to see powerful implications for ourselves and our work in communities:

- If we acknowledge our own emptiness and fullness, as well as that of others, it changes our relationship to each other and to community. The moment we enter any relationship or community with the belief that we are all full and they are all empty—that we are better, that we can fix them, or that we can fill their emptiness up with our fullness—we are arrogant at best and oppressive at worst. But if we recognize that we are half-full, half-empty people who are helping half-full, half-empty neighbors and communities, we can create transformative relationships that will have much greater impact for individuals and communities.
- This also means that we can't use the last conflict, wrong, or stupid thing someone has done to define that person. We have to challenge ourselves, even in the harsh moment when we are staring at others' emptiness, to recognize that they also have fullness and that we also have emptiness. We don't deny the other's emptiness or excuse it, and we don't deny ourselves legitimate anger when we are wronged. But we do still see others as whole, imperfect people like ourselves. I gained insight into this idea when my friend Mark had the unenviable job of eulogizing his cousin John, who had died of a drug overdose. Mark was very close with John, and everyone felt the tension when Mark got up to speak. But Mark broke through the awkwardness and lifted John up with a profound yet simple statement: "You can't define someone's life by the stupidest thing they've ever done." We should never permanently close the door on others by defining them only by their emptiness.
- This really calls on us to reject any situation in which there is an "us" and a "them." The moment we become all good and others become all bad, we abandon responsibility, accountability, and

truth. It is an easy thing to do, deflecting our own responsibility by focusing on others' culpability. But personal conflicts are often like car crashes—not just one person is responsible for the conflict, or for fixing it. Accountability, as Peter Block says, means first owning our role in creating any problem before we focus on the contributions of others.[3]

- It works the other way, too—if we put people on a pedestal for their fullness, then we can get incredibly disappointed and angry when we inevitably see their emptiness. That's a trap we must avoid. As leaders, we have shortcomings and we will fail. And those who inspire us, those we seek as mentors, those we partner with, and those we organize will be as imperfect as we are. We need to be patient with our own leaders and mentors and recognize that they're just as fallible as we are.

From the Proverbial Glass to Community Practice

The idea of half full and half empty applies to communities, too. Fullness and emptiness may look different in wealthier and poorer communities, but they are both there. Jody Kretzmann often illustrates this point by acknowledging that many of the pathologies stereotypically associated with the West Side of Chicago—addiction, domestic violence, gambling, theft, graffiti, child neglect, drunkenness—also exist on Northwestern University's campus, just north of Chicago, where he teaches. Yet Northwestern's students and faculty are generally defined by their assets, and residents of the West Side are generally defined by their deficits. Some neighborhoods are statistically safer, of course, but no neighborhood has a corner on assets. Moving from defining other people and other communities as half empty to acknowledging that they, like us, are also half full is the first step of this work.

Jody Kretzmann and John McKnight developed their approach in the late 1980s and early 1990s by visiting some of the economically poorest communities in America in addition to

Chicago's West Side—places like South Central Los Angeles, East St. Louis, and the South Bronx—looking for what was working. They noticed that those places with a better quality of life for residents had leaders and neighbors who saw the communities differently. These residents saw their own communities as having assets that could be connected to solve problems and care for each other. The biggest problem, as John and Jody began to understand, is best summed up in a story they often tell about Edna Johnson, a resident of the South Bronx, who told them, "We are in a prison—not a prison of iron bars, barbed wire, and the rest, but a prison in people's minds. When I tell someone I am from the South Bronx, a whole set of negative and hopeless images emerges in that person's mind, and I become part of that."

The Needs Map

From this insight, John and Jody developed the model of a *needs map*, which documents the sorts of images Edna Johnson describes, images of what many people see when they think of these communities—crime, drugs, poverty, vandalism, truancy, and other social ills.* A needs map labels the people in such communities as being *teen mothers*, *ex-offenders*, *illiterate*, *mentally ill*, and *at-risk*. Yet those of us who serve these communities are labeled *volunteers*, *philanthropists*, *care providers*, and *experts*. The resulting message—"We are full, you are empty, and we are coming to fill your emptiness"—can exacerbate rather than ameliorate social ills. It produces clients, not citizens or leaders who can solve problems in their communities.

In my early years at Public Allies, I too had to remove the needs map from my head, a map that had been built up

* McKnight and Kretzmann have since regretted using the term *map* because they did not intend for people to map anything, especially the social services, in a neighborhood. The term was meant as a metaphor for how images of and beliefs about a community come to mind.

from years of seeing the "inner city" of Milwaukee as what the evening news and prime-time cop dramas showed: unsafe, poor communities of color. As a recovering addict and former drug dealer who wanted to be seen for my assets, I had to recognize that it was incumbent on me to see the same assets in others. Yes, needs and challenges do exist—no denying that. But there is so much more in communities, and the reality is that even in our poorest neighborhoods there are many residents and many associations sustaining families, children, and community every day—there is hope. Unfortunately, however, too many people see these communities as war zones and imagine that they could become crime victims just by crossing whatever neighborhood boundaries exist in their minds. For example, when I was working on a volunteer event with some college students a few years ago, I asked one student to visit eight nonprofit youth organizations in Milwaukee to distribute tickets. He hesitated and, with a deer-in-the-headlights look, half stuttered, "Will I be safe?" All he saw was the needs map; he had never been exposed to anything else. He went, reluctantly, but returned two hours later, ecstatic: "Those groups were so cool! I didn't know stuff like that existed. People were so nice. At one of the places, they hugged me when I came in." Unfortunately, though, most people focus on the fear that the sirens on the nightly news conjure up, instead of accepting the logic that tens of thousands of people live and work and care for each other in these communities every day.

Communities are half full and half empty. People in communities do have needs, and those needs often can be met through services. But we rarely think critically about the services that exist, or about the unintended consequences they may have for the people served and their communities. In medicine, when a cure makes an illness worse, the patient is said to have contracted an iatrogenic, or doctor-created, disease. Likewise, leadership and service that seek to do good can have iatrogenic effects in communities when leadership and service are rooted in the needs map, and these effects can bring negative consequences:

- They can lead people to be labeled and to internalize the labels that others use to define them—a form of internalized oppression that can limit hope and the belief that things can be better.
- They can encourage the labeled people to rely on "professionals" to serve and fix them rather than relying on each other, and relationships among neighbors, friends, and family members—relationships that are the fabric of community—can break down.
- Philanthropic and governmental resources may be directed to the helpers rather than to those who need help, a practice that often reinforces social and economic disparities.[4]
- They can foster dependency of community members on service organizations, which are rewarded for serving more people, not for making the community stronger and more self-sufficient.

These are the challenges John McKnight was referring to when he wrote about how communities are disabled by the helpers who intend to make them better (see Chapter Four).[5] Imagine that social services came with a list of potential side effects, just like prescription drugs: "If you use this service, professionals will tell you lots of other things that are wrong with you, you may become depressed, you may become more detached from your neighbors and your family, and you may come to see your condition and your community's condition as hopeless." Of course, there are many important and needed services that are consequential in people's lives, but they can also lead to unintended consequences for their clients and communities.

One of my great early lessons came through Public Allies' practice of neighborhood walks. Whenever a Public Allies office started up in a community, one of the first things we did was to walk through some of that community's toughest neighborhoods and ask residents if they knew any young people whom they saw as potential leaders. Our first such outing in Milwaukee engaged only seven of us: Tim Webb and Mike Canul, staff members from the Public Allies national office; Brian Young, a friend of mine from college; Kimberly Tuck, a superenergetic volunteer I later hired to help start Public Allies Milwaukee; two high school students from the community whom Kimberly had mentored; and myself.

We divided up to walk the eastern half of Milwaukee's Sherman Park neighborhood. I eagerly knocked on door after door and asked, "Do you know any young people in this neighborhood who are potential leaders?" People looked at me like I was crazy, and most often they replied, "There are no young people like that around here." I didn't get many names.

When we all met up four hours later, I was deflated, and I questioned this whole idea. Tim joked a little about how dire it seemed, and then he straightened me out: "While we didn't get a lot of names, we sent a message. No one walks through these neighborhoods asking them about the positive. We probably shocked people, and some probably didn't trust you. The only people who come knocking are cops and social workers." Then Mike returned with the two high school students. They were giddy with excitement and surprised us with a long list of names. We asked how they had done it, and Mike said, "We went to the beauty salons and then hit the grocery store. They even made an announcement over the loudspeaker. The salon ladies knew everyone." We were off to a great start in identifying potential leaders.

I walked away from the experience with two powerful lessons. The first is that the deficit mind-set is strong and is internalized in communities. Some white guy holding a clipboard and asking about potential young leaders isn't going to penetrate that by himself. But if more organizations and leaders build relationships with a community's residents, asking them about and engaging their assets, this can change. The second lesson is that local residents know right where to go and can be quite creative in identifying assets. It would not have occurred to me to visit beauty salons and talk to the women, but it did occur to two kids from the community.

Our next neighborhood walk engaged over sixty volunteers from inside and outside Milwaukee's Mid-Town neighborhood. This walk began a three-year partnership with the Mid-Town Neighborhood Association, in which Allies worked with residents on a variety of projects that brought local leadership, voices, and service to the center of community-building activities. Relationships built on a foundation of assets can create conditions for positive change.

Identifying and Mobilizing Assets

We've seen that ABCD is about defining a community on the basis of its assets. If one can identify and mobilize assets rather than just trying to fix deficits, more effective and lasting change will result.

As stated earlier, being asset-based does not mean denying that deficits exist. Our glasses are indeed half empty and half full. The question is, how do you begin building relationships with others that place emphasis on their fullness? If you are like me, it is easier for you to talk about your emptiness with people who acknowledge your fullness. It was the belief in me of people like my sponsor, my peers in recovery, and other friends, who were quite aware of my emptiness but recognized my fullness, that changed my life. I am far more defensive about my shortcomings when I am with someone who seems to be looking for them than I am when I am with someone who, I trust, believes in my fullness. Communities operate the same way. If you build relationships with people that are based on their fullness, you will gain the trust and understanding that will make it easier to work on their emptiness (and yours). If you imagine the community you want to live in and start building it, that can be more powerful than trying to meet various needs. It means thinking differently about communities: How do you do your work? Whom do you do it with? What are your shared goals?

An asset-based approach changes the power dynamic and puts residents—citizens—at the center of building community. At this center lies a rich and often untapped array of assets that can be mobilized to build strong communities. There are three primary assets in a community: the gifts and talents of *community residents*, the *associations and social capital* that bind community residents together, and the *institutions* that engage local residents as stakeholders or open their institutional resources to the community.

Community Residents

At the heart of an asset-based approach are two fundamental principles: that every member of a community, no exceptions, has gifts and talents to contribute to the community, and that communities are places where all people are able to contribute their gifts and talents. If one believes in engaging all people in building community, then it becomes important to find ways to help people contribute to their community—not just through formally organized efforts but as neighbors. Important within this approach is the fact that we are all fallible and have limitations as part of our human condition. We can accept people's limitations as part of their humanity or believe that their limitations must be fixed. Systems often pursue cures for every limitation, whereas communities recognize us for our gifts and accept our limitations.

It is especially important to consider those who are "strangers" and often feared, ignored, or marginalized in a community. If one can bring those who are marginalized into the community, everyone can be part of the community. Community leaders are not viewed as those with positional power but as those with the most relationships in the community and as those who can create opportunities for people to network, collaborate, and pursue common goals. Reggie and Sharlen Moore of Urban Underground have helped Milwaukee see African American and Latino youth, especially those who are part of hip-hop culture, as assets. Steve Ramos has done that, too, in Washington Heights, and now he is engaging immigrant youth on the margins of his community. Peter Hoeffel of the National Alliance on Mental Illness reprimanded me recently when I referred to someone I knew from recovery as a paranoid schizophrenic: "He is not his disease. He is a person with paranoia and schizophrenia." Peter does not define people by their labels but seeks to engage those he serves as partners with dignity and assets.

Associations and Social Capital

The fabric of a community is woven from the relationships among its members and neighbors. These relationships are another important and often overlooked community asset. There is often a range of groups that come together in communities, from informal groups (for example, the ever-growing group that meets at the same coffee shop every morning, the friends who meet at the playground to watch their children, those who gather to play card games) to more formal ones (book clubs, sports teams, church choirs, self-help groups). What distinguishes an association is that it exists by the choice and decisions of its members and that no one person or institution controls it. Alexis de Tocqueville saw three powers in associations: the power to define a problem, the power to decide how to solve the problem, and the power to be a key actor in implementing the solution.[6]

Associations aggregate the assets of individuals around common interests and can be mobilized in support of larger community goals (for example, we see associations all over highways through "adopt a highway" programs, and associations raise funds, volunteer, or help in other ways unrelated to their purposes). Fostering associational life in a community, working with associations to achieve community goals, and building relationships among residents are powerful ways to strengthen a community. In fact, relationships are often more important than programs.

Associations are also a means of building social capital, the connections among individuals and the norms of reciprocity that arise from them. Robert Putnam has found that the more social capital or relationships one has, the more likely one is to be employed, to be safe, to live longer, and to participate in volunteer and political activities.[7] Relationships are an outcome for communities—the more, the better. For example, as Jane Jacobs illustrated many years ago in her classic *The Death and Life of Great American Cities*, and as recent research reinforces, safe neighborhoods are an outcome of residents knowing each other across generations, of people being outside on their porches, and of people walking around on the streets.[8] Social capital may take the form of bonding among people with common characteristics or interests, or it may take the form of bridging, in which people come together across different backgrounds, beliefs, interests, or groups. The bottom line is that relationships are an outcome that is not only effective in building stronger communities but also essential in building solutions to social problems involving such factors as education, health, and poverty.

Institutions

Institutions, including governmental agencies, businesses, and nonprofit organizations, can be community assets, but often they are not. Many service organizations are like UFOs that have landed in a neighborhood, and their staff members have little relationship to neighborhood residents or other groups in the neighborhood—schools, houses of worship, and neighborhood groups—who are serving the neighborhood's residents. Many service organizations also present themselves as "safe havens" from the community, defining themselves in opposition to the community that lies outside their walls. Such an organization offers few opportunities to people living in the neighborhood to participate in the organization's governance, its management, its volunteer programs, or its advocacy mission. These organizations bring in outsiders to do the important work. For an institution to be an asset, it must open its doors to the community, finding ways that it can support the community beyond its specific mission and involve community residents as direct stakeholders. It must also build community and social capital for people, not just offer services.

Often people believe that the ABCD approach sees all organizations that serve communities as assets. That is false. As McKnight reminds us, the professionalization of services and how they are normally delivered can actually disable communities. Institutions take the personal out of it. They are structured to maintain continuity, managed to create efficiency, and focused on sustaining themselves and their interests, not on building community capacity to sustain solutions. According to Harry Boyte, Jane Addams, the great social reformer, warned in 1902 "about the emergence of a class of professional 'experts,' as she described them, who saw themselves outside the life of the people. In her view, detached expertise reinforced existing hierarchies based on wealth and power and created new forms of hierarchical power that threatened the everyday life of communities."[9] She proved herself quite prescient.

The trouble is that care and engagement are nuanced, often inefficient, and even unmanageable. That is, care and engagement are necessarily bumpy and inconsistent. It's these bumps that "professionalization" tries to smooth out. Many nonprofit organizations see the people they serve only as clients and see themselves as experts who can fill the emptiness of people and neighborhoods in the community. They gain expertise in providing some isolated intervention or even a few interventions, regardless of whether these are the interventions that people need and regardless of whether people need something else that the organizations don't provide. They fail to build collaborative relationships at the neighborhood level. In practice, this may mean that, for example, a nonprofit youth worker does not know the teachers, pastors, community organizers, and local elders in the neighborhood. But consider the research conducted by Peter Benson and his colleagues at the Search Institute, a group that has spent fifty years developing evidence-based strategies for developing youths into healthy, successful adults. Benson and his colleagues have shown that neighborhood-level relationships and coordination among them are critical to improving the lives of young people.[10]

Social services are themselves assets when they recognize and mobilize a community's assets, when they build relationships among residents, when they facilitate collaboration with associations, organizations and institutions, and when they engage community members as partners, leaders, and experts. The greatest service that can be provided is one that helps citizens understand and express their unique gifts and talents and work with fellow citizens to improve their communities.

My own experience of recovering from depression and addiction clearly demonstrates the value of these three assets. The institutions—in my case, inpatient treatment and outpatient counseling and therapy—were important, but on their own they would never have been enough. Inpatient and outpatient treatment, although important, were completed after seven months, and therapy, when I sought it, was only one hour a week. It took me five years to gain self-esteem and belief in my future, and that came mostly from relationships—from people who believed in me when I didn't believe in myself, and who were there for me when I stumbled or needed support. And it was associations (my twelve-step groups) that had the greatest impact because they were where I built relationships and friendships that helped me gain self-esteem, create a sober lifestyle, find housing and a job, and accomplish much more. Without a community of support, institutional services would not have been enough. The tools I learned from others in the groups and support networks were more important than what I learned from books or treatment.

Two Solutions, Two Paths

To sum up the difference between ABCD and the traditional approach, the traditional path to community problem solving identifies needs and creates services to meet those needs. Those services are typically fragmented, fund outside helpers, target isolated individuals, and attempt to fix them. An asset-based path identifies assets, connects those assets, and helps people contribute their assets to build a stronger community. ABCD represents a major shift in power, from people as clients of services to people as producers of solutions. Peter Block contends that there is an addiction to problem identification and problem solving that prevents people from accepting a certain amount of fallibility and from focusing on building relationships and community.[11] Community builders are those who accept fallibility and become able to recognize all these assets, to connect them, and to mobilize them, because a more engaged community will be a more successful community.

Today there is great belief that rigorous metrics, focused outcomes, and evidence-based interventions are the best means of solving problems. More effective service is important, but it also tends to operate from a needs map and ignores the reality that problems are often complex and not solved by one program or intervention. The trend toward more effectiveness and better management in the nonprofit sector is necessary but not sufficient to move the proverbial needle on some of our most persistent public problems—those involving health, education, economic security, and other areas. That is why we see more and more programs in our communities, while the same problems remain and even get worse. Building effective organizations is not enough to solve problems. We must build effective communities.

The nonprofit sector has been changing in recent decades as a generation of social workers and activists has retired. That generation often did a great job of building community but a lousy job of managing organizations and results. The social workers and activists of that generation have been followed by CEOs from the ranks of a generation of MBAs and development directors who have focused on building their organizations like businesses. Their innovations, their focus on organizational effectiveness, and their focus on results have often led to better outcomes. But often those outcomes have not added up to citywide change. In order to be effective at transforming not just a few lives but a whole community, such efforts need to blend with community-building efforts. As Jeff Edmondson of Cincinnati's promising Strive Partnership states, "Silver-bullet efforts don't create better outcomes. Partnership building is the key to sustainable improvement."[12]

Benson and his colleagues believe that community-building strategies focused on assets are essential. Their recent report reviews what has been learned during the past decade in the field of youth development, especially about the shift from focusing exclusively on the negative (disadvantaged family backgrounds, risky behaviors, substance use) to focusing on positive youth development (building developmental assets in youth that will help them succeed despite their shortcomings). The lessons learned about what works are not about program models but about community. Here are a few of those lessons, summarized from their research:[13]

- *Change in contexts changes young people*. Efforts that emphasize transforming the environment they live in and the adults and systems that interact with them are more important than "fixing" kids. This does not mean just adding programs—research shows that "proven" programs placed in toxic or unhealthy environments often fail.
- *When youth themselves take action to improve their contexts, their efforts are empowering and also improve the contexts in which*

they and their peers live. These efforts should integrate service, leadership, and engagement in a way that is normative, not as an add-on to adult-driven service. Cumulative impact over time and across contexts is most effective; one-off service activities are not. Young people should be engaged in all phases of planning and leadership.

- *Increasing the number of developmental opportunities or assets for youth across settings is what matters most*, not increasing specific opportunities or assets in a single setting. It is best when development happens in multiple settings—at home, at school, in youth programs, and in religious organizations.
- *Communitywide efforts to build youth assets are as important as those at the level of the organization, the family, or the individual*. Benson and his colleagues offer an example from public health, whereby "improved sanitation, work environments, and immunization programs as well as safety measures have done more to improve health than improvements in one-to-one medical treatment." Success won't come from individual organizations' strategic plans but from community plans that cross boundaries.

For several years I conducted workshops for youth workers in America and from around the world through the Asset-Based Community Development Institute. I would begin by giving them a copy of the Search Institute's forty developmental assets for youth, a list of cumulative assets showing that the more assets a young person has, the more likely he or she is to become a successful adult. I asked the youth workers to identify the five assets that had been most powerful in their own development. I then asked them to identify the five they most often produced among the young people they worked with. Almost every participant over the years had two lists that were misaligned. Relationships had usually had the biggest impact on their development, but their programs focused on behaviors and services, not on relationships or on helping their community.

Research into youth development, education, public health, crime, and other areas demonstrates the importance of community building—engaging citizens as problem solvers, recognizing and mobilizing various community assets and connecting them, fostering greater collaboration among individuals and institutions, and building leadership among community residents. Community-building activities are essential to solving problems and are probably more important than silver-bullet programs that seek to change a community through a relatively small group of clients at one organization. That explains why so many great individual programs in communities fail to add up to aggregate change. Building assets and building community are essential if we want to move from *organizational* impacts to *community* impacts. Doing otherwise is doing the same thing over and over again and expecting different results—a definition of insanity.

Marc McAleavey

Marc McAleavey is a community builder in Indianapolis. He got his start at Broadway United Methodist Church, one of the great examples of an institution that has been a catalyst for community transformation. Broadway United's Zawadi Exchange (*zawadi* is Swahili for "gift") is a program focused on identifying the gifts, talents, and skills in the Mapleton-Fall Creek neighborhood, known for crime, blight, and decay. The program seeks simple outcomes—getting to know neighbors, understanding their gifts and talents, and working toward building connections and relationships centered on exchanging those gifts and talents. Marc, whose title was "illustrator of gifts," worked with De'Amon Harges, a neighbor whose title was "roving listener."

One of the first things Marc did with De'Amon was reach out to area youths. As they approached high school students in the neighborhood, they found many with a strong interest in health. They invited the students to a meeting and also invited doctors and nurses from the congregation and the neighborhood. The result was the Blood Pressure Posse, a group of youths who were trained to go through their neighborhoods doing simple biomedical diagnoses and educating older neighbors about health. Marc explains, "The neighbors listened to them because they were kids from the neighborhood who cared, not representatives from institutions."[14] The youths also organized walking clubs for neighbors with diabetes and worked with neighbors who gardened to supply healthy fresh food to those who needed it. The state department of health is currently looking at ways to further expand this program.

Late one night, at one in the morning, Marc was awakened by "a swarm of brawling youths, perhaps seventy-five of them, who were beating the crap out of each other WWF-style." The next morning, Marc met with De'Amon. They suspected that a new gang, the Buddha Boys, was at the center of the fight. De'Amon reached out to the gang members and found that each of the kids had talents to share, and that most of the kids had joined the gang hoping to make more money.

Marc and De'Amon began meeting with neighbors and businesses to see if they could find jobs for these youths. They did not introduce the youths as gang members but instead described them in terms of their skills. They did not find jobs for everyone, but they made an impact, and the Buddha Boys gang was no longer a problem in the neighborhood.

Marc is now the executive director of Public Allies Indianapolis, which is a program in partnership with the Indianapolis Neighborhood Resource Center.

Abundant Communities

In 2010, Peter Block and John McKnight combined and refreshed their analytical insight into communities as the solution, not the problem. "A neighborhood," they wrote, "can raise a child, provide security, sustain our health, secure our income, and care for vulnerable people."[15] But they see this insight contrasting more and more with the dominant paradigm: "People hold to romantic beliefs that a system can produce care, a doctor can produce health, a school can educate a child, the police can keep us safe, and that therapists and social workers can wash away our cares and woes."[16] What Block and McKnight believe is that each of these outcomes is within the power of communities—the power that comes from identifying and connecting a community's assets.

A community, by definition, is both a place and an experience of connectedness. Communities are built around the recognition of fallibility; institutions are built around the elimination of fallibility. Living "in community" is being willing to live with people's imperfections, which is different from living with people's transgressions. We have a choice to accept and forgive people's mistakes; we have no choice about the fact that people have imperfections.[17]

As McKnight wrote fifteen years ago, once we define a condition as a need, we have to fill that need.[18] Institutions say, "You are inadequate, incompetent, problematic, even broken. We will fix you." And, unfortunately, many leaders think the idea of a strong community is something that's sort of nice—a luxury, if you have the spare time, though not really important, vital, or necessary. They still see themselves as full and the community as empty. Block and McKnight believe that abundant communities are built from the following elements:

- Citizens choosing to exercise their power rather than deferring and delegating it to others
- Citizens showing hospitality and care in a community where everyone belongs
- Citizens recognizing that community grows out of their possibilities, not from the specialized expertise of professionals and systems
- The recognition and mobilization of assets, especially the assets of those on the margins of the community

The capacities that need to be developed are kindness, generosity, cooperation, forgiveness, acceptance of fallibility, and mystery (because not every question can be answered, and not every problem can be solved). Sorrows are no longer secret but are revealed and shared, which uplifts both the teller and the listener. Community depends on this sharing. Local citizens looking at neighborhood assets are the primary group with the power to change lives, heal wounds, and produce healthy communities.[19]

Block and McKnight see leaders in the "abundant" community as "community connectors," who view assets as raw materials, associations as the way to connect assets, and hospitality as the way to widen the inventory of assets. Community connectors make this happen by connecting the assets, social capital, and associations in a community and working with institutions to be more citizen-centered. They welcome the community's "outsiders" and help people who have often been defined by their deficits to act on the basis of their assets.

We aspire for our Allies to become community connectors. One way we teach the Allies to be community connectors is through the team projects they undertake, in which they practice their skills, learn how to work with diverse groups, and facilitate collaborative efforts among citizens and organizations. For example, our Public Allies site in Miami uses the "study circle" process developed by the group Everyday Democracy. Allies in Miami engage the clients of local nonprofit organizations in efforts to identify issues of concern in their communities, identify potential solutions, and lead the effort to implement those solutions. The Allies serve as facilitators and offer resources, including a small grant of up to $2,000 to support the projects that participants create.

Lori Deus

In 2009, Lori Deus organized a study circle project in the West Grove community of Miami, a poor African American neighborhood established by immigrants from the Bahamas in the nineteenth century.

Ms. Donna, a local leader, had taken Lori on a walking tour of the neighborhood, where Lori saw homelessness, drug use, and prostitution. She also noticed something else: "The neighbors came up to Ms. Donna and talked with her and each other about their day-to-day lives, just like in the small town where I grew up, in the Appalachian Mountains. It was a community despite these hardships."[20] She also noticed that it was a very spiritual community, with over thirty churches in the neighborhood.

Lori worried about how she would relate to and be able to help this community, but her supervisor reminded her, "Your job is not to figure things out for the people in West Grove but to give them a means of figuring it out themselves."

"Here was the little white girl from Appalachian Georgia with a southern accent, coming into an African American community, and people didn't want to talk with me," Lori says. "They were skeptical at best, angry at worst. They thought I wanted to study them."

Then she built a relationship with the pastor at St. Paul African Methodist Episcopal Church, who told her, "You realize, don't you, that they think you're part of the problem." She answered that she did. The pastor decided to help her, and they built the largest and most sustainable of the study circles formed that year.

It was a challenge to shift the perspective of the residents from seeing themselves as having needs to recognizing and building on their assets. People questioned whether Lori really would listen to them, support their leadership, and keep her promises.

The residents decided that their first project would be to reenergize a "shower ministry" for homeless people in the neighborhood. The project had been teetering and was not reaching many of the people who needed it.

Lori found it odd at first, but it turned out to be a great way to connect with residents at the margins of their neighborhood. The residents partnered with a church and set up a place to shower in a building across the street. Each homeless person had a bin with his or her name on it that could be used at each visit. Neighbors laundered and mended clothes for the individuals who came to shower, offered them meals, and invited them to ministry; if they wanted to, the homeless people could worship—fresh, clean, and fed. The group used the funds from a small grant to pay the water and power bills.

Lori says, "It was not all sunshine and roses. There were challenges along the way, but my job was to facilitate and follow their lead."

One day, a couple of community residents invited her to a barbeque at one of their homes. She was honored. When she got there, she realized it was a party for her. The residents gave her a scrapbook with their stories and photos of each of them. They wanted her to remember them.

She certainly does. In fact, she still helps out her friends in West Grove. Now she is the community engagement coordinator at the Human Services Coalition of Dade County, where she continues to build leadership and community among low-income people.

Applying the Model at Public Allies

At Public Allies, we aim to create leaders who can be community connectors. We also implement our leadership model and practice its principles throughout every aspect of our program—in our recruitment and selection of the Allies, in our process of partnering with groups to develop service projects for our Allies, and in our leadership-development methods.

Recruitment and Selection

We recruit Allies for their credibility and commitment, not their credentials. We look for assets where many people don't; we see potential in people that others wouldn't see if they only looked at degrees, résumés, or club memberships. We see potential in those who've excelled at school and those who've dropped out or been adjudicated. We see potential in those who have been activists and volunteers with community organizations and in people who have been active at their houses of worship or active in their neighborhoods without a connection to a particular service activity or group. Our criteria and process are set up to identify a wide array of potential assets. That is how we ended up bringing together into one Ally class a high school graduate, a teen who had aged out of foster care, graduate students, a mortuary school student, a cell phone salesman, an eighteen-year-old father, community activists, a 911 call operator, a transgender individual, and a garbage collector. (Yes, in one class!) We find assets beyond labels, degrees, or titles.

To find these people, we look in all parts of a community. We build relationships with community organizations, schools, community organizers, pastors, and others who know young people. We also turn to our Allies and alumni, who are a growing network of recruiters. We hang flyers as if we were advertising a band gig or a poetry slam. We then invite alumni and other diverse volunteers to help us interview and select candidates, hoping they will bring to the process perspectives we might miss. This attention to community-based recruitment and broad selection has led us to become one of the most diverse, homegrown, and selective AmeriCorps programs in the country.

Our approach does present challenges because we place our Allies to serve full-time in other organizations, which interview and select our members. Many times these organizations want the young people with the best credentials, and we have to advocate for Allies whose assets and potential might not be as apparent to the host organizations.

Here are questions, based on our experience, for leaders seeking to engage people in building community and service opportunities:

- If you are recruiting community members or volunteers for a project or program, how do you define the criteria for candidates? Who helps you define those criteria? How can you ensure that the project or program works culturally for the people and community you seek to engage?

- How do your materials and messages represent the community? Do they say you believe your community is a place filled with assets or a place filled with needs?

- Where in the community do you publicize your activities? Are you meeting people where they are—on Web sites, through radio programs, at clubs, and so on, that diverse community residents use?

- How can you engage others from the targeted community in recruiting people to participate in your effort?

- Once community members come through the door, how do you orient and support them so they feel empowered and connected?

- How will you measure the success of your engagement?

Service

Public Allies partners with local community organizations to identify how we can help them expand and enhance services to meet local needs. We especially look for opportunities to help organizations improve their capacity to serve, empower residents to become more engaged in community efforts, collaborate with other organizations and associations, and expand services to more residents. Because our partners design the projects and employ the Allies, we cannot tell them what approach to use. We hope that they share some of our values and approach, but we don't force them to do so. If a partner does not use an asset-based approach, we encourage the Ally to learn what works and what doesn't work in the partner's approach. We can always learn from the assets, experience, and wisdom of our partners, too.

One of the ways we've built an asset-based approach into the Allies' service is by encouraging them, as part of their service, to recruit volunteers. Many groups engage volunteers, of course, but we add a community-building twist: we encourage our Allies to recruit at least half their volunteers from the neighborhoods or client bases of the organizations where they are placed. In addition, we have them focus on engaging their volunteers to serve four or more times so they are engaged in a more sustainable way. In 2009, our Allies recruited 31,000 volunteers to join them in service, and 60 percent were from the neighborhoods served or were "clients" of the partner organizations. We also encourage Allies to foster collaborations among organizations in their communities and to seek ways to work with other groups. We ask Allies to report on how many collaborative relationships they have formed and on what the results were. Typically, each Ally develops half a dozen linkages among such organizations.

Here are questions we think are helpful to leaders creating community service or engagement efforts:

1. How do you decide what is needed? Who can help you identify needs, consider how best to serve them, and determine what outcomes to pursue?
2. Who else works on the same issue or serves the same people you serve, and what is your relationship with them? How can you collaborate with other groups in your community in ways that benefit residents?
3. How can your project identify and mobilize local assets? How can it build social capital and connect community members?
4. How can you engage as citizens and partners people normally seen as clients?
5. How is your effort accountable to the community, to the people you work with and serve, and not just to funders or political leaders?

Leadership Development

Public Allies builds leaders in the context of a community. There are five ways in which we use an asset-based approach to develop the Allies.

First, the assets of the Allies are the most powerful teaching tool. The cohort of Allies—a very diverse group of young adults, most of whom come from the communities they are serving—learn from each other's backgrounds, perspectives, neighborhoods, and service.

Second, as part of their leadership-development experience, we offer Allies leadership opportunities in planning, facilitating, training, and evaluating. We follow the best practices in adult education and accelerated learning, which means focusing on the whole person, creating a positive and interactive learning environment, mixing content with activity, fostering collaboration in the learning environment, and allowing each learner to accept responsibility for his or her development (see Chapter Eight).

Third, we do not engage with our Allies, especially those who've faced more challenges in life, as clients who need to be fixed. Rather, we build on their assets and encourage them to take responsibility for their own development and wellness.

Fourth, we call on local community leaders and practitioners to train the Allies in our curriculum so that they not only learn skills or practices from people with expertise but also gain relationships and resources in the community.

Fifth, we teach and reinforce the asset-based approach through our leadership-development curriculum itself, which creates many opportunities for our Allies to reflect on how they practice this approach at their placement organizations and in their communities.

We believe that those who conduct the training and education of community members and leaders will benefit from considering the answers to these questions:

1. Whom do you identify as potential leaders?
2. How can your development efforts stimulate peer learning and engage the group's experience? How do members participate in each other's learning?
3. How are participants oriented to the community and to each other?
4. What relationships and resources do they gain access to through the training?
5. How do participants learn to practice community-building approaches?

The Cornerstone Value

Recognizing and mobilizing community assets is the cornerstone of the Public Allies leadership model. If Public Allies gets this right, the other values will follow. If we see the assets in all kinds of people, especially those on the margins, and seek to engage them, we will be more inclusive. If we consider ways of connecting the individual and organizational assets in a community, we will be more collaborative. If, instead of approaching a community as experts who are there to fix others, we approach it as half-full, half-empty people serving and learning from others who are half full and half empty, we will continue to learn. And if we are as accountable to the people we serve and work with as we are to those who support or sponsor our work, we will have greater integrity.

Recognizing and mobilizing assets is essential to sustainably solving problems in community. We need more practice of this value. We need more citizens stepping up and getting involved and putting their assets together. That requires a greater commitment to inclusion, which is not always easy. That is the subject of the next chapter.

Key Ideas and Lessons

1. Each of us and each of our communities is both half empty and half full. We all have needs and challenges, and we all have assets.
2. When we build relationships based on assets instead of just delivering services to meet needs, we open the door to greater individual and community transformation.
3. There are three primary assets: the gifts of individuals, the social capital and associations through which people are connected, and institutions that engage and support the power of citizens.
4. The focus on effective and innovative organizations is necessary but not sufficient to create sustainable change. Collaborative efforts that engage residents and groups together are the primary means by which real change happens.

5. Leaders in the asset-based model are "community connectors" who are able to recognize, connect, and mobilize the assets of individuals and groups throughout a community.

Exercise and Activities

Along with the questions in the section of the chapter called "Applying the Model at Public Allies," here are a few exercises you can do with a group.

Gift Interview

This simple exercise can help people identify and acknowledge their own and others' assets. It is often done in pairs. Each individual writes the answer to the following questions and then shares them with his or her partner. Once all the pairs have finished, each participant, using the list of his or her partner's assets, introduces that person to the group.

- What two gifts, talents, or skills make you a valuable family member and friend?
- What two skills make you especially good at your paid or volunteer work?
- What talent do you have that not many people know about?
- What are two or three of your favorite hobbies? What do you love to do so much that you can do it for hours without getting bored?

Get to Know the Community

Here are two activities to help people start to see a community differently.

1. Organize a tour of your community with elders or historians. Afterward, when participants are reflecting on the tour, ask these questions:
   - What is positive about the community's history?
   - Where are the challenges?
   - How can residents be involved in addressing the challenges?

   After the tour, you can also form small groups and have each group create a sixty-second commercial about why people should want to be involved in the community. Individuals within the groups can also create personal plans describing how they will apply their knowledge and appreciation of the community's history to their work.

2. Create a community scavenger hunt in which groups are sent out to gather information about a diverse array of assets in the community. When the groups return, ask them the following questions:
   - What was new to you?
   - What challenged your preconceived notions the most?
   - What do you want to learn more about?
   - Has anything you learned prompted you to action? What will you do?

6

CONNECTING ACROSS CULTURES

Susan Edwards: "Diversity Is an Action, Not an Ideal"

Susan Edwards grew up in the suburbs just north of Milwaukee. When she arrived at Public Allies, she had just completed college, had been working odd jobs, and was contemplating law school. One day a friend recommended Public Allies.

"The leadership component really spoke to me," Susan recalls. "It was not just about service but much more. Though I was from a lily-white suburb, I was aware of segregation in Milwaukee and that there were huge parts of the community I knew nothing about. I was interested in a program that would give me an experience with our whole community."[1]

Susan admired and respected her supervisors at the Institute for Wisconsin's Future, where she worked on an economic-development initiative. At her Presentation of Learning, the end-of-year event where Allies describe how they've met Public Allies' learning outcomes, her placement supervisor, a baby boomer and longtime activist, asked an interesting question: "What does my generation of activists need to learn that you learned from Public Allies?"

Susan didn't hesitate. In two short, smart sentences, she nailed what was distinct about Public Allies' approach to diversity and inclusion.

"For your generation," she said, "diversity is an ideal, something to believe in. At Public Allies, we learned it is an action—it is something you do."

She further explained, "Progressive leaders and groups all want to be more diverse, but they haven't figured it out, for the most part.

People talk about the segregation and lack of diversity, but they aren't actively breaking down barriers and creating diversity. Public Allies does that, and I learned to do it. A lot of it came from the kind of group Public Allies selected and the environment they created. We were forced to have the tough and uncomfortable conversations about our differences and what they meant. We'd also find our common commitments and values and build community with that. We'd reflect upon, share with each other, and argue about sensitive issues. We were supported to take risks and maybe say the wrong things. There would sometimes be raw feelings. Then we would break into our teams to work on our projects. You couldn't escape it. You had to work through the difficulty and find ways to work with each other well."

After Public Allies, Susan went to work for the United Food and Commercial Workers Union in Milwaukee: "It was often immigrants and people who had very different backgrounds than I have. Public Allies prepared me well to work in an environment like this. Instead of expecting them to come to where I was, and instead of projecting my values and beliefs on them, I was able to approach folks where they were, listen to them, acknowledge them, and build relationships with them. As a white female college graduate from the suburbs, I never felt out of place working with working-class immigrants and others. I got that from Public Allies and will always bring that with me."

This approach is the essence of diversity and inclusion work. It is about actions and results, not beliefs and intentions. Too often, *diversity* and *inclusion* are words in values statements or principles in strategic plans. Too rarely, we see diversity and inclusion as results. We need results. Our nation is becoming increasingly diverse, yet research shows that residents of diverse communities don't know how to work well together on public issues, and that the nonprofit organizations that serve our communities also struggle to engage and develop diverse leaders. Recent events in our political culture demonstrate that we still have a way to go to dismantle various forms of oppression. We need leaders who can create opportunities for diverse citizens to realize their potential and work together.

Public Allies employs three key strategies to build such diverse and inclusive leaders. The first is to select people with very diverse backgrounds and talents. The second is to help emerging leaders confront issues of power, privilege, and oppression within themselves, their communities, and our larger society. The third is to use that awareness to advocate for and build inclusive communities. Doing this work can be hard, but it is also quite rewarding. Inclusive leadership, as your knowledge and relationships expand, can be joyous and inspiring and can lead to better results in your work. You will see these strategies unfold in the course of this chapter, but first let's explore the environment in which they must work.

E Pluribus *Ouch!*

Our communities, like America itself, are best when we create a place for everyone. At Public Allies, we believe that everyone has assets that can contribute to our community, and we value the different perspectives, talents, and skills that people bring. Unfortunately, we still have a long way to go in building such communities.

In a recent study titled *E Pluribus Unum*, Robert Putnam found an inverse relationship between civic engagement and diversity—that is, in communities with greater diversity, less engagement was found across different racial and ethnic groups, and even among members of the same group.[2] Putnam, as mentioned in Chapter Three, calls this the "turtle effect"—people hiding inside rather than engaging with their neighbors and fellow community members. It appears that in many diverse communities people don't know how to build relationships and work together cross-culturally. Diversity on its own does not automatically lead to inclusion.

Nonprofit organizations are vehicles by which citizens come together to solve problems and improve their quality of life. One would expect these groups to have an exemplary record on diversity and inclusion and to be beacons showing our society the way forward. Instead, nonprofits have a troubling record on diversity. Too often the photos on the cover of the annual report (the people served) and the photos in the back (the leaders who serve them) don't match. As mentioned in Chapter One, recent studies have found that 80 to 90 percent of nonprofit executive directors are white and that there is a glass ceiling for women in the field—the bigger an organization is, the less likely it is to be led by a woman. The lack of leadership diversity drives a gap between nonprofits and the people they serve. This deficit yields a lack of awareness, action, and results. It means that staff themselves often don't know how to work together and engage communities effectively beyond "serving" them. Transformation is lacking.

Public Allies' program has been part of the AmeriCorps network since its inception, and we are proud promoters of volunteering and community service. This field offers a good example of the barriers that well-intentioned groups face in achieving results in diversity and inclusion. According to past data from AmeriCorps, two-thirds of AmeriCorps members are white, and about the same percentage are current college students or graduates. The view of who should serve is shaped by organizations led overwhelmingly by white graduates of elite colleges. A recent review of the leadership of three prominent organizations in the field found that, on average, 85 percent of their boards and 74 percent of their management are white, and yet their service is concentrated in low-income communities of color. It is therefore no surprise that throughout the service world recruitment messages such as "Take a year off" or "How will you spend your gap year?" are prevalent. In a nation where only 20 percent of young adults complete college, and where 75 percent of the people in that group graduate from public universities, how many people have the ability or privilege to "take a year off" or have a "gap year"? There are more than four million young adults disconnected from school or work. These young adults are living gap *lives* and are looking to take a year *on*. Community service offers skills, work experience, social skills, understanding of different cultures, and other benefits that are needed by people of all backgrounds—those who come from privilege and those who are more disadvantaged. We need everyone.*

Beyond the exclusive messages about "gap years" and "years off," community service is also often presented as something the "haves" *do to* the "have-nots." The message is often about helping the poor, serving the less fortunate, making a difference in others' lives. The images of need are often images of children or families of color, creating a message that certain people are the helpers and others are the helped. As we saw in Chapter Five, this deficit orientation promotes the notion of certain communities as needy places filled with needy people who need outsiders to come in and help them. The deficit-based message is clear: the community is empty, you are full; come fix it. The poor are passive objects of service. Few service groups promote their work in a way that represents communities as places filled with talented and committed residents or other assets, and rarely do they approach such communities as sources of volunteers or servers who can partner with them to make a difference.

Even the language we use to describe community service and volunteering creates a barrier for some young people. A few years ago, one of our D.C. Allies was sitting on a panel at a conference of funders. The topic was getting young people involved with community service and civic engagement. The Ally, a young African American woman from southwest D.C., was asked if she had volunteered while she was growing up. "No," she answered bluntly. "I never had a chance to really do that." The room looked astonished and worried about the fact that she or anyone had not had the chance to volunteer.

The Ally was asked, "Do you think if your school or other community groups had asked you to volunteer, you would have?"

---

* Philanthropy for Active Civic Engagement, a network of foundations, produced an excellent report in 2010 on how service and civic engagement can be a ladder of opportunity for young people; see *Civic Pathways Out of Poverty and Into Opportunity*, available at www.pacefunders.org.

She replied, "I don't know. I was really busy back then. I was helping my sister with her kids after school and spent my weekends helping out at my church."

If someone outside this Ally's community had come in even once a week to help kids after school and had helped out at a local church, that person would have earned a community service award. For this Ally, that was just life. I have seen this story played out again and again over the years, particularly among those who come from low-income communities and communities of color. We ask them to describe how they've been involved in their communities, and they say, "I haven't been that involved" before rattling off an impressive list of ways they've been good family members, group members, neighbors, and friends. Many see volunteer community service as something an outsider *does to* their communities. It's no surprise, then, that community service can be viewed negatively because it is associated with punishment—something judges or schools force you to do.

Former Campus Compact CEO and Public Allies board member Liz Hollander shares a similar story from her efforts to expand service initiatives and service learning on college campuses. "Historically Black colleges and universities often had service and 'giving back' as core expectations for students," she says. "It had been part of their culture since their founding, but they did not have formal service-learning programs, nor did they have the resources to write up their good work. As a result, they were often disrespected or disregarded by the higher education service community."[3]

In the same way, one might find incomplete data on volunteer and civic activities among poor people and people of color. According to data from the Corporation for National and Community Service, white people reportedly volunteer at a greater rate (28 percent) than African Americans (19 percent), Asian Americans (19 percent), and Latinos (14 percent).[4] The National Conference on Citizenship's Civic Index also finds that, in general, people who have higher education levels are more likely to participate in civic activities.[5] From our experience, I would guess that much of the informal work that takes place within families and among neighbors is missed by such studies.

This analysis is not meant to discredit community service and volunteering. Public Allies works to get more people of *all* backgrounds volunteering and serving, including those from more privileged backgrounds, and our communities need the help. Nevertheless, such service and volunteer efforts need to be more diverse and inclusive in terms of how they define needs, how they describe communities, whom they invite to serve, how they partner with the communities they serve, and how they are accountable to the communities they serve. We believe that both reflecting on and *acting on* these questions can make service and volunteering more inclusive and impactful.

The need for citizens to get engaged is real, and this need does, unfortunately, have racial overtones. Despite substantial gains won by the civil rights movement, our nation continues to have odious racial disparities in areas such as education, health, justice, and poverty. Some argue today that the underlying issue is class more than race, and that argument has some merit. Many different kinds of people experience challenges and needs. But, all things being equal, race matters. In education, Latino and African American students fall far behind their white counterparts. In the justice system, research clearly shows racial disparities at every level of the system. And researchers have documented in myriad ways—for example, using race testers to mail résumés, complete loan applications, and pursue housing—that people of color often face persistent discrimination.[6] Although discrimination, for the most part, is not as overt, sanctioned, or violent as in the past, it still exists through rules that disadvantage people whose experiences or backgrounds are different, through subconscious bigotry, or through overt acts of hate. Dismantling the oppression that underlies such discrimination is something that must be proactively addressed and is essential to a just society.

Our culture can be quite corrosive in confronting these topics. We still struggle to live up to our nation's founding principles, to be a nation where all men and women, created equal, have inalienable rights to life, liberty, and the pursuit of happiness. Too often, these rights are seen as a zero-sum proposition, and people resist, sometimes violently, steps toward greater equality. As I write this, I can reflect on ugly public battles during the past year over gay marriage, gays serving openly in the military, immigration reform, the opening of an Islamic cultural center in New York City, the birthplace and citizenship of our president, burnings of the Qur'an, and bullying of gays as well as other well-publicized hate crimes. And our nation continues to become more diverse—2011 is the first year in which Caucasian babies are the minority in America.[7] Electing Barack Obama president of the United States was a milestone, but the hope for healing was quickly diminished as our nation became further polarized over a variety of issues that sometimes sparked incidents of bigotry and hate. The struggle to live up to our founding principles continues to be just that—a struggle.

Diversity

We need leaders who can dismantle oppression, acknowledge and bridge differences, and bring diverse people and groups together to solve problems. Many people, talking about power and influence, talk about the proverbial table where decisions are made. At Public Allies, we recognize that if you change the people who come to the proverbial table (diversity), then the table itself must change (inclusion) if people are going to work well together. This means co-creating, not controlling.

The first step is committing to diversity as a goal. There are many good reasons to seek diverse people and perspectives. Some of us commit to diversity because of our commitment to social justice and our belief that everyone should have equal opportunity, especially those who face historical or current barriers based on race, gender, sexual orientation, and so on. Others among us appreciate the new experiences and lessons we gain when we are engaged with people who bring different personal and cultural backgrounds as well as new perspectives. And still others among us recognize that if we want to serve or engage a diverse constituency, community, or customer base, we must have people working with us who understand those groups. There is evidence that greater diversity yields greater innovation and effectiveness. Scott Page, a University of Michigan economist, has shown through complex experiments and mathematical models that diverse groups often outperform more homogenous groups of "the best and the brightest."[8]

If you are committed to diversity, then you have to be aware of the lack of diversity and act on it. You have to look at your personal and professional networks, at the groups you belong to, and at the organization where you work and see whether they are diverse. You have to consider what perspectives you are missing that could help you or your groups better understand an issue or a potential solution. Too few people are aware of or bothered by the lack of diversity in their personal and professional lives. They dismiss diversity as something difficult to bring about, and they say they've tried. It is not hard, in fact, but it does take more than trying. You must be intentional about expanding your networks and learning how to engage new people, constituencies, and communities. For us at Public Allies, this means that we recruit diverse candidates, build relationships with leaders and groups in all parts of our community, develop our application process and selection criteria to be culturally relevant to diverse communities, and create an inclusive environment for diverse individuals when they are selected. By recognizing diverse assets within individuals, recruiting through outreach to diverse leaders, organizations, and communities, and valuing the learning that comes from diverse backgrounds and perspectives, we are able to build a diverse group of Allies.

In our society, unfortunately, we rarely see truly diverse groups, companies, organizations, and communities. But if you seek more diversity, you have to be willing to change. You can't keep doing the same thing and expect a different result. Diversity does not mean adding a few token people of color. It means that you yourself or your group will learn and adapt with new people. Oliver Wendell Holmes Jr. is reputed to have said, "Man's mind, once stretched by a new idea, never regains its original dimensions." Something analogous can be said about groups and diversity: once a group becomes more diverse, it will never regain its original shape, and the new shape will lead to innovation and change.

Ava Hernandez

For Ava Hernandez, diversity is "the way it should be. It is a vision of how we want community to be. We just don't see it enough elsewhere, and we wish it was everywhere."[9]

Ava is originally from a large New Orleans family and now works for Public Allies Milwaukee, where she directs training and learning.

"When we interview," she says, "we consider what each Ally might uniquely bring to the group. It goes beyond race. We see the value in having people who may have been to jail, may be HIV-positive, may have been teen parents, may have dropped out of school, may be recovering from addiction, or may have faced other social problems. We also look at other distinct backgrounds and interests—someone might be from a rural community, might be a deacon at her church, might wish to work with the elderly, or might be a performing artist. We look for people who we think will do a good job, and then we consider—because we have so many applicants—the unique assets each person might bring to the group. We find that having such a diverse mix of backgrounds and interests makes the learning and leadership development far more extensive and fulfilling for everyone."

Ava acknowledges that it's "not always easy, as there are people we see as assets that our partners don't, so we have to persuade and negotiate to place some of our Allies. This most often happens around educational background. But in almost every case where we've convinced an organization to take an Ally they were hesitant about, the partner has been grateful at the end of the year that they took the chance."

At Public Allies, we've learned that bringing such a diverse group of leaders together is critically important, but it is distinctly difficult work to make such diversity a real asset for everyone. Making diversity an asset is how we change the "table" itself. One of the big mistakes that groups and organizations make in well-intentioned efforts to add more diverse people involves wanting these new people to join the existing culture. The group wants to bring in a new perspective but ends up marginalizing that perspective because, rather than expanding or reshaping group norms to engage the newcomers, the group expects the newcomers to adopt the existing norms. The goal is to gain from each person's full contribution, which can be stifled if a group doesn't change as it becomes more diverse.

Diversity is not the same as inclusion. Groups can be diverse but exclusive. For example, we had a local site that at one point was selecting only Allies who shared the existing group's ideology. The people at this site shunned people they perceived as having come from privileged backgrounds or holding more conservative views. They lost the opportunity for Allies to have additional perspectives to consider and learn from. That is not the kind of community we aim to create. We want to benefit from having diverse backgrounds, beliefs, and experiences at our table, and we also want to ensure that the diversity we've created leads to productive and effective collaboration. Everyone brings assets to the group, and all of those assets are needed. To maximize those assets, however, one must build an inclusive environment, and that means addressing, head-on, issues of power, privilege, and oppression.

Power, Privilege, and Oppression

Power. Privilege. Oppression. These are difficult and loaded words. The reality is that without understanding these three concepts and being aware of how they operate individually, institutionally, and societally, you cannot really build cultural competence and a commitment to diversity and inclusion or work for justice. Addressing diversity and oppression means looking at all the forms oppression takes and at the intersections of racism, sexism, heterosexism, classism, and other forms of bigotry and hate. The important thing is that the conversations happen among diverse people, and that people are pushed to discuss difficult issues with each other—to question our own assumptions, to become aware of how people's different experiences have shaped them, to be aware of how we perceive others and are perceived by others, and to be aware of how these dynamics play out in the larger society. And this is at the heart of our second strategy—we help emerging leaders confront the issues of power, privilege, and oppression.

Oppression exists when there is both prejudice (an assumption or belief that someone or some group is inferior) and power. Power can come in many forms. It may entail having certain privileges, many of which we don't even think about, that give us more opportunity than others have. When we enjoy our own privilege but are naïve or ignorant about opportunities to share it, or when we refuse to share it, then we have power. There is also power simply in having and making a choice about whether to dismantle oppression or not.

There is no such thing as working passively against oppression. Either we are working to dismantle it or are we colluding with it through our silence. This notion was captured best by Martin Niemöller, a Lutheran pastor, in 1946, after he had spent eight years in Nazi concentration camps:

> First they came for the communists, and I didn't speak out because I wasn't a communist.
>
> Then they came for the trade unionists, and I didn't speak out because I wasn't a trade unionist.
>
> Then they came for the Jews, and I didn't speak out because I wasn't a Jew.
>
> Then they came for me, and there was no one left to speak out for me.[10]

I learned a similar lesson when visiting South Africa in 1997 with the Rockefeller Foundation to study the work of that country's Truth and Reconciliation Commission. There, I saw that many citizens, while not direct perpetrators of apartheid or of gross violations of human rights, realized how their ignorance, denial, and silence had contributed to apartheid.

One framework for understanding oppression is to see it as a cycle that we experience over time. It includes the following elements:

- Accumulating biases through myths, stereotypes, misinformation, and erasure of information (as in history books that ignore or demean groups)
- Having our biases reinforced by friends, family, schools, media, and our larger culture
- Internalizing oppression by believing biases about ourselves and others, seeing differences as exclusively negative, or seeing ourselves as inferior or superior to others
- Acting with prejudice, accepting privilege, or behaving on the basis of internalized oppression
- Not making waves or challenging the status quo, thereby perpetuating biases, myths, and so on[11]

We can interrupt this cycle and dismantle oppression by unlearning biases, understanding the impact of this cycle on ourselves and others, and taking action to stop the cycle in ourselves and others.

I grew up experiencing this cycle. From my neighborhood, my school, the television shows I watched, and the larger culture, I developed biased and bigoted beliefs about people of color, gays, and others who were different from me. On the rare occasions when I met a person of color, I would think that this person was an exception—one of the good ones. I felt bad when others used racial epithets but didn't think twice about using homophobic ones. When I went to treatment for drug addiction, I was confronted for the first time in my life with a group of people who were very different from myself. I thought myself smarter, more sophisticated, and superior to many of them. My counselor and my group confronted me: How could I, a drug dealer and addict, look at other drug dealers and addicts and feel superior? I had to own who and what I was. I began building relationships with people and opened myself to a new, uncomfortable world. Those lessons put me on the path to Public Allies.

Over time, I came to understand the privilege that supported my recovery and success. I had been busted at parties in the suburbs, where police would take names and phone numbers, turn the names over to the school, and call parents. Ten miles south, the same parties would have produced paddy wagons and police records. Other times I had talked my way out of trouble in ways that would not have been possible if I hadn't been a white guy from the suburbs. My parents had health insurance and the ability to copay, which allowed me to go to treatment. There were several recovery meetings in my community that I could go to and meet people who were like me. I had support from family and friends. When I had to panhandle and find places to crash each night during my "gap year," I did better than others on the street. And with two college-educated parents and five siblings who had gone to college, I always expected that I would find my way to higher education. I experienced great struggles with depression and addiction that challenged and shaped me, but my various kinds of privilege gave me a leg up on turning my life around and finding success personally and professionally.

The Tracing Center on Histories and Legacies of Slavery offers definitions of oppression through the lens of racism.[12] We live in a society marked by what the Tracing Center calls *structural racism*—racism that is embedded in the fabric of our culture so that outcomes in key areas are worse for people of color than for white people. Within that environment are various forms of racism. There is *intentional racism*, which is overt actions by people who are proud of their racism. There is *implicit racial bias*, which is the unconscious biases and stereotypes that many of us hold about other groups. *Internalized oppression* is the negative attitudes that a group's members hold toward themselves and other members of their group (for example, a 2006 study found that 75 percent of whites had an implicit prowhite/antiblack bias, and that blacks were evenly split between prowhite and problack bias).[13] *Privilege* is made up of all the unearned advantages that give certain groups a greater chance at success. Class differences are a key part of this equation. Nevertheless, when all else is equal in terms of economic status, African Americans and other marginalized racial and ethnic groups face disadvantages. It is the Tracing Center's position that in order to understand structural racism, one has to understand the role history has played in privileging and disadvantaging particular groups. For example, the GI Bill, the Federal Housing Administration, and other federal policies that built the American middle class in the twentieth century discriminated against African Americans and other racial minorities for decades. This discriminatory treatment created disparities that still exist today.

We believe that Allies must wrestle with the oppression that exists in themselves, their communities, and their society before they can focus on building more inclusive and just communities. Allies participate in a variety of workshops and activities to do this. Our program begins with their reflections on their own life stories, and Allies often share information about the personal impacts of their backgrounds, including factors related to race, class, religion, sexual orientation, gender, and other characteristics. There are also workshops on various "isms" that explore how particular forms of oppression operate individually and collectively and how to be aware of and dismantle them.

These conversations can be difficult to begin. One exercise that many Public Allies sites use to launch this conversation is the Privilege Walk. It begins with all the Allies holding hands in a line at one end of a room. A facilitator gives a series of instructions, and each person determines whether he or she should move forward or back one space (we say *space* instead of *step* because some people in our groups have not been able to walk). Everyone remains silent throughout the exercise, looking around and reflecting after each movement forward or backward. Here are some of the instructions:

- If your parents spoke English as their first language, move one space forward.
- If, as a child, you had a bedroom of your own with a door, move one space forward.
- If you were discouraged by teachers or guidance counselors from pursuing activities, careers, or education at the school of your choice, move one space back.
- If, when you were a child, your home had more than thirty books in it, move one space forward.
- If both of your parents completed college, move one space forward.
- If one or both of your parents did not complete high school, move one space back.
- If your family never used public assistance for food or housing, move one space forward.
- If you easily find greeting cards for people of your skin color, move one space forward.
- If you have ever feared that showing affection for your girlfriend or boyfriend in public could be dangerous, move one space back.
- If you have never had to hand a grocery store cashier food stamps for your food, move one space forward.
- If you have never been followed by a security guard at a store, move one space forward.
- If you have seen the owner of a purse close it, move it, or clutch it tighter as you approached, move one space back.

- If you do not need aid in order to read, hear, or transport yourself, move one space forward.
- If you have never been harassed or disrespected by someone because of your sexual orientation, move one space forward.
- If you have ever been stopped or questioned by the police or other people about your presence in a particular neighborhood, move one space back.
- If, while attending school, your religious holidays were regularly recognized by your school, move one space forward.
- If you can enter and exit buildings and bathrooms without trouble, move one space forward.

The joined hands break apart early, and by the end of the exercise, the group is scattered all over the room. As Allies reflect on where they are and where their peers are, there is often a great feeling of discomfort for everyone, from those furthest back to those furthest ahead.

There is always a long conversation after this exercise. The facilitators ask questions like these:

1. How did it feel to be in your position at the end?
2. How did you find yourself reacting internally during the exercise?
3. What did you think and feel when you looked around at the end?
4. Was there anything that surprised you about people's positions?

In Baltimore last year, one Ally, a white man who had just graduated from a private college, resisted the exercise: "We spent all this time bonding as a team, and now we've pointed out all our differences and how separate our experiences are."

Laura Bumiller, our senior program manager, grabbed the opportunity. She responded, "It is important to highlight, understand, and even celebrate our differences. When you ignore difference, you don't treat people as individuals, which is almost as bad as making assumptions about them.

"We start with life stories so Allies begin to see both commonalities and differences and understand their motivations and values. There are differences we were born with and others we learned. This exercise helps Allies wrestle at a deeper level with those differences and with various forms of oppression and privilege. Out of this, we begin to see how our different backgrounds and perspectives become assets to the group. It is what gives people sources of power—your experience and story is a source of power."[14]

A few months later, the Ally who had resisted the exercise was in a discussion with a group of Allies about race. When the staff sought to wrap it up, he fought back and said that not everyone had been fully heard and that he wanted to hear the opinion of everyone who wanted to speak. Laura later told me, with a smile, "He went from 'Why are we going there?' to 'Why *aren't* we going there' in four months."

Ebony Scott, our program director at Public Allies Chicago, shares a story about a college-educated African American woman in a workshop who challenged the idea that African Americans could be privileged. Her team was working in a low-income African American neighborhood, and she thought herself the best person to present the team's thoughts about their project to the community residents. The residents pushed back hard at her, wondering who she, a college-educated girl from outside the neighborhood, thought she was to come in and talk to them about their community. It was an awakening for her about the many layers of power and privilege in communities.[15]

To open up these kinds of conversations, Public Allies creates an environment that supports the participants as they take risks and express themselves fully. Feelings of frustration, guilt, anger, apathy, and confusion surface. Some feel vulnerable about the many barriers and challenges they've faced, and others feel guilty for being so far ahead. We discuss these questions openly. We push people to express what they are feeling and reflect on why they feel that way. Ava Hernandez tells me, "Sometimes there is a natural desire among our staff to help everyone come to peace by the end, but allowing people to depart with some anxiety and ambiguity is not a bad thing. These issues are tough and must be wrestled with over time and with each other."[16]

Through these exercises, Public Allies has opened a door that will lead participants to a new way of working together. The goal is not to make people feel bad or to "rank" levels of oppression but to acknowledge it and be aware of how oppression influences ourselves and others and consider how people experience various barriers and opportunities in their lives. They gain understanding and empathy for each other's perspectives and feelings. That awareness is one key to being more inclusive leaders. A second is the skill that leaders gain through having difficult conversations about power, privilege, oppression, and race in the safety of the Allies group. They become able to initiate and facilitate such conversations themselves.

The Privilege Walk is one way of starting the discussion; there are many other ways available. For example, we've had Allies walk through public places holding hands with someone of the same sex, or in interracial couples and groups. They are asked to notice how they feel and how they and their peers are viewed. Allies reflect on the relationships they had growing up and the ones they have currently. They consider diversity among their friends, among the people they've invited to their homes, among the people they worship with, among the people on the sports teams or other groups they belong to, and among those they work with. These exercises help them be more empathetic toward others' experience, aware of how they perceive others and are perceived by others, and more aware of how inclusion takes intention, attention, and effort. They learn that inclusion does not often happen naturally or automatically.

David Weaver founded Public Allies Cincinnati in 1998 and was our national vice president of programs from 2002 to 2005. He is now vice president of programs at Bridges for a Just Society in Cincinnati (formerly the National Conference of Christians and Jews), a human relations organization that operates Public Allies Cincinnati. Explaining what he thinks is unique about our approach, Weaver says, "People develop a world view growing up that holds assumptions about how our society and the systems we interact with works. We push people to understand how they developed their world view, learn about others' world views, and reflect on how their world view creates and blocks opportunity for others. We look at all forms of oppression and how they interact. Leaders who want to lead a whole community need to understand how race, class, gender, sexual orientation, and other forms of oppression work internally, interpersonally, and institutionally, so they can dismantle them. It is about creating opportunities and experiences for people to recognize differences and to figure out how they work together for something new across their differences."[17]

David Weaver created opportunities for Public Allies staff, too, to wrestle with these issues. Six years ago, on a February night in a wooded area near a camp in Ohio, I was lying in the snow shivering from fear as much as from cold. My Public Allies colleagues were nearby, but I could not see them in the dark. We were being auctioned off as slaves by actors/facilitators who were screaming at us and demeaning us. I looked at one of them and was ordered never to look anyone in the eyes, a power dynamic that generated a very submissive posture in me. After we slaves had been marched by our owners into the woods and had sat down outside a cabin in the snow, two rescuers came to take us along the Underground Railroad. We then hid, ran, hid again, were captured, escaped from the slave catchers, and eventually made it back to the camp.

Despite the fact that we had been oriented to the exercise as a role-play, the experience was emotionally intense for all involved. The facilitators gave us scarves that we could take off at any time if we needed a break from the acting. Afterward, sitting with an interracial group and discussing the exercise, our emotions were frayed as we spoke of how this experience is relevant to our lives today. I reflected on how it must have felt to be treated that way all day, every day of one's whole life. I had participated in antioppression exercises and trainings before, but this exercise helped me connect even more to the horrors and scars of oppression and gain insight into how different people experience the legacy of oppression.

David McKinney, our vice president of programs, was also there, and he reflects on his experience: "When our group escaped, we were posing as a choir, and the rescuer handed me a paper that he said was from a church, and I opened it to read to the group. He stopped [me] and reminded me, 'You can't read.' It made me recognize my privilege as an educated African American male and think about who lacks that privilege today. For many of us, it brought up experiences we've had with racism, heterosexism, anti-Semitism, and sexism in our own lives and [helped us] to understand their roots."[18]

After these experiences, participants have to think about what to do with what they have learned. They consider and discuss how they can dismantle oppression within their own minds, within the groups or communities to which they belong, and in the larger society. How can they take whatever privilege they have or have gained and use it to create opportunities for others or work for greater inclusion and social justice? Katrina Browne, our Public Allies co-founder, sets an inspiring and humbling example.

Katrina Browne

While in divinity school, Katrina Browne discovered a terrible family secret: her ancestors, the DeWolf family, had been the largest slave traders in North America. Katrina was devastated by this information, but she had to admit that there had been clues throughout her life that she had ignored.[19]

She decided to use her experience to explore power, privilege, and the generational impact of slavery and oppression. Katrina wrote letters to over two hundred living descendants of the DeWolf family, inviting them to join her for a trip to Rhode Island, where their ancestors had been based; to Ghana, where they had traded rum for captured Africans; and to Cuba, where they had owned sugar and coffee plantations and sold people into slavery. Nine members of her extended family agreed to join her. Most never answered, and some responded with hostility.

Katrina and her team filmed their journey, which resulted in the Emmy-nominated documentary *Tracing the Trade: A Story from the Deep North.* The film aired nationally on PBS in 2008. The documentary shows Katrina and her relatives learning about the conditions the enslaved people endured in the slave forts of West Africa, on the ships, and on the plantations. They discover the huge extent of the North's complicity in slavery. As they learn how their family's privilege, and America's, was generated, they struggle with frustration, guilt, anger, and other emotions. Their mortification is palpable, and one of the most poignant moments comes when they all discuss the role of privilege in their lives, especially the fact that half of them have attended Ivy League schools, as have all but one of their fathers.

Katrina used this experience to build the Tracing Center on Histories and Legacies of Slavery, which is working to engage Americans in continued discussion about slavery, racial equity, and racial healing. Her recognition of the role of privilege in her own life led her to make a commitment to dismantle oppression and help our nation reckon with this past that still shapes us in so many ways. Once we better understand power, privilege, and oppression, we have to work both to dismantle it and not to perpetuate it.

Inclusive Leadership

This brings us to our third strategy. We ultimately want our leaders to convert their new understanding of diversity, oppression, power, and privilege into the commitment to and the action of building inclusive communities. The real work of inclusiveness can be challenging and uncomfortable. It requires us to adapt and change our ways, and perhaps even to relinquish power. But it is also very rewarding and transformational. Inclusive leaders gain relationships and knowledge that allow us to think in new ways about ourselves, our communities, and solutions to the problems we face. We create opportunities for others, and we gain opportunities for our own growth and effectiveness.

Our asset-based approach (see Chapter Five) helps. When we see ourselves, others, and communities as both half full and half empty, we can begin a relationship without oppressive or arrogant power dynamics. The asset-based approach asks us to pay attention to the whole community. It helps us make sure others' assets are being recognized and engaged, especially the assets of those on the margins of the community, or the assets of those whose strengths go unrecognized. This approach leads us to ask whom else we need to listen to and engage. This is the essence of inclusion. It is how we build community.

In our program, most of the community building happens experientially. We match exercises that promote difficult conversations with activities that bring group members back together to recognize one another's assets and to collaborate. David Weaver says, "The Allies learn how to be inclusive from each other, not through training exercises. Because of the diversity of the group itself, they learn about their complexity as human beings and the various barriers, challenges, opportunities, and experiences that shaped them. They surface disagreements, push each other, and learn from each other. They question their own worldview, processes, networks, workplaces, and friends. It is a microcosm of the community outside. Allies learn that their interpersonal relationships set the stage for inclusion, and they can build it step by step, regardless of how much formal power they have. They learn that they each have a responsibility for creating a more inclusive environment."

Hez Norton

Hez Norton, a white Duke University graduate, joined the inaugural class of Public Allies North Carolina in 1994. Hez, who is gay and prefers not to be identified by gender, came out to the Ally class early in the program. Racial diversity was something that everyone was comfortable discussing, but tensions and discomfort bubbled up around the issue of sexual orientation. Hez and two others in the group perceived homophobia. They had experienced it before, but they thought the Public Allies group should be a safe space for them.

"There was constant tension, especially when everyone came together for group trainings," Hez recalls. "A lot of it was rooted in religious traditions being expressed by the African American men in the group."[20]

Two of the Allies spoke up to the group and to the staff about the need to address the homophobia. Hez took a more quiet, long-term approach.

Hez's team service project involved working in low-income housing in an African American neighborhood. Hez's team included several African American men from the neighborhood.

"Being both gay and a 'Dukie,' I was an outsider," Hez recalls. But through their project, Hez and the other team members worked every week on a common goal and learned to rely on each other's different strengths. Often they would blow off steam by talking basketball or playing pickup basketball. "I never felt uncomfortable in my group," Hez reports. "Then, toward the end of the ten months, one of the guys came up to me and said, 'You know, through knowing you, I've had to rethink my feelings about'—he didn't use the word *homophobia*—'my feelings and opinions about gay people.' And I essentially said the same thing to him about my feelings regarding people of color involved in the church. It was very brief but very meaningful. It spoke to me about the power of being in a relationship with people without having to change them. The power of just hanging out together."

Hez doesn't defend the quiet route as the better route: "The other way—the more confrontational way—can work and is sometimes necessary. I was somehow able to give the group more space. I kept thinking, it's the first year of the program, they're all good people, everyone is trying to figure it out."

After Public Allies, Hez founded a statewide, youth-led leadership-development network for gay youth. It was a position that put Hez in contact with far more hostile people ("We're talking death threats") and far more entrenched attitudes. Throughout that experience, the "power of connecting on a relationship level continued to resonate. It was a huge learning experience for me about really leading with relationships and not leading with 'This is the right way!' You have to meet people where they are, be who you are, and build relationships to create change."

Nelly Nieblas

Nelly Nieblas is the daughter of immigrants. She grew up in East Los Angeles and has a physical disability that has required her to walk with crutches her whole life. When she joined Public Allies Los Angeles, many of the Allies and staff were not aware of how people like her are excluded.

"I was constantly waving the flag," Nelly says, "reminding them that I couldn't do an exercise, or that they were making generalizations about people that I was not a part of."[21]

During the year, Public Allies Los Angeles joined another group for a leadership retreat. They organized a series of team-building exercises that required movements Nelly could not perform, so she sat out and got angry. Her program manager came up to her, and Nelly snapped about how the exercises were set up. She wanted to talk to the other leaders of the group: "No one understands, and they still don't get it."

Her program manager made a suggestion: "Maybe you should stop and see if they have been listening. Don't say anything, and see what happens."

When the exercise was over and the group met to debrief, Nelly held her tongue. Then one of her fellow Allies from Los Angeles raised his hand and spoke up.

"These exercises were not inclusive, and one of our members had to sit out," he said. "Did you consider whether everyone could participate when you planned the exercise?"

Then, a little later, a list of upcoming workshops was posted on the wall, and people could sign up for them on a first- come, first-served basis. Nelly got upset again. *Oh, great,* she thought, *I'll get what's left.* But almost before she could complete her thought, one of her fellow Allies came up to her, asked what she wanted to do, and ran up and filled out the forms for her. Nelly realized she had gotten through to her fellow Allies, and that they were more aware of her needs. She did not have to "wave the flag" anymore. She was not invisible.

After Public Allies, Nelly attended the Kennedy School of Government at Harvard University, where, unfortunately, she felt invisible again. This time, she used her experience and her commitment to bring inclusivity to the school.

"It was hard to build relationships," she says, "because I was always the different one, and people, frankly, didn't make much effort to get to know me. I took a course from a popular and well-known professor who, after I spoke up on issues of inclusion, described my disability as 'crippled.' I was marginalized by the professor and my classmates as the 'disability person.'

"I shut up and decided to show the *person,* separate from the label, and show my strengths in other ways. But the Kennedy School was not very accessible, so I created an accessibility committee with some friends, to address issues like ice removal, handrails, and evacuation procedures.

"The dean met with us, and a position was eventually created at the school. It really came from my Public Allies experience. I built relationships with people and used that as the foundation to then organize around inclusion issues. My friends saw my assets, such as my ability to talk to anyone, my public speaking skills, and my negotiating skills. They defined me by those instead of my disability, yet they were aware of my challenges and advocated with me on those issues. That was, unfortunately, not the case of many others there."

After graduating, Nelly returned to Los Angeles, where she worked in county government for two years before becoming director of external relations and public policy at Public Allies.

Ebony Scott, our Program Director in Chicago, describes Hez's and Nelly's stories as the blossoming of inclusive leaders. "Our Allies are able to go into any environment," she says, "and recognize that everyone came from a multitude of different paths and experiences, and that no path is greater or more legitimate than another. They have personal and social awareness. They are conscious of who they are and conscious of how they are perceived. They sense power dynamics and how they play out in a group. They appreciate, value, and celebrate differences, seeing them as opportunities, not barriers. They see assets where others don't. They make sure that groups reflect and represent the communities or constituencies they serve. They make sure that others' voices are heard and their assets are recognized. They listen to what is being said, and listen to what is *not* being said—they look for deeper clues and signals. They know when to push back and when to pull back. They realize that the goal is not just to work with others but to build relationships with them. They invite feedback so they are not just guessing at how they are doing or being perceived. They have the confidence to know the assets and value they bring and the humility to know they don't have all the assets or answers that are needed. They have the right confidence in their core, surrounded by a wall of humility."[22]

First Lady Michelle Obama, our former Chicago director, echoed Ebony's point in a 2009 speech on service:

> We all have skills and talents that make us good friends, family members, workers, and leaders, and we also have needs and shortcomings that come along with those strengths. We can't do well serving these communities, I learned with Public Allies, if we believe that we, the givers, are the only ones that are half full, and that everybody we're serving is half empty. That has been the theme of my work in community for my entire life—that there are assets and gifts out there in communities, and that our job as good servants and as good leaders is not only just being humble, but it's having the ability to recognize those gifts in others and help them put those gifts into action. Communities are filled with assets that we need to better recognize and mobilize if we're really going to make a difference, and Public Allies helped me see that.

> At Public Allies, we endeavored to do this also by bringing these young people together from diverse backgrounds. We worked with African Americans, Asian Americans, Latinos, Native Americans, white, gay, straight, you name it, college graduates, ex-felons—we brought them all together every week to work in a group. And, truly, that's where the magic happened, when you saw those kids from all those different backgrounds really tussling it out and trying to figure out their philosophies in the world in relationship to their beliefs and stereotypes.
>
> The law school graduates realized they had a lot to learn about how communities really work and how to engage people. There's nothing funnier than to watch a kid who believes they know it all actually come across some real tough problems in communities that test every fiber of what they believe.
>
> And then you see the young person with a GED realize that they could go to college because they're working with kids who are just as smart or *not* as smart as them, who *are* going, and they gain a sense of the possibilities that they have. They know that their ideas are just as good, sometimes even better. That's when those lights go off. That's what we think about when we think of asset-based community development—that a kid from Harvard and a kid with a GED are both full of promise.
>
> Everyone learned to build authentic relationships with one another where they could recognize each other's strengths and provide honest feedback on their challenges. They gained a blend of confidence and humility that prepared them to be able to lead from the streets to the executive suites.
>
> You could take any one of those Allies—and it's not just Allies, there are kids like this all over the country—and you could plop them down in any community, and they would know how to build relationships. You know, that's not just important in a nonprofit, that's important in life.[23]

Mrs. Obama's second-to-last statement—"you could plop them down in any community, and they would know how to build relationships"—is what we mean by the ability to connect across cultures. It is still rare for leaders to cross the boundaries that we accept, unfortunately, in our communities. The Public Allies process builds leaders who are comfortable crossing these boundaries. Our leaders learn that crossing boundaries is actually a primary part of their work. And we continue to need boundary crossing in a country where we do not see enough workplaces, professions, and groups that are truly diverse. In fact, our schools are more segregated now than in the 1950s.[24]

I try to cross these boundaries as a leader myself. I pay attention to diversity in terms of whom we hire and the composition of various teams and groups within the organization and in the Ally classes. I've also advocated for diversity and inclusion on every board or group I've been a member of. For example, while on the board of the Helen Bader Institute for Nonprofit Management at the University of Wisconsin–Milwaukee, I initiated an effort to compile and promote data on diversity among local nonprofit executives and set goals for the institute to help increase diversity, and I spearheaded an effort through the Nonprofit Workforce Coalition to work on increasing diversity in nonprofit leadership.

My mentor Lisa Sullivan told me that whatever I achieved, I had to bring other folks with me, so I've tried to live up to that. As I've become more successful and built more powerful networks, I have tried to expand the tables where I sit and be available to other emerging leaders, especially young leaders of color. For example, when I joined President-elect Barack Obama's transition team, I reached out to over a dozen people of color I had worked with in the nonprofit sector—people who might not have been on other leaders' radar—to help recruit them for federal appointments. When I speak publicly about service and leadership, I never shy away from discussing these issues, even if it means challenging the diversity of a group I am addressing. In exchange for the privilege of leading this very diverse organization, I feel a responsibility to promote diversity and inclusion through all my work. And perhaps I am the one who has benefited the most from this focus as I've gained knowledge, perspectives, relationships, and ideas that have made me a better leader and Public Allies a better organization.

Our communities and our country are changing. Soon we will no longer have one group—whites—as the majority but rather a plurality in which no single group is dominant in number, and in which many groups lead. Women's roles and expectations have changed rapidly, and more gays are coming out. David Weaver of Public Allies Cincinnati sums up the call to action very well: "Diversity is unavoidable in the twenty-first century. *Inclusion* is a choice. It can be a positive force, but we have to be intentional about it."[25]

Inclusion helps us live up to our nation's ideals of justice and lets us transform and grow our own leadership. It also makes groups more innovative and effective. Building effective collaboration among diverse groups is the topic we turn to in Chapter Seven.

Key Ideas and Lessons

The process for building diverse and inclusive leaders can be summarized as follows:

1. Build networks and relationships that allow you to bring together people with diverse backgrounds, beliefs, and experiences.
2. Share life stories and learn about each other's communities, experiences, struggles, motivations, successes, and assets.
3. Build a safe environment that supports participants while challenging them to have tough, honest conversations. Set clear ground rules, encourage risk, and help the group persist and move through the inevitable emotional and interpersonal struggles.
4. Participate in exercises that encourage discussion and understanding of power, privilege, and oppression—how they operate

internally, interpersonally, and institutionally, how they are experienced, and how to dismantle them.

5. Acknowledge commonalities and differences. Discuss how those differences can be assets to the group.
6. Build awareness and knowledge of how participants can foster greater inclusion in their own networks, workplaces, and other groups they belong to.
7. Help members build the confidence and approach that allows them to lead and facilitate diverse groups, know when to push back and pull back, and ensure that everyone's voice and assets are valued.

Exercises and Reflections

Privilege Walk

The Privilege Walk exercise described in this chapter is a great way to begin a conversation about power, privilege, and oppression. An exercise like this should take place after a group has started building community through activities like sharing life stories, navigating ropes courses, and other team-building exercises that help them build trust and get to know one another's backgrounds, motivations, values, and goals.

Labeling

Another interesting exercise is to create labels such as *senior citizen, poor, rich, drug addict, hearing impaired, politically powerful, transgender,* and so on. Place the labels on people's foreheads so they cannot see their own labels. Everyone should then go up to every other person, one at a time, and talk to that person according to the label. Each partner in one of these pairs, viewing the other's label, can ask the other to share a fact about his or her life, so that the two can learn more about each other; or each of them can ask the partner a *yes/no* question about his or her own label, to ascertain the status it describes. Assumptions surface through this exercise as people consider how they have responded to information about their own labels and how they have treated others. We ask the Allies, "How did it feel to be treated differently? How did you adjust your response to each label?" This exercise begins a conversation about how people perceive various differences.

Personal Experience

Consider diversity in your professional and personal life:

- How diverse is your circle of friends? your workplace? your place of worship? How diverse are the groups, teams, or clubs you belong to?
- Why do you think that is?
- Do you believe you would benefit from greater diversity? Are there missing perspectives or experiences that would benefit your group?
- How could you bring greater diversity to your personal, professional, and volunteer life? How can groups you belong to be more welcoming of diverse people and perspectives?

7

FACILITATING COLLABORATIVE ACTION

Pittsburgh: Collaborators Who Put the Community First

Each year, teams of seven to ten Allies work on projects that they design, implement, and evaluate. This is a way for them to have impacts on neighborhoods. But it is also where they learn how to collaborate. The process challenges them to work together to plan, set goals, delegate, and share as well as to manage their relationships and neighborhood politics and hold each other accountable.

In 2010, our Pittsburgh Allies chose to work in Larimer, a largely African American neighborhood on the eastern end of the city. When the Allies approached the Kingsley Association, originally established as a settlement house and now a community center serving the neighborhood, Fred Brown, the associate director there, was not sure he wanted their help.

"We get calls all the time from groups who want to come in and help," says Fred. "Well-meaning people come into our community to serve, often to feel better about themselves, assuage guilt they may have about their own privilege, and experience an underserved neighborhood. Then they leave, and their help actually erodes our community's ability to be self-sufficient. So I'm always a little skeptical."[1]

Cynthia James, executive director of Public Allies Pittsburgh, wasn't deterred. She began by building a relationship with Fred Brown.

Fred recalls, "I suggested a different approach than the one she wanted to use—one that may have been against her self-interest, and she was open. I voiced my skepticism about what they were doing, and she never backed off."

He was impressed.

"She wanted to build a relationship, not a project. She was persistent, committed, and kept building a relationship and helping us out," he says. "She even helped facilitate a strategic planning process we were doing at the time. Then I met the Allies and recognized that they were sensitized to the community and didn't have outside agendas."

Fred watched the Allies in action and thought this kind of "help" looked different: "They weren't just in the community, they were part of the community and true partners. Some even lived here. I saw that we would benefit from having the Allies, and they would benefit from the project, too. It was a win-win."

The Allies spent three months immersing themselves in Larimer. They walked door to door, surveying over two hundred residents in their homes about their community and about how local residents and groups could help improve it.

Matt Bartko, the program manager (and Public Allies alumnus) who coached the Allies team, says this effort was intentional: "We encouraged the Allies to build relationships and understanding in the neighborhood. We worked with Allies on how to ask good questions and focus the conversation on assets and solutions, not complaints. Allies decided to walk together in racially diverse groups so they could gain greater credibility with the neighborhood and not just be seen as outsiders."

The Allies met with many neighborhood groups, securing their meeting space from Mt. Ararat Baptist Church and learning about the neighborhood from resident leaders at the Larimer Consensus Group, a neighborhood association. As they got to understand Larimer, they also recruited other partners to contribute their resources to the neighborhood, including a youth volunteer group and a community gardening-development group.

The Allies used the survey results to organize a neighborhood summit. About seventy-five residents met for a day in intergenerational groups to discuss the assets in their community and develop a vision for their community.

"It was not the groan zone that these meetings often become," says Matt. "It was a positive and energetic experience, where residents were really imagining together what they could help create."

The result?

"The residents were empowered in ways both emotional and practical," Fred explains. "We have improved services, increased participation and ownership from local residents, and have emerged with new neighborhood leaders. We went from having twenty to forty people at our monthly neighborhood meetings to having forty to eighty people.

"The Allies brought a lot of capacity to our neighborhood," he continues. "They did not overpromise. They leveraged residents and other assets in the neighborhood. They created partnerships that paid quick dividends and could be sustained. They were a reservoir of information because they had experience working on different issues and parts of the community. And they were sensitive and respectful of neighborhood politics. And the Allies are still involved today, after the project has ended. Most nonprofits talk about collaboration and partnering, and it means 'Help me.' They use neighborhoods as their laboratories. Their project isn't necessarily what we want; it is not sustainable, and they build their volunteer or organizational capacity, not our neighborhood's capacity. Public Allies put the community first."

This story illustrates two keys to collaboration: self-awareness and teamwork. Our Allies built awareness of themselves and those they were working with, built trust and team skills with each other and with other neighborhood groups, and brought together groups and residents to solve neighborhood problems.

Leadership is inherently a collaborative process. Leaders inspire, persuade, and engage others to work *with them* on common goals. As two leadership experts, Kouzes and Posner, make clear, a prospective leader without constituents is alone and incapable of leading, and constituents without leaders have no one to fire their passions or guide them by example.[2]

This chapter explores Public Allies' three-part approach to building collaborative leaders:

1. We believe that effective collaboration begins with knowledge of self and awareness of the ways in which others

work and lead. This awareness helps build our emotional intelligence to manage relationships effectively.

2. Building teams is about building trust. Exercises and processes can help prevent common pitfalls, such as artificial harmony and gossip.

3. We have to think about community in a collaborative way. Just as an individual leader can't create much change without engaging others, individual organizations can't create change without greater collaboration. We believe that if leaders and communities really want to move the needle on issues such as education, health, and poverty, using approaches that have collective impact is probably the most promising way to get results.

Awareness of Self and Others

To work with others effectively, we must first understand ourselves—our strengths, our limitations, our learning styles, our work styles, our needs, our personal missions, and our grounding motivations and values. Such self-knowledge helps us to have confidence about our purpose and what we can best contribute to our purpose. It also gives us humility when we realize we can't do it all, and that we need others in order to achieve our goals.

The Allies' principle that everyone is half full and half empty grounds us in the fact that we bring assets but also limitations. As we saw in Chapter Five, if we accept our own and others' half fullness and half emptiness, we can build more honest relationships. This helps us avoid defining someone only by his or her emptiness or last wrong, and it banishes "us" and "them" dynamics. It also prevents unrealistic expectations of our leaders and colleagues, which only lead to disappointment when leaders and colleagues inevitably show their emptiness. These understandings help us own or accept our own limitations and be more forgiving of others. Add to this the principles of diversity and inclusion—avoiding assumptions, understanding and valuing differences, understanding the dynamics of race, class, gender, and other differences, and holding ourselves accountable for inclusion. Awareness and values combined facilitate the collaborative approach.

But achieving this level of awareness, understanding, and values is work. The average person rarely has learned all these lessons by the time he or she is asked to work in a diverse group. That is why we spend so much time on the interplay among self-awareness, teamwork, and collaboration at Public Allies.

One of my interesting *Aha!* moments came when I realized the relationship between fullness and emptiness. Back in 2003, my management team did a simple exercise. On Post-it notes, we wrote what we liked best about working with each other and what we did not like. We then placed the notes up on a wall and grouped them by similarity. We realized that the things we liked and didn't like about each other were connected. For example, people commented on my ability to craft a vision, synthesize scattered information into a bigger picture, and inspire others. They also struggled with my lack of focus on details, my disorganization, and my talking too much. This pattern emerged across the group as we saw both sides of being a great process person, a great mobilizer, and a great detail person. Connecting these dots opened a new way to value our strengths and understand our shortcomings.[3]

Personality and Leadership Styles

This connection between strengths and shortcomings is reflected in many personality inventories. At Public Allies, we've used tools such as StrengthsQuest and the Myers-Briggs Type Indicator® (MBTI) to assess our work styles. The MBTI® assessment, based on work by the psychiatrist Carl Gustav Jung, assesses each person's style on the basis of the following factors:

- Do you prefer to focus on your outer world or your inner world? Extraverts (E) put their energy and attention into and on the outer world of people and things. Introverts (I), who are not necessarily shy or reclusive, focus on the inner world of ideas and images.

• Do you prefer to focus on the basic information you take in, or do you prefer to interpret and add meaning? Those who are Sensing (S) types pay more attention to information that comes through their senses, whereas those who are Intuitive (N) types tend to pay more attention to patterns and possibilities in the information they receive.

• When making decisions, do you prefer to look first at logic and consistency or to look first at people and special circumstances? Those who put more weight on objective principles and impersonal facts are Thinking (T) types, whereas those who put more weight on personal concerns and the people involved are Feeling (F) types.

• In dealing with the outside world, do you prefer to get things decided or do you prefer to stay open to new information and options? Those who prefer a more structured and decided lifestyle are Judging (J) types, whereas those who prefer a more flexible and adaptable lifestyle are Perceiving (P) types.

Each person is scored with four letters (one from each pair), which reflect the relative strength of each preference, and is assigned to an overall type (there are sixteen types).

For example, my score over the years has tended to be ENFP, with stronger preferences for Intuition and Feeling and slighter preferences for Extraversion and Perception. Without going into great detail, I can say that some of the strengths of an ENFP type include enthusiasm, imagination, optimism, spontaneity, authenticity, systems thinking, and making quick connections among ideas and people. But these are accompanied by such weaknesses as dropping projects, getting distracted by new possibilities, becoming frustrated with mundane details, needing to be liked, and manipulating others with the gift of gab. This description—the pluses as well as the minuses—fits me well.[4] Early on at Public Allies, I had a colleague I really struggled to communicate with. When solving a problem, I was more likely to throw out ten ideas and see if others agreed with any of them and then try to build consensus immediately. She was more likely to sit and think deeply about the problem as she tried to surface what she thought would be the best options. I was Extraverted; she was Introverted. We solved problems in different ways, and we learned that we had to accommodate each other. So, for example, we could meet and brainstorm ideas for solving a problem and then set up a follow-up meeting to gather additional input and make decisions. I could throw my ten balls in the air, and she could have time to generate and think through her options.

Tools like the MBTI® assessment help us understand and communicate with others. As Tina Morrow, our executive director in Delaware and a certified MBTI® administrator, explains, "We use it with the Allies and their supervisors as well as among Allies to open a conversation about work styles. They see the strengths of each of the main styles and also how to work with each style. The tool helps Allies learn about themselves, recognize different styles in others, and learn to bridge those differences and work better together."[5]

In addition to tools such as the MBTI® assessment and StrengthsQuest, exercises can help us become aware of our diverse leadership styles. The Leadership Compass exercise is adapted from the Native American medicine wheel, which represents the idea that health comes from balance. Likewise, for a group to be healthy, it must also have balance. In this exercise, we imagine the room as a compass, with four leadership types as poles (most people have elements of each of these styles, but there is one more dominant style):

- East: *Visionaries* are big-picture people. They are generative and innovative, enjoy experimenting, and like solving problems. They can also lose sight of process and details, struggle to follow through, and have difficulty sustaining passion after their initial enthusiasm begins to wane.

• West: *Analysts* (Teachers) tend to be very detail-oriented and are excellent at planning, documentation, systematizing, and quality control. They can also be averse to risk, paralyzed by analysis, indecisive, and insensitive to people's passions.

• North: *Mobilizers* (Warriors) like challenges, persevere through obstacles, are decisive, and are good at organizing and motivating people for action. They can also overlook process, be argumentative, and be impatient.

• South: *Nurturers* (Healers) pay attention to how the work is done and want to make sure everyone is heard and engaged. They listen and facilitate very well and are observant of group process and values. They can be so focused on process that they can lose sight of goals, be risk-averse, avoid conflicts, and allow individual feelings to divert a group's work.

In this exercise, participants choose a compass point, and we don't allow them to straddle groups. Once people go to their own compass points in the room, they discuss with others who share their style the assets of individuals with this particular leadership style. Then they think about the assets of the other styles as well as about the qualities of those styles that they themselves need in order to be successful in any endeavor. They take notes and report out. For example, the Nurturers describe what they bring to the table, and then each of the other three groups describes the assets of the Nurturers.

It is affirming to hear your group's assets acknowledged, and to recognize why different styles and skills are valuable. Each person recognizes that he or she is needed and needs the others. We each bring pieces of the puzzle. Differences are indeed assets!

After the exercise, we discuss the balance in the room. What does it mean to have a team that has only three of these leadership styles? How can an unbalanced group compensate?

Darren Thompson, a community health worker in Milwaukee for a large local hospital, and chair of a Native American community health center, is a member of the Ojibwe Nation. When he was an Ally, he found the exercise rewarding, personally and culturally. "I was proud that something from my culture had influenced Public Allies' leadership beliefs," he says, "and that it was being shared with my class. I felt pressure to be good at everything. It made me feel good to understand myself this way—that I don't have to be all of these things. It helped me realize I do need others as well. Now, when I'm in a group, I think about the different styles each person brings."[6]

I've also used this approach when looking at my teams. A few years ago, our management team had become bogged down in process. The leadership compass revealed that we had several Analysts, one Nurturer, one Visionary, and no Mobilizer. The group needed more entrepreneurship, experimentation, and action to offset the emphasis on process, planning, and systems. So for my next executive hire, I sought someone who would bring more of a Mobilizer-type leadership style. The goal is not dominance of any one style but balance that produces better results.

Besides those mentioned here, many different tools and exercises exist to help group members achieve greater self-awareness, develop greater understanding of others, and discuss how to benefit from style differences. What's important is that leaders and teams engage in the process so they can build confidence in what they know and do well, humility about what they don't, and respect for the help they need from others.

Feedback, Leadership, and Collaboration

An old friend used to say, "When I am the best source of information about how I am doing, I'm in big trouble." It is good to assess how we are doing on a regular basis by asking for feedback.

One way to test our perceptions of our skills, leadership styles, or values is by seeking feedback. Allies receive several workshops on giving and receiving feedback, and they participate in 360-degree reviews and feedback circles (see Chapter Eight). Learning to give and receive direct feedback is one of the most important skills for collaborating effectively.

Building awareness of ourselves and testing it through feedback allows us to become more "emotionally intelligent," to use the phrase coined by Daniel Goleman. In his seminal study *Emotional Intelligence*, Goleman argues that we have, in effect, two brains—one rational and the other emotional—and that both determine our success in life. He draws extensively on brain and behavioral research, and he builds on work by the Yale psychologist Peter Salovey, who defines emotional intelligence as having five components. Goleman identifies five domains of emotional intelligence:

1. Being aware of feelings as they happen
2. Managing our emotions as we respond to people and situations
3. Marshaling our emotions to motivate us in the service of a goal
4. Having empathy, or recognizing emotions in others
5. Handling the emotions involved in relationships

Our abilities differ within these domains. For example, someone may be quite adept at handling his own anxiety but inept at soothing someone else's upsets.[7]

The exercises and tools we use at Public Allies help our participants hone their emotional intelligence. These improvements make them both better leaders and better people. As they build greater self-awareness and awareness of others, they do better at working with others in teams and groups. Emotional intelligence is essential to good teamwork and collaboration.

Building Teams

Team building and being a team player are essential leadership skills, but the process doesn't happen automatically. At Public Allies, team-building retreats, workshops, and training help Allies learn to work effectively with others. Experiential opportunities, such as team service projects, strengthen Allies' collaborative muscles the most.

Our Public Allies program year begins with a "core training" retreat. There are no screaming sergeants or push-ups, but group members work together to overcome many personal and physical challenges.

The retreat typically begins at a sleepaway camp, where members participate in a ropes/challenge course for two or three days. This activity encourages Allies to take risks, be vulnerable, listen to each other, support each other, and solve problems together. They run around blindfolded, undo knots, climb trees and jump, squeeze through tight holes, fall into each other's arms, get frustrated, argue, hug, and cheer. The effort breaks through initial posturing as people adapt to a new environment and can't lean on their normal personality or social crutches. Participants start to see each other beyond initial judgments and recognize how groups can work better together.

During this time we typically also make life maps (see Chapter Two) to further help Allies get to know each other and share about themselves. Through this exercise, Allies learn about each other's backgrounds, motivations, challenges, assets, and values.

Combined, these two exercises help eliminate assumptions, break down prejudices, and create intimacy and empathy. According to Tina Morrow, our Delaware director, "Life maps help feed our group dynamics. It helps us get out of the 'polite' state quickly. At the end of the exercise, people feel they can connect to everyone in the room in some form or other. It starts to build a sense of community."[8] Life maps are just one way of helping the members of a team learn about each other's authentic selves so they can build trust and begin to learn to work together. Without such authenticity, groups can fail to come together and build that trust in each other's motivations, perspectives, and purposes.

In addition to learning how to function as team members, Allies receive team-building training in such skills as facilitation, giving and receiving feedback, and conflict resolution. The training and exercises also challenge Allies to consider earlier lessons—what it means to be inclusive, to value and understand the roots of difference, to embrace the notion that everyone has assets to contribute, and to accept that they and their teammates are half empty as well as half full.

In the middle of the year, there is another sleepaway retreat. Many Public Allies sites use this occasion to recenter their teams. After the initial "honeymoon," when Allies all learn to like and value one another, they inevitably begin to slide into dysfunction. Some of this dysfunction occurs through overt conflicts, and some of it happens quietly. The group starts to acquire "elephants in the room" that no one talks about—conflicts get buried, motives get questioned, domineering team members gain too much power, someone isn't pulling his or her weight. These are normal events in teamwork, but they infect and sour the group. The first round of 360-degree reviews, which comes right before midyear, opens up some of the dysfunction, but the retreat is where we dive in deeper. It is during this critical retreat that Allies learn much more about what it means to be authentic in a group so the group can become a stronger team.

Various authors have described the process by which a group of individuals becomes a team. M. Scott Peck, in *The Different Drum*, describes four stages a group moves through on its way to becoming a community:[9]

1. *Pseudo-community*, when people pretend things are great and avoid conflict
2. *Chaos*, when differences emerge and people fight, rebel, try to heal differences or convert others, and so forth

3. *Emptiness*, when people let go of the barriers inside them that block them and begin to communicate authentically
4. *Authentic community*, which is not an "end" but an ongoing process of accepting and rejoicing in differences, a condition in which problems are no longer avoided but are instead resolved

The process Peck describes is parallel to Bruce Tuckman's better-known "forming-storming-norming-performing" model of group dynamics. Both processes share the assumption that conflicts must be surfaced, that they usually are symptoms of individuals' own challenges, and that they need to be overcome in order for people to work together.

Some of our sites adapt Peck's community-building process for their midyear retreats. The exercise begins with everyone sitting in a circle. Ground rules for the experience (such as speaking in "I" statements and not interrupting) are established, and then there is silence. After a bit of silence, anyone who is moved to speak is invited to speak. At some point, chaos appears. Two trained facilitators monitor how much chaos to allow before moving to the "emptying" phase. Among the challenges they try to address in this process are the "fight" impulse (making accusations and being defensive), the "flight" impulse (ignoring or dropping difficult issues), pairing (allying with others and separating from the larger group, or ganging up on others), and being dependent (looking to a leader to step in).[10]

According to Kate Flynn, executive director of Public Allies Milwaukee, "The primary benefit of this process is developing emotional intelligence skills, an understanding of group process, and what true community looks like." Kate has been through the process six times and worked hard to keep it central to the Allies' experience. "It creates a space for profound personal introspection that some folks may never experience in the same way again. The experience is also deeply meaningful to the group. When conflicts arise, individuals rely on what they gained from the retreat to resolve issues."[11]

Alisha Klapps, a Public Allies Milwaukee alumna who participated in the process in 2010, found herself shutting down somewhat: "While I was there, I viewed it as a negative experience. However, as time has passed, I look at it differently. It brought me to a place where I recognized that reflection needed to be part of my life. My team had lots of conflicts at the beginning. We didn't click. And then we brought it to life at the retreat. We threw it all out there. We aired our dirty laundry. And after that our group started to grow in a better direction. We understood each other better. I wish I could do that in every place I am."[12]

In the same room with Alisha was another Ally experiencing something different—Nelson Rivera. "It was a tremendous experience to be able to open up about stuff," he says, "stuff I could not even open up to with my mom and dad. I was able to release a lot of things that were bothering me, a lot of tension from a personal matter that was really blocking me. I was able to tell these thirty-five people about it and receive so much support. You could feel the warmth and deep understanding. I had never opened up like that before. It was such a loving and nonjudgmental atmosphere." Unlike Alisha, Nelson felt an immediate change: "After that exercise, I was able to detach myself from negative issues and refocus my energy toward positive life-changing ideas I know I'm capable of. At Public Allies, you do so much work on yourself without even realizing it. I would want my kids to go through it."[13]

Vanessa L. Llanas had sat in the same circle six years earlier, and she remembers it vividly. "It doesn't take a lot to move me to speak," she says. "So of course I was one of the first people to speak. That provoked one of my classmates to say to me—I'll never forget it, she was across the room, and she was crying—'I just don't understand how you can be moved to speak so much.'" When the exercise ended, Vanessa started asking her quieter colleagues to explain how they felt, and she learned that just because someone doesn't speak, that doesn't mean they have nothing to say. "I have taken that lesson with me," she says now.

"This helped me pursue work as a community organizer—the importance of getting to know someone one on one, and getting to know their story and assets. I try to remember lessons like these whenever I'm working in a group and getting frustrated. I try to step back, be quiet, and observe instead of jumping in."[14]

I've found this process useful myself because my first such retreat helped reveal how fear was driving my leadership style and my lack of trust in others. I had to learn to let go, and my teammates had things they had to let go of, too.

A decade later, we hit another challenging time, during a strategic planning process that explored a major reorganization of Public Allies' national and local relationships. Dana Burgess O'Donovan of the Monitor Institute, our consultant, realized we needed help working things through, and she introduced us to the book *Difficult Conversations*, by members of the Harvard Negotiation Project. Their book helps a group move toward becoming a team, and their process involves five steps:[15]

1. Sort out what happened, understand your emotions, and determine what's at stake for you.
2. Check your purpose and decide whether to raise the issue that concerns you.
3. Describe the problem in terms of the differences between people's stories, holding up each story as a legitimate part of the conversation, and explain your purpose.
4. Explore others' stories and your own.
5. Invent options to meet everyone's most important criteria, look to standards for what should happen, and talk about how to keep communication open as the group moves forward.

All the types of processes described here help team members address difficult issues together and build their decision-making muscles. When there are tough problems to solve, it is good to step back and do the team- and community-building work that will produce more effective solutions.

Team Service Projects

Many of the skills, books, and exercises discussed here have helped Public Allies staff and Allies learn how to work in teams, but the real learning is experiential. For our Allies, experiential learning comes through team service projects.

At the beginning of the year, we split Allies into teams of seven to ten people to undertake projects that they design, implement, and evaluate together. To select team members, we use their backgrounds, personality profiles, and staff observations, seeking to balance different personalities and leadership styles on each team. The projects are focused on achieving a community impact while teaching Allies how to collaborate effectively with diverse groups.

Each team has a Public Allies program manager whose job is to support and coach—not to step in, lead, or solve the team's problems. Like the community-building facilitators, they allow some level of chaos to develop before they step in to help the team resolve it and move on. The conflicts and challenges are teachable moments and help the Allies build their own capacity to solve problems and work effectively with others.

Here, to complement the example of collaboration in Pittsburgh that opened this chapter, are two more examples of team service projects:

- In Delaware, a team of Allies worked with a church on the west side of Wilmington to address the issue of a park that had become dangerous because of drug use and other crimes. The Allies, after spending two or three months meeting with local community groups and surveying neighbors door to door, helped establish a summer baseball league to bring positive activity and neighbors back to the park. The project was very successful and is being sustained by local groups.
- In Connecticut, the Bridgeport team worked with the Bridgeport Neighborhood Trust to help rehabilitate two

six-family buildings for low-income families. To help mobilize the community, the Allies organized a photo exhibit at a branch library of local families telling their life stories. The exhibit brought dozens of families to the library. Then the Allies launched their Buy a Brick, Build a Home project. The effort raised funds from local residents and businesses. In the end, twelve families ended up with affordable housing, and the neighborhood built new relationships and resources.

These two team projects, like the one in Pittsburgh, built relationships in a neighborhood. But the process also teaches Allies how to build and maintain relationships with each other. The teams experience many interpersonal and external challenges while accomplishing their goals. They have to deal with people who are too dominant or apathetic, with people who are controlling and want to do it all, and with others who don't pull their weight. They have to resolve disagreements about goals, tactics, and the quality of their efforts. These are common challenges that Allies will also face as they become the leaders of the future. The skills they learn as they overcome these challenges will serve them well. All communities need people who know how to build trust, focus on collective results, facilitate difficult conversations, give direct feedback, help people understand and participate in difficult decisions, and hold high standards for everyone on the team. And these skills are essential for ensuring *functional* collaborative work.[16]

Collective Impact

Self-awareness and interpersonal collaboration also extend to the formal and informal organizations that constitute communities. Just as none of us has all the skills and assets to lead all alone, no one organization or program can solve problems all alone. Public Allies believes that social change is possible only through efforts that build community capacity, including collaborations among citizens and groups across various boundaries—racial, class, sector, issue focus, and so forth.

Milwaukee has experienced massive growth in new schools, after-school programs, youth organizations, and nationally replicated programs. We've seen rapid growth of professional certificate and graduate degree programs in nonprofit management, education, and youth work, and major philanthropic investments in nonprofit management capacity. Despite these investments, I recently woke up to read some troubling news in the morning paper—that our state's African American fourth graders had the worst reading scores in the country.[17] How is it that the good work of fine people has not added up to genuine impact?

The problem lies in the fragmentation of the nonprofit and public service sectors. The issues that lead to poor performance among fourth graders are integrated into their lives, but our institutions try to solve them piecemeal. For the past few decades, we've been chasing a theory of change that incentivizes solving problems as follows:

1. Target a narrow need in a community, isolate it, and create an intervention for that need.
2. Believe that this limited intervention will lead to long-term change in the life of every person the intervention touches.
3. Once there is evidence that the intervention produces positive short-term outcomes, replicate the intervention with more people, on the theory that doing so will have the cumulative effect of solving the community's problem.

This theory sounds logical, but decades of efforts have shown that interventions based on this theory of change simply do not work. We see positive results from programs, but often the change produced is not enough or cannot be sustained. People's lives are complex, and so a student's challenge in school may be related to issues of housing, safety, mental health, physical health, nutrition, social capital, or economic security. The services a family needs to get on track are divvied up among dozens of disconnected organizations. Short-term gains from tutoring, for example, will be lost if they are not connected to other improvements in a child's life. There are many programs that are rigorous in pursuit of specific outcomes, but programs must collaborate and integrate their activities in order to create real and sustainable community change.

John Hagedorn, an urban sociologist at the University of Illinois–Chicago, has written insightfully and provocatively about his time working with the civil rights and education activist Dr. Howard Fuller in the late 1980s to reform the child welfare system in Milwaukee.[18] The fragmentation of the system confounded him. He notes that the clients were unpredictable and that their problems resisted the routine treatment prescribed by bureaucracies; he also points out that there were more than forty county, city, state, school, and private nonprofit workers directly serving one family.[19] For example, he tells about calling a meeting of the various social workers and staff members from the schools and agencies that were serving the children of a troubled immigrant family. He also invited the children's mother. The social workers shared a litany of challenges that the kids were facing—they were often dirty, ill behaved, not prepared for school, and so forth. Then Hagedorn turned to the mother and asked her what she thought the main issue was. She answered without hesitation: "I don't have any electricity in my house." Hagedorn discovered that both the school's social worker and the social worker from the state's department of social services had known this for weeks but done nothing about it. The school nurse didn't even understand how electricity was related to hygiene! Hagedorn asked who was going to call the electric company and get the family's power turned on. The professional helpers all gave their narrow job descriptions, and getting this family electricity wasn't included. Hagedorn had to order it done himself, and he concludes from this experience that "while the family's problems went far beyond electricity, the point is it wasn't anyone's job to look at the family's problems as a whole."[20]

About a decade ago, Public Allies had teenagers map the assets in their neighborhoods, using the Youth Mapping initiative developed by the great youth-development innovator (and Public Allies board member) Richard Murphy. These teens worked for a summer, interviewing neighbors, friends, and leaders in their own neighborhoods. They were surprised to find that school principals, teachers, community organizers, community elders, nonprofit leaders, neighborhood associations, youth workers, neighborhood business owners, and pastors did not know each other. For example, the head of a youth agency would know other agency heads across the city but not the other people in the neighborhood who served the same kids. The teens thought it was odd that if a kid was troubled at school, the teacher or the principal didn't contact the after-school program, the family's pastor, or others in the neighborhood.

This fragmentation of services and effort is why we have a lot of activity and "outcomes" but no real solutions. John Kania and Mark Kramer of the Foundation Strategy Group have addressed these challenges, arguing that "large-scale social change comes from better cross-sector coordination rather than from isolated intervention of individual organizations" and noting that funders and nonprofits are so used to focusing on isolated, independent actions that they miss the bigger picture: "Funders, faced with the task of choosing a few grantees from many applicants, try to ascertain which organizations make the greatest contribution toward solving a social problem. Grantees, in turn, compete to be chosen by emphasizing how their individual activities produce the greatest effect. Each organization is judged on its potential to achieve impact, independent of the numerous other organizations that may also influence the issue," and the result is that "nearly 1.4 million nonprofits invent independent solutions to major problems, often working at odds with each other."[21] The volume of resources going to solve problems grows, but the problems aren't solved.

To make matters worse, recent trends in social innovation are all about increasing the size of organizations and their particular interventions (grant makers like to call this "going to scale") rather than about comprehensive community solutions. Once again, the common model for social change is to isolate a need, fill it, and replicate the intervention to solve the problem. What Kania and Kramer suggest instead is an approach they call "collective impact." This is a long-term approach in which groups come together with a centralized infrastructure, a dedicated staff, and a structured process, and it leads to a common agenda, shared measurement, continuous communication, and mutually reinforcing activities among all participants. It calls for a core group of community leaders who decide to abandon their individual agendas in favor of a collective approach to solving a community problem.[22]

As an example of collective impact, Kania and Kramer cite Cincinnati's Strive Partnership. Strive seeks to address the needs of youth, "cradle to career." In Cincinnati, more than three hundred local leaders—university presidents, school district officials, nonprofit leaders, philanthropists, and business leaders—have come together, guided by fifty-three success metrics for youth. These metrics include fourth-grade reading and math scores, graduation rates, and readiness for kindergarten. Fifteen Student Success Networks have been formed at each point along the continuum (for example, early childhood, mentoring, job training). These networks bring the players together to set a coordinated plan under one set of metrics for the community as a whole. According to Kania and Kramer, "The leaders realized that fixing one point on the educational curriculum—such as better after-school programs—wouldn't make much difference unless all parts of the continuum improved at the same time."[23]

Jeff Edmondson, president of the Strive Partnership, has described to me how this process works:

> We've learned that the only way to build sustainable change is to focus on collaboration among all the stakeholders. It took a lot of time to build trust among groups—the school district, nonprofits, the teachers union, and others—who had distrusted each other for years. Now resources—both existing dollars and new dollars—flow to the collaborative action plans and common performance goals that lift the whole community.[24]

Khalilah Slater Harrington, an alumna of Public Allies Cincinnati, leads much of the collaboration among community groups and schools at Strive. Khalilah tells me her skills as an Ally are being put to work every day: "At Public Allies, I learned how to work well with people I didn't always agree with." She now works with a team of coaches to support the twelve Student Success Networks in building trust and teamwork with each other. "The process takes time," she says. "Given the economy, some groups initially come to the table hoping for money. Then they realize there isn't necessarily a pot of gold at the end of the rainbow, but they remain engaged because they realize we have to all improve outcomes for kids, even if we don't have more money. I approached this with an asset-based community development perspective—we've got to leverage the assets that exist and look for new ones. Some network members felt, 'Ours is the best at this service or that,' and we'd say, 'Great. Show us your data.' Then we had to get past the posturing, to a point where we could share a common plan, common measures, and transparent data to have collective impact. It took time to work through issues and build that trust, just like on my team service project."[25]

Strive Partnership is an impressive and promising example of collaborative approaches to complex social problems, such as problems involving educational success and poverty. The organization admits that its community engagement has not been as effective as its building of partnerships among providers, but it is continuing to seek ways to increase ownership for these results in the communities themselves. The success indicators tracked by Strive are on the rise across the board. And these collaborative efforts require a different kind of leadership. Jeff Edmondson describes Khalilah as having "incredible emotional intelligence. She has an invaluable ability to build relationships and see through different lenses. She helped us understand that engaging the community is not about how the community perceives our work but about how they own it."[26]

David Chrislip and Carl Larson wrote about this way of leading back in 1994: "Collaborative efforts cross many boundaries—public/private/community. No single organization can solve problems."[27] Elsewhere they state that collaborative leaders "are not heroes who tell us what to do, but servant leaders who help us do the work ourselves."[28] They argue that we fail to solve problems in part because of our inability to acknowledge and work with complexity and ambiguity, a capacity that requires us to recognize that we do not "know" what to do and must instead experiment and learn our way into solutions with others: "No one recognizes that the capacity for renewal is rooted in the community rather than in programs or individuals. It is the people who live there."[29] Chrislip and Larson describe many characteristics of collaborative leaders, including those that follow:[30]

- The capacity to safeguard group process, tolerate frustration, and facilitate interaction
- The ability to identify relevant stakeholders and interests and their potential for agreement
- The ability to evaluate the community's capacity for change and where change might best be leveraged
- The ability to avoid the tyranny of consensus, the worship of process, and endless meetings while relying on peer problem solving
- The capacity to inspire commitment to action toward clear results

- The capacity to secure broad-based participation and to sustain hope

In short, a leader's role is to convene, energize, facilitate, and sustain the process. These are the collaborative skills Public Allies seeks to develop among our participants. Our leaders need to be able to build collaborations among individuals, teams, and communities to solve pressing problems. And it is their values that guide that process. Leaders must build relationships with people by sharing and listening to everyone's stories, interests, motivations, and values. They must know how to build trust as well as to surface challenges and conflicts and resolve them. They must be willing to make compromises and sacrifices for the larger good, maintaining a commitment to real change that goes beyond individual or group interests. Combining these qualities with emotional intelligence, asset-based community development, and inclusion, leaders have the skills to collaborate effectively in a group or in the whole community.

Being collaborative is a *commitment*. I am always inspired by the impacts our alumni continue to have in their communities, but I am most inspired when they are collaborating with each other and bringing others together to have greater impact. That is the kind of leadership we need. In Chapter Eight we will turn to another value that makes collaboration possible: the commitment and humility to continuously learn and improve, especially by seeking the support, counsel, and feedback of others.

Key Ideas and Lessons

1. Teamwork begins with self-awareness and awareness of others' work and leadership styles.
2. We can't be good at everything. We need to build teams with others who bring different styles and talents. We then have to work on valuing and working through those differences.

3. Building teams requires intentional processes so that people can learn about each other, focus on relationships and not just on work, move past artificial harmony, and learn to work with each other. These processes include giving feedback and disagreeing, productively.
4. Collaboration is necessary to solving community problems. It is rare that one organization can solve problems without collaborating with others. If we want to address long-term problems in a community, we must have all the stakeholders coordinating and collaborating on shared, communitywide goals.

Exercises and Reflections

This chapter has already introduced a number of activities that can be used to foster collaboration, such as ropes courses, feedback exercises, and exploration of personality types and leadership styles. Here are some questions that can be used for reflection on collaboration and collective impact.

Teamwork

Describe an effective team or group you were part of. What made it work well?

- How was leadership practiced among the members? What was your role?
- Did the team have a good balance of personality and leadership styles?
- How did the team motivate commitment and deal with people falling short of expectations?
- Are you more of a visionary, a mobilizer, an analyst, or a nurturer?
- What do you find most rewarding and most challenging about working with the other three leadership styles?
- Why do people like having you on their team? When do people struggle with you?

Collective Impact

Consider the community where you live, work, or worship, and think of all the groups in the neighborhood that work on youth development, for example, or on public health or housing.

- Do these groups meet with each other to do any type of common planning or programs?
- Do they have shared goals for improving the community? Do they share data with each other as a way of identifying successes, gaps, and areas for improvement that they can address together?
- As they do their work, do they also engage other nonprofits, houses of worship, businesses, schools, and citizens from the neighborhoods they serve? Do members of the community feel that they have a say in the goals, programs, and metrics used by these groups?

8

CONTINUOUSLY LEARNING AND IMPROVING

Melia Dicker: Reschooling Herself

Melia Dicker grew up in Sonoma, California. Her family was one of several Asian American families in a predominantly white community. She was a high achiever growing up and continued her record of achievement at Santa Clara University, where she obtained a degree in psychology.

After college, she felt that something was still missing and that she had more to learn: "I'd perfected the formula for success in school—follow other people's rules and reap the rewards. I'd gotten all A's."[1] But her achievement had been driven more by the fear of failure than by a love of learning. She felt stifled by the achievement game, and she thought that school hadn't really prepared her for success in life: "After I graduated, there were no tests to ace, no teachers to tell me I was good enough. I had to make my own rules, but I had no clue how."

A friend from Santa Clara University shared with Melia her transformative experience with Public Allies Silicon Valley, and Melia thought this could be the experience she needed.

Melia's Public Allies placement was as an after-school coordinator in the Mountain View-Whisman school district. Despite challenges with the bureaucracy and an unsupportive supervisor, she connected with the students and worked hard for them.

Through service, coaching, feedback, and reflection, Melia had numerous *Aha!* moments. For example, in her team service project, Melia fell back on the superachiever role she had often assumed for group projects in school. Her idea of collaboration was telling her teammates, "I can handle it," not trusting that others could do as good a job as she could. So she took control and figured her team would be grateful for her effort and the quality of her work. They weren't.

When she received her 360-degree evaluation feedback, she was stunned. She had rated herself highly for her collaborative skills, but others had not. Then, during an exercise when Allies shared direct feedback with her, she realized that "the behaviors of competing, taking control, and showing that I could master a task myself were always rewarded growing up. I learned that I had to create opportunities for others to step up, that things actually worked better when I listened to others and we did the work together. For the first time in my life, I took a back seat, and it turned out well."

Reflecting on and preparing for her required end-of-year Presentation of Learning helped her figure out the kind of leader she wanted to be: "I realized that real leadership is about inspiring the best in others, not achieving a goal by yourself. I found that the differences in our group were strengths, and that working together did get us to better results in the end. It was a shift in how I'd thought about leadership before."

She also made a big decision. At her placement, she had seen that kids were struggling to see school as engaging, relevant, and interesting. She reflected on her own experience and realized how narrow her own education had been while she was so focused on achievement rather than learning. Building from her Public Allies experience, she co-founded Spark, a nonprofit that places middle school-aged youth in apprenticeships in their dream jobs so they can experience different career opportunities.

"It was a different approach to learning," she says, "one that I think young people really need and that I got only later in life. I based a lot of it on what we did at Public Allies—blending education with real-world experiences."

After launching Spark and helping lead it through its first few years, Melia decided to undertake a unique experience to explore education and learning. "Reschool Yourself" was her personal project of revisiting her education and considering how she would do things differently if she had a second chance. She went back to her old schools and classrooms, spending about a week in each grade, from kindergarten to college. She triggered old memories by doing whatever the students did—in the classroom and on the playground—and by sorting through old photos, yearbooks, and journals at home: "My goal was to face painful regrets and let them go, and to reconnect with the playfulness and creativity I'd had naturally as a kid." She blogged about the experience and is now working on a book.

Melia learned many lessons: "First, I first took this on as a project, and my 'achiever' side took over, so I was trying to do this perfectly and write about it perfectly. I realized I needed to let go once again." She also learned that mistakes are part of the learning process: "You have to be able to laugh at yourself. I was so fearful of failing growing up, and I wish I had seen that as part of learning because failure is probably the most powerful way we learn. And there were these kids–the type I'd looked down on when I was in school–who saw the system for what it is. They understood the system, and they didn't buy into it. They didn't always follow the rules, and they didn't get A's, and they didn't care. I didn't see them as smart when I was in school, and now I see that they were perhaps the smartest ones. Slowly, I learned to take care of myself and do things that I love every day. By sharing my experiences, I hope to encourage others to reshape their own learning and self-image at any age." Through the journey, she changed career directions, met her husband, moved across the country, and took on new hobbies.

After this experience, Melia co-founded the Institute for Democratic Education in America (IDEA). With the political drive to improve test scores and cut extracurricular activities in K–12 education, she felt the need for a movement to bring learning back to education, with a focus on building citizens for the twenty-first century: "So much of what is happening in schools is either based on old models that are obsolete or so constrained that it doesn't build thoughtful, responsible young people. Education should not be about memorizing answers or pleasing teachers but about being critical and collaborative and knowing what questions to ask. It is about connecting real-world experience, responsibility, group learning, and working across difference. I was book-smart coming into Public Allies and came out people-smart. I gained responsibility as well as social knowledge and accountability to others. That is what education should be about."

Melia is a continuous learner—on steroids. She has taken responsibility for continuously learning and improving. She used feedback to learn and grow. Through reflection, she processed her experience and applied it to her work and her life. And she has used what she learned to support learning among others.

Leadership is not an end; it is a process. Leaders need to be confident in what they know and humble about what they don't. They need to ask for help and feedback. As John McKnight once told me, "It is more important to have the right questions than the right answers." I often see leaders who are fearful of failure and fail to admit mistakes and ask for help. They believe leadership is about showing they can do it all and handle it all. I know because I was one of them.

Our Allies are taught the value of being continuously open to learning and improving, and they are given tools to make this a lifelong habit. Here is what we do to promote these outcomes:

1. Create an effective learning environment and community
2. Provide coaching and critical feedback to support learning
3. Facilitate critical reflection to help leaders learn from their experience

The goal is to develop habits of mind that lead Allies to challenge assumptions, consider others' perspectives, ask good questions, seek feedback, ask for help, reflect, and continually seek ways to learn and grow. In other words, we develop more leaders like Melia—people who are constantly learning and thinking of better ways to grow and make a greater difference.

Creating an Effective Learning Environment and Community

When I go to conferences and trainings, I am amazed by how poorly event planners and organizers understand adult learning styles. They focus on how to transmit information, not on how the audience will learn or process it. They often overprogram the day with panels and speakers. Then, on the day of the event, speakers go overtime, PowerPoint presentations repeat a speaker's words, and audience members may, at best, get a few chances to ask questions. I once went to a conference where, between individual speakers and panels, thirty-six speakers talked at us in one day. I had to keep leaving the room, and I wasn't alone. A group of us sat in the hall and complained, probably missing some really interesting ideas. But it was too much information, and, as a result, I retained little.

This "sage on the stage" model limits learning and networking and leaves participants bored and sapped of energy. It's a good thing that so much coffee and so many sugary sweets are often put outside these conference rooms because we need them to survive these stifling, boring experiences. I always imagine that event planners are type-A personalities who achieved straight A's in school, love structure, follow the rules, and want to make every minute productive. They were the kids who got to class early, sat in the front row, loved lectures, stayed after to ask the teacher more questions, and frowned upon the class clowns like me. So I made up a rule at Public Allies, only half in jest: "No one who received over a B average in high school should organize a meeting." I want the attention-deficit folks to design my learning experiences. We need to be engaged and to have space to reflect and speak with each other. I've heard musicians say that the pauses, the silences between notes, are as important to music as the notes. In learning, the silence between the lessons is powerful, too.

Building an effective learning environment and community is pretty simple. Our approach is grounded in three theories:

1. Howard Gardner's theory of *multiple intelligences* teaches us that there are multiple ways the brain accepts and retains information, that we have different interests and abilities, and that we have diverse ways of inputting and learning information.[2] Gardner offers seven areas of intelligence that we all have to varying degrees: linguistic, mathematic, musical, special, kinesthetic, interpersonal, and intrapersonal.

2. *Accelerated learning* theory builds on adult education theory. It creates a learner-centered, interactive, collaborative

learning environment. The approach of accelerated learning is one that "supports learning at multiple levels, the emotional, the mental, and the physical, and taps into and develops the inner wisdom we all possess. It incorporates the arts and music, a sense of play and experimentation, simulations, improvisation, story and metaphor . . . into a cycle of learning" that helps learners move beyond limiting beliefs to tap into their potential, widen their perspectives, and learn more quickly and easily.[3]

3. The theory of *learning organizations*, a concept developed by Peter Senge, teaches us to create a learning community in which people discover how they can create their own reality.[4] It is based on five disciplines:

a. *Understanding systems thinking*, which allows one to see the proverbial forest, the trees, and the patterns among them
b. *Developing personal mastery* of skills and knowledge
c. *Challenging mental models*, the ingrained assumptions that influence how we understand the world and take action
d. *Building a shared vision* with the group for what it wants to do and be
e. *Employing team learning* so that the intelligence of the team exceeds that of its individual members

Combining all three theories, we've sought to build learning environments and communities that have the following characteristics:

- A focus on the individual and group learning of Allies, using a blend of activities and experiences
- Use of our Allies' diversity—their backgrounds, neighborhoods, demographics, placements, and issue expertise—as the biggest asset for learning, and creation of an environment that draws those lessons and differences out
- Creation of clear, relevant objectives for every learning experience so that Allies know what they will learn and how they can apply it

- A blend of activities that allow Allies to interact with information, connecting it to their experience and current work
- Facilitation of reflections and follow-up activities to support the retention and application of lessons

Let's look at each of these.

Focus on Individual and Group Learning

Traditionally, there is often much more focus on teaching than on learning. At Public Allies, we recognize that people learn in different ways, and that learning is an active experience, not a passive one. Research cited by James Whitmore indicates that three weeks after training, we retain 70 percent of what we have been told, 72 percent of what we have been told and shown, and 85 percent of what we have been told, shown, and invited to experience; three months after training, we retain 10 percent of what we've been told, 32 percent of what we've been told and shown, and 65 percent of what we've been told, shown, and invited to experience.[5] It's clear that lectures by speakers will not be well retained by the majority of listeners. If we focus instead on learning, we will blend activities that support, reinforce, and retain learning.

I learned the difference between teaching and learning back in college. I had a logic professor, Michael Liston, who in our second semester challenged us with difficult work but also offered many more office hours than any other professor I had. I was in his office one day and apologized for taking so much of his time. He replied, "Don't apologize. I'm not doing my job if you're not able to do it." The night before our midterms and our final exams, he reserved a classroom for the evening and allowed pizzas so that students could come and practice with him. That was the first time I saw the distinction between someone teaching me and someone helping me learn.

I had another professor for an economics seminar, Bill Holahan, who elated us briefly on the first day of class: "You are all going to get A's this semester." Before the high-fives commenced, he added a qualifier: "And you'll get those A's once all your papers are A papers, whether that comes before or after the end of the semester." As I rewrote some of my papers two, three, four, or five times, I both mastered the information at a much deeper level and became a much stronger writer (he subsequently told me that some students never completed their A's). These memorable professors were focused on learning. Their approach to learning offered a sharp contrast with the lecturers who talked, took a few questions, examined us, and moved on, whether we had mastered the content or not.

At Public Allies, we focus on individual learners by creating a learning environment that supports their learning. We help them create individual development plans, coach them on their development, offer feedback, arrange for interactive learning activities they can apply in their work, and ensure many opportunities for reflection. Leadership development is a comprehensive experience, not a set of classes.

We support group learning by using the Allies' diverse experiences, perspectives, and knowledge to enrich the learning experience. Those differences sometimes make learning uncomfortable—people may disagree with the presenter or each other, get defensive, struggle with the applicability of a lesson, and face other challenges.

The learning environment must be safe and supportive of those challenges. Overall, our Allies don't begin the year at the same starting line, and their experience varies by topic. If someone believes he is already an expert in some area, he should be engaged in helping others learn and should be challenged to find something new in the lesson.

We also find truth in the moral of a Sufi Muslim parable that John McKnight and Jody Kretzmann have often told: "You will learn only what you already know." We find that this is often the case because training elicits reflections, connections, and ideas from Allies that pull from their experience and knowledge base.

For example, when we start training in asset-based community development, the Allies quickly grasp their own assets and the assets in their neighborhoods. We find that this knowledge appears to them as common sense. But many professionals unlearn simple ideas such as these as they get steeped in institutional and bureaucratic norms. When I train experienced professionals in asset-based community development, they often remark that the approach is more like something they have forgotten than like something they are learning for the first time.

When we say that Allies are responsible for their own learning, we mean that we expect them to co-create the learning space they need in order to be productive. To that end, we expect them to arrive on time, fully participate, wrestle with concepts and try to apply them, take risks, challenge their peers, provide feedback and solutions in a timely manner, and seek out training and education to further their knowledge and skills. We can set the stage for learning, but they have to own it.

Use of Diversity

In Chapters Six and Seven, we saw how differences can make us more productive. They are also valuable for learning.

When our Allies talk about social issues or approaches to public problems, they are able to learn from their different backgrounds, beliefs, and experiences in ways that are incredibly enriching. The Allies come from different neighborhoods, races, economic classes, educational backgrounds, sexual orientations, and family circumstances. They work for different nonprofit organizations in different neighborhoods on different issues (such as education, health, poverty, and the environment). When the Allies meet each week, all the knowledge and all the experience of the group are drawn on in ways that multiply each individual's knowledge.

An Ally graduates from the program understanding multiple perspectives, knowing about multiple issues, connecting with multiple neighborhoods, understanding different approaches to solving problems, and aware of diverse assets in the community. I would argue that, apart from the framework of our five core values, what they learn from each other is more powerful than anything else they learn in the program.

Clear, Relevant Objectives

The learning process actually begins before a training, with the preparation and even the naming of the training or learning event. Once a topic is introduced, participants begin to think about what it means and what they might learn. To facilitate that early engagement, we use what we call "value-added titles." For example, rather than just "Public Speaking," we'll use a title like "Public Speaking: Tips and Tools That Will Prepare You to Have Confidence and Comfort Before Any Group." We also often let Allies know the learning objectives for each training or activity.

The objectives for any learning event or experience should be clear and relevant to the learner. For our trainings and learning experiences, we aim to create objectives that are SMART—specific, measurable, attainable, results-focused, and timely. A training objective that states, "They will understand asset-based community development" is not SMART. Instead, a SMART objective would state, "Allies will demonstrate that they understand definitions of neighborhood assets, have the ability to survey, identify, and analyze neighborhood assets, and are able to build relationships and collaborations in a community, using this approach." The title and objectives help members see the relevance and applicability of what they will learn, and they enter training with an eye to how this will help them as leaders.

Blend of Activities

Allies learn by doing, talking, observing, and thinking. Trainings should, as much as possible, allow a variety of presentation and group activities. We make sure lessons include practical examples of how the information or skills can be put to work. Allies learn from each other, not just from the presenter. A rule many of us like to use is that for each minute of lecture time, there should be two minutes of group activities and discussion. We help Allies draw on their experience and knowledge and share those in relation to the topic. We recognize that with multiple intelligences, what works for one person may work *only* for that person. Therefore, we design trainings with diverse perspectives and learning styles in mind. And to truly deepen learning, reflection is necessary.

We prepare our rooms and our trainers to support learning. The preparation of a room signals to people what kind of experience they may have. The setup should reflect how people will interact and how information can be taken in, both visually and via the speaker or facilitator. Chairs may be in rows, groups, or a large circle. There may be flip-chart paper with key concepts on the wall, or paper and markers around the room. The arrangement will signal to learners what they should expect.

Our model stipulates four leadership roles for a successful learning experience:

1. Trainer: the person who leads the learning activity that day
2. Designer: the event coordinator, who ensures that the design of content, delivery, and the environment will produce outcomes
3. Subject-matter expert: someone with expertise in content, who may or may not be the leader of the training
4. Facilitator: the manager of time, materials, evaluation, and the environment during the learning experience

One person can play all these roles, but the roles must be played. We rely heavily on outside trainers who bring subject-matter expertise to Allies. Sometimes they have excellent facilitation skills, and other times they do not. Before a trainer comes into our space, our staff will meet with him or her to discuss the training, including the value-added title, the objectives of the training, how those objectives tie in to Public Allies' learning outcomes (our five values), ways of making the training relevant to the group, and the training plan, which includes presentation, room setup, materials, timing, exercises, and any pre- or posttraining work.

Todd Wellman, an alumnus of Public Allies Milwaukee who helps train our staff across the country in this model, explains it this way: "Presenters have to think like a tennis instructor. A tennis instructor can hit the ball hard and fast, but when playing with a beginner [he has] to hit slow and direct so the learner can hit back. The instructor also has to walk off the court sometimes so the learners can volley with each other. So a trainer or expert must meet the learners where they are and play with the different levels in the room."[6]

Support for Retention and Application of Lessons

Training is an event, but learning is a process. Too often, however, training is seen as an end. Learning continues through the evaluation and debriefing of a learning experience and is best retained when it is revisited after the original lesson. Evaluating training is not the same thing as evaluating learning. Evaluating whether someone has learned a lesson requires time, reflection, and specific questions about the application of knowledge. Follow-up work might include coaching sessions, virtual learning or e-courses to further or refresh learning, live chat sessions, critical reflections, self-reviews, or other opportunities that help one continue to process and apply lessons. For example, we've found that in delivering trainings in asset-based community development to groups, it works best if we have conference calls or webinars one month, three months, and six months afterward, where learners can share how they are applying the lessons of the training. When workshops are presented without such follow-up, the results are not sustained after people return to their heavy workloads.

Eagle Rock

The way one establishes the learning environment and the learning process speaks to the commitment to learning. No organization has influenced our approach to learning more than the Eagle Rock School and Professional Development Center of Estes Park, Colorado, the gateway to Rocky Mountain National Park.

Built in 1992, and fully supported by the American Honda Corporation, Eagle Rock has been able to build an innovative educational curriculum for young people who've struggled or failed in traditional school systems. It has won awards and drawn thousands of educators to learn from its model. Around 90 percent of Eagle Rock students graduate from high school, despite the fact that they were not succeeding in other schools.

Eagle Rock is learner-centered and uses a curriculum based on the theory of multiple intelligences, on individualized instruction, and on experiential learning through projects and service where learners apply their lessons. The school builds individual integrity, citizenship, artistic expression, communication, intellect, spirit, physical health, and ethics. According to Robert Burkhardt, head of the school, "We expect students to become autodidacts—teachers of themselves. We help them discover their passions and then clear away the debris between them and their passion, using it as a tool for development and transformation. In contrast to our approach, most schools make all the decisions for kids: *Sit down. Shut up. I'll tell you when I want to hear from you.* That approach is centered on what the adult teachers need. We create a space for students to step up and lead by serving and teaching others."[7]

Eagle Rock students create Presentations of Learning each trimester. They appear before a panel of outside leaders and their Eagle Rock community to demonstrate personal and academic growth, link their learning to their past learning, and project their future learning goals. For fifteen minutes, students present themselves as learners to this panel and to an audience composed of their peers, staff members, family members, and friends. First the panel and then the audience ask questions of the students, forcing extemporaneous thinking and responses. It's a good learning experience as well as an accountability tool for the whole school. All presentations are videotaped so that students can watch their past presentations and see their skills grow over time. To graduate, students who have mastered all their requirements do a final one-hour Presentation of Learning.

Back in 1995, Public Allies Milwaukee graduate Dan Condon was selected for a teaching internship at Eagle Rock. He returned a year later to work for Public Allies Milwaukee and shared with us a lot about Eagle Rock's model: "Eagle Rock holds high expectations, recognizes that people learn differently and have different assets, and believes that every young person, no matter how disenfranchised, can learn and do more than they think they can do. It is really aligned with Public Allies."[8]

In 1997, a group of program staff from across the country formed the Eagle Rock Group, which met at Eagle Rock to develop Public Allies' first curriculum. The group developed what eventually became our five core leadership values, developed our approach to training and learning, and adopted the Presentation of Learning as our main assessment tool for demonstrating the learning outcomes. In 2001, we formed a partnership with Eagle Rock whereby twelve Allies each year serve as teaching fellows, helping support the education of the students while building their own leadership and becoming certified as teachers. They often disseminate Eagle Rock's model in their future teaching and youth work.

Individual Development, Coaching, and Feedback

To support Allies' individual learning, we use specific tools to help them grow. They begin each year by creating Individual Development Plans, which lay out their personal and professional goals beyond Public Allies and the steps they need to take during the year to achieve them. Allies have worksheets to guide their thinking about their educational, career, and personal goals. They are invited to think five to ten years out and to consider what they want their relationships as well as their family, health, spiritual, and professional lives to be like. Then they consider what they can start doing now to achieve those goals. They pick goals that they can achieve in a set period of time, consider what resources and relationships they have to help them meet those goals, identify their needs, and use timelines to connect actions to their needs. These plans are iterative. Allies' experiences in their apprenticeships, their team service projects, and the feedback they receive from their supervisors and teammates help inform their personal development goals. To help Allies develop and achieve their plans, Public Allies uses a coaching process.

We use coaching because it focuses the Allies on taking responsibility for developing their goals and solutions and then taking steps to achieve them. This is something that we believe leaders must learn how to do. Coaching helps the Allies access their wisdom and experience and shape it into practical actions, solutions, and ideas. According to James Whitmore, "Coaching is about unlocking a person's potential to maximize their performance. It is helping them rather than teaching them."[9] The goal is to support the responsibility of Allies to solve their own problems, not to offer solutions to their problems.

A coach is not a manager or a supervisor, and coaching is not about reviewing performance. It is about learning. A coach does not give advice, provide answers, act as a therapist, or supervise performance issues. A coach is an empathetic and intentional listener who asks questions that help coachees draw on their own wisdom and on their own resources to solve problems and meet goals. A coach avoids questions that lead a coachee to defend his or her actions, assign blame, or speculate about others. A coach asks, "What are the steps you can take right now to achieve your goal? Tell me about a time that was helpful to your growth. What happened? What was the result the last time you faced this situation?" Coaches also listen for what is *not* being said, and they pose questions to help coachees take on more responsibility: "Have you gone to your supervisor on that? Have you given your teammate that feedback?"

The typical coaching process we use includes four steps:

1. *Celebration.* A coach invites the coachee to share the story of a victory related to his or her work. For example, an Ally shares that she attracted 50 percent more community residents to a community event than attended last year.

2. *Discovery.* What did the coachee learn from the celebration stage? What would he or she like to reinforce? What could

be different for the future? For example, the Ally shares that she invited local business owners, and this energized them and spread the word about the event to customers.

3. *Intention.* On the basis of the discoveries, Allies consider what they will do, how they will do it, what they have to work with, and how they will prioritize. In this example, the Ally says she wants to reinforce one-to-one meetings with local businesses and get other staff from her agency more engaged; after coaching, she decides to make her priority the business outreach.

4. *Action.* The Ally creates a list of SMART goals, to achieve the intentions that remain on his or her priority list. In this example, the Ally decides to meet with eight business owners in two different neighborhoods over next two weeks.

The meeting closes after the coachee shares what he or she has learned or discovered and what he or she will do as a result.

The individual development and coaching process builds throughout the year as Allies gain clarity by using the process, setting goals, creating specific actions, bringing in feedback they've received, creating more complex actions, integrating personal values and visions, and seeking different perspectives. A program manager may help an Ally apply lessons from a recent training, engage his or her supervisor better, work more effectively in a team environment, and pursue education and career goals. This process keeps the responsibility on each Ally but supports that responsibility so that Allies can better achieve their goals.

I've also used a coach for several years—sometimes weekly, sometimes monthly, depending on the challenges or issues I'm dealing with. I've found the coaching space to be a safe place to process what I am doing and learning, to think about my relationships with co-workers and board members, to assess my priorities, and to set goals for myself and my performance. I've also used coaching to help me with conflicts, to allow me a place to vent, to practice difficult conversations, and to think through tough decisions. I would not be as successful without that support.

I have grown and gained much from having that space to reflect, prioritize, learn, and choose actions and strategies for my learning and goal achievement.

Feedback

Individual development and coaching are enhanced by direct feedback. We provide a variety of trainings to help Allies learn to give and receive feedback. Allies learn that when giving feedback, they should pay attention to the following areas:

- *Timing.* They learn to be aware of the other person's state of mind and readiness to listen.
- *Being specific.* Allies learn to use specific examples and to choose a few themes so as to not overwhelm the receiver.
- *Maintaining balance.* Even though it may be necessary to describe a shortcoming, Allies learn to affirm the receiver's assets. We must put into practice our belief that individuals are both half empty and half full.
- *Being considerate.* By separating the other person from his or her behavior, Allies learn not to hurt but to help the individual learn, grow, and improve the situation, relationship, or team.
- *Making "I" statements.* They learn to deliver feedback by using statements of this kind. That way, Allies accept responsibility for the feedback they are delivering. A simple model is "When you . . . , I feel . . . ," or "I need you to . . . , or else . . . may be a consequence."

Receiving feedback is also a skill, and it requires practice. In receiving feedback, it is best to avoid being defensive. Listeners should use rational judgment to decipher the relevance of the feedback after having received it, and they should also understand their own boundaries so they can let people know if they have hit the limit on how much they can hear. Listeners should also give themselves an opportunity to process and remember the feedback by taking notes and by taking time to reflect on the feedback or discuss it with a coach. Receiving feedback requires active listening, which means listening without judgment and defensiveness, paying attention to body language (so that the person giving feedback sees that the receiver is listening), and repeating what was heard, for clarification.

We sometimes pair Allies so they can practice listening. One speaker talks for five minutes about something that has been going on in his or her life. After the five minutes are up, the listener is invited to paraphrase what he or she heard and to ask a question or make a comment. Then the speaker is given five more minutes. Allies find it is hard to listen for ten minutes, and hard even to speak that long.

Allies first receive feedback through a 360-degree assessment, during which fellow Allies, the placement supervisor, and Public Allies staff members review how the Ally is practicing our five values. It is not a performance review but a tool to support learning and growth. I've participated in my own 360-degree review processes for more than a decade now. Like the Allies, I complete a self-assessment, and then I am reviewed by our senior managers, my assistant, and my board. The experience helps me check on how I am leading, learning, growing, and supporting others. It also helps me identify goals and priorities for my own growth each year, informed by those who work with me every day.

Getting feedback on a regular basis is also important. For example, as a CEO, it is hard for me to receive good feedback because of power dynamics (people don't like to dis a boss to his or her face). I have to remember to ask for feedback more regularly because people don't often volunteer critical feedback to their bosses. Even when I do request it, there is usually a little hesitation on the other person's part. One particularly instructive moment always stands out for me. During a team meeting seven years ago, a new vice president, Dawn Hutchison, asked me about my process for planning a board meeting. I responded to her quickly, and a little defensively, by describing what had generally been an ad hoc process as if it were a specific process. I thought I was quite convincing. Then she stopped me, saying, "You obviously just came up with that. Why didn't you just answer, 'I don't know. What do you think?'" I was stunned. She was right. "Thank you," I said, "for driving into my blind spot—and honking." That phrase has become one I often use when people see something I don't, or when they step up and speak up on something that they're better at than I am.

The Gift Seat

After Allies have received the feedback from their 360-degree reviews, they are asked to apply what they've learned about giving and receiving feedback. The Gift Seat is a powerful exercise for this purpose. Allies sit in a circle with all the people who reviewed them. The ground rules are simple: everyone will both give and receive feedback, the person currently receiving feedback can only reply "Thank you" (it is a listening exercise), and there is no talking over, interrupting, or attacking. Each Ally in turn asks the group such questions as "What strengths do I bring to our team? What do you enjoy about working with me? What about working with me do you find challenging? Is there anything you'd like to share about me that you don't think I realize about myself?"

Danise Sugita, an alumna of Public Allies Silicon Valley who is now a program manager there, describes the experience. "I was really nervous because I'm self-critical and tend to beat myself up. After I received the feedback, I realized I liked it a lot. The group told me that I needed to be more assertive, that they wanted to hear more about my point of view and thought I was too silent and neutral in meetings. Harder than receiving feedback was giving it. I didn't want to hurt others' feelings but learned that it is not helpful to someone to withhold feedback and not hold them accountable. I learned that they will respect you more if you are up-front."[10]

Melissa Aguilar had been an insurance agent before joining Public Allies in 2007, and she now works at Centro Med in San Antonio, Texas (she was hired permanently by the organization where she apprenticed through Public Allies). She likewise found the process nerve-racking but powerful: "It was uncomfortable at first. But, you know, people are only saying what they see and how you've treated them or how you've reacted to them. It's not a bad thing. I can be short, and sometimes I overreact and snap at somebody. So it's good that I have to keep my mouth quiet and let everyone else talk. You get both positive and negative comments, and that can be uncomfortable. At the end of it all, however, you feel closer to your group, and it opens a discussion about things that need to be addressed. I still use it today as I try to get my current team on the same page. I've learned to approach people in a way they prefer, waiting for the right time, being an active listener, and focusing on our common goals. I'm not afraid to ask people to do things, nor to constantly seek feedback: 'What do you think? How else would you do it?' And with that, I'm more open to others' ways of doing things."[11]

Carson Henry, a 2005 graduate of our Delaware program who is now associate executive director of YMCA Youth & Family Services in Silver Spring, Maryland, explains that he'd never before "had a group of people sit down and literally look me in the eye and tell me everything they liked and didn't like about working with me." He wishes that the 360-degree review process and Gift Seat exercise had been used in every other setting where he has worked. "I've learned to give people feedback in a manner where they can understand it's not a personal attack," he says, but an opportunity "for them to develop and grow. If I hadn't been a beneficiary of the 360-degree review and Gift Seat, I would have fallen on my face many times by now."[12]

We often viscerally fear sharing our mistakes and shortcomings. It is natural for us to fear that vulnerability. But the interesting thing is that they really aren't secrets. I once did a presentation in which I made a list of things I suck at. Here is the partial list:

- Interpersonal conflict
- Personnel management
- Patience with process
- Administrative paperwork
- Being punctual
- Small talk
- Active listening
- Trusting my instincts
- Delegating responsibility
- Making unpopular decisions

I shared this list with my wife, with my employees, with my board, with Allies, and with public audiences. When I stood before my staff, I was terrified to share the list, but then I realized something immediately afterward—none of this was a surprise! No one stood up and said, "Paul, I thought you were always good at handling conflicts" or "You are always on time, and I never have to nag you on timesheets" or "You never doodle or check e-mail during conversations" or "Paul, you never take on too much, and you delegate so quickly." The point is that our shortcomings are not secret, even though we pretend they are. I actually felt relieved after making and sharing my list, and I've shared it dozens of times since. I am half full and half empty, like everyone else.

Of course, owning your shortcomings is not an excuse or a license to keep sucking at them. But by sharing your shortcomings and being more aware of them, you can pay more attention to improving. In fact, owning them opens the door to learning in three ways. First, you can be less defensive about the feedback you receive, and you can recognize that you do indeed have your faults. Second, you can open yourself to the fact that you need others who are good at the things you are not good at—you need to work with others who compensate for your shortcomings, and you need to seek learning and growth in those areas. And, third, you can more authentically hold others accountable. For example, not long after I shared my list, I had an argument with a colleague about some work that had been done poorly. My colleague was very defensive. Finally I asked, "Can't you just admit that you suck at this?" It was harder for my colleague to back out of that challenge, knowing I had published a whole list on the Internet of things I suck at.

Asking for Help

Giving and receiving feedback and owning our shortcomings and mistakes are critical for learning. So is simply asking for help. When I look back at all the people I've worked with over the years, the biggest difference between those who succeeded and those who did not is the humility to ask for help. I've seen people who think that by doing everything themselves they are proving that they are worthy of being a leader or earning affirmation of their skills. They don't ask for help, admit mistakes or weaknesses, or delegate. They often burn themselves out, feeling underappreciated for all their effort. They are infected with what Roger Martin calls the "responsibility virus" (see Chapter Four) and want to be heroes. But leadership is not about what you do; it is about what you inspire *others* to do *with* you. A leader is one who engages and mobilizes all possible resources to achieve a goal. *Leadership is not about the leader but about the goal.* This is what Melia Dicker learned, as we saw in the story at the beginning of this chapter.

When I started Public Allies Milwaukee at the ripe young age of twenty-four, I did not know anything about how to build or lead an organization. My colleagues were also young and inexperienced. We succeeded in building an excellent program because we assembled a group of mentors and advisors we sought help from constantly. We asked for help, and people gave it freely. We've continued that tradition to this day.

Here's a great example. In the heat of the 2008 presidential campaign, I woke up one morning to find an *Investor's Business*

Daily editorial circulating in the blogosphere, claiming that Public Allies was part of Senator Barack Obama's secret plan to build a Red Army of radicals that would grow to be a $500 billion federal program if he got elected. (If only!) Glenn Beck followed up, as did other right-wing pundits and bloggers, describing us, for example, as running Marxist reeducation camps that train impressionable young people to hate America, distribute needles and condoms, help illegal immigrants, and promote a homosexual agenda. We were worried about further attacks as YouTube videos sprouted up, comparing our "reeducation camps" to Hitler youth camps and more. After meeting with my management team, I contacted my government relations consultant, Patricia Griffin, along with Tom Sheridan, a lobbyist and friend; Linda Stephenson and Pat Griffin, two former board members with expertise; and Bill Graustein, my board chair. We all got on the phone a few hours later with Erik Smith, a communications guru Tom had enlisted, and they calmed me down, helped me plan for communications inside and outside the organization, and helped us manage our way through the crisis. I also called David Eisner, President George W. Bush's appointee to run the Corporation for National and Community Service, and he agreed to weigh in if the attacks grew. (Fortunately, they died down, despite many vicious and threatening calls and messages.) Once again I learned that my role, as a leader, is to mobilize help, not to solve problems by myself. And you can't mobilize people without asking them for help!

Critical Reflection and Presentations of Learning

Critical reflection is an important part of learning. People need time to process learning. If you learn something and then run off to another activity, task, or experience, you will lose sight of what you have learned. Reflection allows people to step back, think about what they have learned, perhaps journal about it, and maybe discuss it with another person or small group. We use critical reflection to help Allies examine motives, assumptions, ethics, behaviors, and beliefs on a regular basis. Allies may journal during reflection, discuss lessons in small groups, restate lessons in their own words and experience, write imaginary dialogues about a topic with someone they admire, and more. To help Allies process a training, for example, we might ask, "What was new for you in the lesson that you hadn't thought of before? What challenged you in the lesson? What more will you need in order to apply the lesson effectively? What will you do differently tomorrow with what you learned?"

We use Eagle Rock's Presentation of Learning model for Allies to reflect on and share their learning at the end of the program year. (Allies also do a miniversion at the midpoint of the year.) The presentations must demonstrate how the Allies have achieved our five learning outcomes (that is, how they have practiced our five core values) and how they will apply them in the future. The presentations can be spoken, sung, acted, or even danced. Last year, one Ally made a book with her own drawings, based on Dr. Seuss's *Oh the Places You'll Go!*, and called it *Oh, the Lessons You'll Learn!* Another Ally performed a skit in which Allies stood on a train, reading different books and articles and reflecting on what they were reading in ways that related to each value. The Allies present before fellow Allies, Public Allies staff, their placement supervisors, guests, and a panel of community leaders. The Allies prepare a packet that is sent to the panel members beforehand, introducing themselves as learners. In the packet, they share their impact, growth, future goals, and a reflection that we also borrowed from Eagle Rock, in which they write ten before-and-after statements following the model *I used to be . . . Now I am . . .* Here are some examples:

- I used to be insecure about my abilities and ideas compared to others. Now I am confident of the ideas I have to offer.
- I used to be someone who thought community service was going to only be a hobby of mine. Now I am looking forward to a professional career in public service.

- I used to be someone who did not want to disappoint or let down others when it came to their expectations of me. Now I am learning to say no, to take care of myself, and to own my priorities first.
- I used to have no knowledge of what it takes to develop a grassroots project. Now I'm fully aware and capable of creating a community project from the ground up.
- I used to be very talkative and would take the lead on everything. Now I leave room and allow other people to take charge.
- I used to have limited understanding about disabilities. Now I am comfortable with identifying them and being aware of language used to discuss people with disabilities, and I notice if buildings and activities are accessible.

These before-and-after statements are enlightening, but even more so are the live presentations. They last fifteen minutes and are followed by fifteen minutes of question-and-answer time with the panel and audience. On a warm June Friday last year, I was privileged to sit and listen to nine Allies share their learning. They showed videos, performed songs, quoted poetry and scripture, and offered other creative expressions. But *what* they expressed was far more impactful.

Quin'Tara shared her lesson that it is better to ask than to guess: "Guessing raises tension and division. You've got to ask people about things and not make assumptions or hold unspoken expectations."[13] She also spoke of the difference between individual integrity and group integrity: "Personally upholding your end is not enough. You have a responsibility to support the overall team's performance."

Gustavo shared his experience of trying to mobilize residents to attend an event by distributing flyers in a neighborhood. Very few people came to the event. He realized that he had to build relationships first, and he learned how to organize and lead: "The biggest asset in a community is the people and their desire to make things better. You have to get behind people, and then they can get anything done."

Alisha reported that her team had been "toxic" at first and that she had questioned her own leadership ability. But in the Leadership Compass exercise (see Chapter Seven), she realized that her leadership style is that of a nurturer, and that she could step up: "I realized that being inclusive, bringing people together, and striving for consensus are valued assets. There was a need for my skills at the table."

Dale talked about becoming less stubborn, more forgiving, and more trusting. He learned that in a conflict "it is not about how well you get your point across, but what you are willing to sacrifice." He also recognized that "if you want to learn something, you have to act. You can't wait for it to come, or for someone to do it to you. I was given a chance to do things I didn't know I could do."

Kanjana spoke of how crucial teamwork skills were to her, since she had always been a high personal achiever. "It is important to go through uncomfortable situations," she added, "in order to build good relationships. I used to feel that the product was the most important part of a project, and now I see the value of team process. My 360-degree review helped me find those blind spots and recognize how important it is to understand how others view you."

In 2004, I led Public Allies through a very important but difficult restructuring. We shifted from the model of a national organization with local branches to a franchise-like model in which local nonprofits and universities operate most of our local programs. The change dramatically drove down operating costs, increased program capacity, and maintained program standards and branding. But it was controversial because our local sites went from running themselves, with little oversight, to working for other organizations and being managed more closely. Leading through this change was the biggest personal and professional leadership challenge I had ever undertaken. I was fortunate that our consultants used a data-driven process that brought a divergent team of local and national staff to the same conclusion—that this was the way to go. But it was a painful and difficult experience, especially for someone who hates making unpopular decisions, is conflict-avoidant, and is not good at process.

About a year later, in July 2005, I was invited by my friend Cheryl Dorsey, CEO of the Echoing Green Foundation, to speak to her program's fellows. Cheryl suggested that I share with the fellows some of the best practices that had led to Public Allies' great success and growth. I began preparing such a speech, but I felt dishonest and a little empty inside. As I reflected on the most important things I had learned from mentors, I realized that I had usually learned most from their mistakes, their challenges, and the barriers they had overcome. I realized that the only useful thing to share with these fellows would be our biggest mistakes and challenges.

I created a presentation titled "The Worst Practices of Social Entrepreneurship," featuring a photo of me wearing a dunce cap. I began by sharing my list of things I suck at. I made the point that we as leaders aren't perfect. As we build our organizations, it's good to clarify our shortcomings because they aren't secrets to anyone else, and admitting this makes it easier to ask for help. Then, using as a frame the findings of a 2005 study by the Bridgespan Group on the obstacles faced by fast-growing organizations, I reviewed the fourteen biggest mistakes or challenges my organization had faced over the past dozen years in areas such as fundraising, board development, fiscal management, personnel, and program strategy.[14] It was a freeing experience, and the group really appreciated it. Several fellows came up to me afterward, and I felt like a priest at confession. Everyone shared a story of a mistake or a challenge that he or she was dealing with.

I have done this presentation over a dozen times since then, and there is always a line of people waiting to confess afterward. I find it unfortunate that in many cases I am the first person they are sharing their challenges with. They don't have coaches, mentors, or colleagues to share with. They are afraid to admit mistakes, shortcomings, and imperfections. This is very sad for leaders. Remember, *we are all half full and half empty*. We can be stronger, more centered, and more authentic if we are real and if we share our reality. That is why leaders need to open themselves to learning, coaching, feedback, reflection, sharing, and asking for help.

Leadership is a process and must involve continuous learning and development. We are responsible for owning our need for learning; supporting others' learning and growth; seeking feedback, coaching, and support for our development; and reflecting on our practice, mistakes, successes, and lessons so that we can improve and better help others. Leadership is not about us—it is a collaborative act in service to others. We have a responsibility to learn what we need to learn and request all the help and feedback we need in order to accomplish our shared mission and goals.

It is that larger sense of responsibility and accountability that bring us to the last of the five values, and to the subject of the Chapter Nine—integrity.

Key Lessons and Ideas

1. Leaders are responsible for learning and improving so that they can do their best working with others to accomplish shared missions and goals.
2. Leaders must create effective environments and processes for others' learning and growth.
3. Leaders should regularly seek feedback, coaching, and other help to identify ways to continue improving.
4. Reflection is essential if leaders are to step back and consider their behavior, relationships, ethics, priorities, mistakes, and lessons.

Exercises and Reflections

This chapter contains many tips for creating effective trainings and developing processes for feedback, coaching, and so forth. Here are some additional reflections.

"Things I Suck At"

Make a list of ten things you suck at—things you are either not good at or just hate to do.

- How does it feel to look at the list? Do you become more anxious?
- Which items do you believe people close to you are well aware of?
- Which items on the list do you believe people are not aware of?
- Consider sharing your list with a few people you trust. Ask them to tell you, from their own experience, if your list is accurate. What, if anything, do they think should *not* be on the list? Is there anything they would add?

Self-Improvement

- What are three shortcomings or challenges that are getting in the way of your goals?
- Whom do you talk to about your challenges? Whom do you seek feedback from? What makes you comfortable sharing challenges with another person?
- Are there people you have reached out to, either to help you compensate for those challenges or to help you improve your performance in particular areas of challenge?

9

BEING ACCOUNTABLE TO OURSELVES AND OTHERS

Leif Elsmo: Putting All the Pieces Together

Leif Elsmo grew up in Racine, Wisconsin. He was completing a degree in political science and philosophy at the University of Wisconsin-Milwaukee and working at a shoe store when he got involved in Public Allies Milwaukee and became one of the first Allies at that site. He served at the Mid-Town Neighborhood Association, working on economic development and job placement in one of Milwaukee's poorest African American neighborhoods.

Leif made a big difference and built strong relationships in Mid-Town, which was not easy. Several fellow Allies had warned him about the neighborhood.

"Some people in the neighborhood were angry," he says now, "and had a right to be. I needed to listen to that, and it was hard at times. I did, though, because I was there for them. They tried to push me away, but I came back, and maybe by the third or fourth time, or when I brought a representative of the mayor's office to meet with them, they realized I was serious. My idealism really helped me. There were not a lot of people coming into the neighborhood looking to build on assets. I really believed we could make a difference, and I didn't have a savior mentality. I was not the solution. They were."[1]

When he graduated from the program, Michelle Obama, executive director of Public Allies Chicago, hired him to join her staff—a working relationship that would continue for almost fourteen years. Leif had been a leader among his fellow Allies during his year at Public Allies Milwaukee, and he had often pushed the staff to practice what they preached. But when the shoe was on the other foot, Leif called and apologized: "Man, you guys had a tough job that first year, and I was a pain in the ass. I'm sorry."

Today Leif is executive director of external relations at the University of Chicago Medical Center. Together with Michelle Obama and Asim Mishra, another Public Allies alumnus, he built a model for community engagement that integrates our five values. It employs asset-based community development, inclusion, collaboration, continuous learning, and accountability to the community.

The medical center first had to overcome the historical baggage of being an ivory tower. It needed to break down the walls between the hospital and the community. Leif and his team began with the hospital staff, many of whom commuted in and out of the neighborhood every day, knowing nothing more about the neighborhood than what was in the news. The nurses, doctors, and administrators were introduced to the rich history, culture, and assets of the neighborhood through tours, service projects, panels on community issues led by local residents and leaders, and important neighborhood events that the hospital sponsored. Leif explains, "It was not about visibility but presence. We went about being good neighbors. Over time, we grew from fewer than two hundred employees volunteering in the neighborhood in 2002 to over a thousand in 2010."

This engagement deepened their thinking about how to have a broader impact on the health of the community. The medical center was already one of the largest Medicaid/Medicare providers in town, but Leif's team knew that there were many other providers who served the health needs of the neighborhood.

"We couldn't act alone if we wanted to make a difference long-term on health in the community," he says. "We needed to find the talented practitioners who were in the community. We needed to work with block clubs, community organizations, youth groups, and faith communities to support community health. We shifted the hospital's point of view from being only patient-centered to being also community-centered. That's a big shift for an academic medical institution."

They created the South Side Health Care Collaborative, with about thirty federally qualified health agencies and clinics that worked on affordable care. They also built new partnerships with the county and individual providers. Their specialists started going out to the community to serve people, not just waiting for them to come in.

These successes over time led the University of Chicago Medical Center to make a much bigger leap. Its recently launched Urban Health Initiative aims to make the thirty-four neighborhoods on the South Side of Chicago one of the healthiest communities in America by 2025 through outreach, research, community education, and patient care. And the medical center is holding itself accountable to the neighborhoods it serves. Staff members meet regularly with a variety of community leaders and groups for feedback. Every six months, the medical center also hosts a community summit to report progress on goals, to share lessons learned, and to invite feedback from an audience of more than two hundred community members.

"We listen to the community," Leif says, "and then we figure out what resources we can pull from the hospital but also from the schools of social work, public policy, and business, for example. We provide grants for research driven by local community residents, which they drive with support from our researchers. It allows us to learn what is important to our neighbors and work with them to solve problems. We have built a lot of trust through the process."

Leif's biggest influence to date has been Michelle Obama.

"I learned so much from her," he says, "especially about integrity. She pushed me in all the right ways and always got the best out of me. She walked her talk. She has such a deep love for people from all walks of life and was so inclusive in how she thought about how everyone could contribute—those who wanted to help from outside and the community residents themselves. She upheld the integrity of our team, too. We went on retreats at least twice a year to really check in on how we were working together, communicating, and developing. She instilled in me that we had to be optimistic that we could get big things done, and sensitive about the promises we made to communities. We had to fulfill what we said we were going to do because communities have been failed so many times. In the short time her husband rose from state senator to U.S. senator to president, I saw her remain true to herself, and she remained true to us and to the community. It is the example I continue to be guided by today."

Leif's story illustrates how you put it all together. Public Allies' leadership values are not one-offs but are an integrated system for effective community leadership. You will lead effectively in any environment if you recognize and mobilize assets, if you cross cultural boundaries and bring diverse people and groups together, if you build teams and facilitate community collaboration, if you seek feedback, coaching, and support to learn and grow, and if you hold yourself accountable to your own values and to others.

Integrity is what holds the picture together. Integrity means integrating our mission, our values, our ethics, our relationships, and our actions. It is how we take responsibility for our actions, our words, our commitments, and our need to learn. Integrity is about holding ourselves accountable to the people we work with and to those we serve. And it is about honoring all those who've inspired, influenced, taught, and mentored us along the way. We look at integrity through the lenses of being true to ourselves, holding ourselves accountable to others, holding ourselves accountable to those we serve, and honoring those who have contributed to our life journeys and our leadership journeys.

Being True to Ourselves

Leadership requires a strong inner core. It is important for a leader to have a clear sense of the purpose and values that drive his or her decisions and actions. We've all seen the leader who seems to shift with the wind and follows fads, dollars, or popular opinion, without a clear sense of what his or her core is. But many of the leadership books discussed in Chapter Three make the case that leaders must be clear about their core purposes and values before they try to influence and engage with others. One reason we emphasize life stories so early in the process at Public Allies is that we want Allies to be able to make sense of their experiences, their motivations, and their purposes. Such clarity will be the foundation of their leadership. We believe it is important for leaders to be clear about why they lead, what values their work is grounded in, and what their personal missions are. We encourage Allies to practice our five core values, but we also encourage them to clarify their personal values, which come from life experiences, beliefs, ethics, and moral traditions.

To help Allies reflect on and clarify their particular callings, we ask them to write personal mission statements. We lead them through exercises to explore their intentions and aspirations, the inner urges they want to fulfill. We help them imagine the futures they want to live in and identify how they can contribute to those futures. We also help them reflect on how their past experiences have shaped them, their values, and their visions for the future.

A personal mission is a bit like a personal brand in that it is about how we want to present ourselves to our world—what is the promise we offer through our work? Steven Covey offers a good model for developing your mission: "It focuses on what you want to be (character) and to do (contribution and achievements) and on the values or principles upon which being and doing are based."[2] Through exercises, Allies reflect on and develop their own moral and ethical codes as we ask them, "What are the values and beliefs that will drive how you carry out your mission?"

Dr. Howard Fuller, a civil rights and education leader who has mentored me for many years, distinguishes between one's work (the mission) and one's job (one's current employment). I have friends who have worked at two or three different organizations, but their work—their approach to their work and the kind of impact they pursue—remains the same. I am fortunate to do my work at my job. Public Allies really felt like a calling for me and engaged my passion instantly. It crystallized my personal twofold mission:

1. To create as many opportunities as possible for people—especially those who have been marginalized or have faced barriers in their lives—to lead and participate in our democracy and create a more just society for all
2. To pay forward, and pay back, the love, care, and support I've received from family, friends, and mentors who believed in me despite my challenges

I carry out the first part of my personal mission on every board where I serve, in every coalition I join, and in every campaign for which I volunteer. I ask how we are engaging diverse people, listening to new voices, being real about communities and how they work, and pushing for greater social justice for all people. As for the second part of my personal mission, I am very rigorous about my life-work balance and do not let work or my iPhone, for example, interrupt time with my children or other loved ones unless the matter is truly urgent (and I have the same expectations for our staff). Several of my older mentors have told me that if they could do it all over again, they would spend more time with their children and loved ones. No mentors have ever told me that they wished they'd worked ten more hours every week. I've taken their words to heart. I am grateful because I'm able to do my work at Public Allies and maintain a fulfilling life beyond work. I've been able to flex my time so that I can both work hard and maintain personal relationships and hobbies.

Being clear about our stories, our missions, and our values allows us as leaders to form a compass that can guide our decisions and actions. Clarity helps us focus and say no to those things that don't align well with our work, because we can't do it all. Being clear does not mean being perfect practitioners of our missions and values—we are, after all, human. It means that we strive to be guided by them in our work. It is not about becoming self-righteous, judging people by our own standards, or evaluating others' missions or values against ours. Our core is our core, and we must have the humility to accept that what works for us might not work for others. And we must also have the humility to know that we will stumble as we strive to achieve our missions and values—in fact, if we don't stumble, our missions and values may not be aspirational enough. Leadership is a process, and our core, while clear to us, must evolve with practice and call on us to continue learning. That clarity allows us to grow.

Dr. Fuller has been a great teacher for me in all aspects of this value. He defines his mission as making sure that the least powerful in society gain traction and greater control over their destiny, with a particular focus on African Americans. He believes that core principles are the most essential aspect of a leader:

> Your core principles should never change. We may change strategy or tactics, but never our core principles. I have colleagues and friends I've disagreed with vehemently over the years, but we have a fundamental respect for each other because we trust each other's core. We need to face feedback and criticism from friends who've crossed boundaries but share our principles. I've made decisions to pursue strategies and alliances with people whose world views I disagree with, in pursuit of what I believed were the best interests of low-income and working-class people. I've made mistakes at times, but I've always made decisions based on my principles and created space for critical debate and feedback. When you are clear about your core, you've got to be straightforward, honest, and consistent with others in pursuit of it.[3]

Being Accountable to Those We Work With

Being clear about our own purposes and values allows us to build credibility as leaders, develop ourselves, and work better with others. Leadership, at its root, is an act of both personal responsibility (the decision to step up and be accountable) and social responsibility (the decision to work with others toward shared goals). As leaders, therefore, we must also be accountable to those we work with.

We saw in Chapters Seven and Eight the importance of taking responsibility. We also discussed the intensive work of building effective teams and considered the need for leaders to seek feedback and support. All of this has to do with how we hold ourselves accountable to others. We create processes for Allies to develop and practice the habits that we hope they will continue as leaders for years to come. The bottom line, in a way, is that if we have to be held accountable *by* others, we are not leading. We must hold *ourselves* accountable *to* others. We are responsible for the goals and commitments we make, the actions we say we will take, the words and ideas we express, the timelines we set, the attitudes we present, the things we need to learn and improve, and the resources and support we need. Leadership means not waiting for others to do something to us or for us. It is about stepping up and owning our responsibility for what we need to do. We work extensively with Allies to help them build that sense of accountability and recognize the responsibility they have to others and to the group.

This aspect of integrity is something that emerged over time at Public Allies. When we initially distilled our ten learning objectives down to core values, we had only four values. Over time, however, we recognized that something was missing, and it turned out to be accountability. In our zeal about empowering leadership and learning, we had frowned on words like *accountability*, *professionalism*, and *management*. Unfortunately, however, we found ourselves using our four existing values as an excuse for poor performance or poor attitudes. For example, staff who were not meeting fundraising goals or who failed to document important program data or who ignored regulations or who did not implement program requirements they didn't agree with also did not think they should be subject to critical feedback or consequences. They would complain, "Your feedback is not asset-based" or "That requirement goes against my values" or "Public Allies is not meeting my needs." As a result, we added our fifth value: integrity. The key measure of integrity is accountability—how leaders step up to fulfill promises made to others and to themselves, including the implicit promises that flow from personal values. That balance is important. It is about both accountability for performance and accountability for how one pursues the goals. The ends and the means both matter.

We build that sense of responsibility and accountability through what we call *responsibility-based management*. Public

Allies staff balance the roles of performance coach (managing and supporting the Allies' performance on goals) and development coach (helping them develop their leadership skills and values). Cris Ros-Dukler, our COO, explains the process:

> We have to be clear with people about their goals and expectations. Then they have to own the responsibility for making those happen. The supervisor can coach them, cheer them on, and help them remove obstacles to their success, but the Ally is responsible for their result. If they are falling short or facing barriers, they need to go to their supervisor and others for help. We must manage and support them to own their responsibility and hold themselves accountable for their performance and growth. That responsibility and accountability is required of leaders. When we focus too much on development and don't balance it with performance, we can get trapped. We can get stuck putting our development needs before the needs of the organization or the community. It is not leadership to put our needs ahead of everyone else's. Yes, we all have assets, and leaders need space to learn and develop, but we must do so with responsibility to the larger effort and goals. Sometimes people's assets are not the best fit with their job. They may love the organization, but do they love their particular role and responsibilities? We must help leaders take responsibility for both their performance and learning. Their accountability to themselves and to others means they have to make sure they can do both.[4]

Cris's words remind me of Peter Block's point about accountability, mentioned in Chapter Four: that "the ultimate act of love that is called for from those who hold power over others" is to "confront people with their freedom" to create their experience and "accept the unbearable responsibility that goes with that."[5] As also described in Chapter Four, one can either make the problem bigger or make the solution bigger. A leader is not a victim of problems but one who seeks solutions to problems.

David Veliz

David Veliz knows something about responsibility. He was a twenty-year-old single dad with a GED when he enrolled in Public Allies New York. Before that, he had held jobs that involved parks maintenance and landscaping or lab work.

"I had accepted that there were limits on my professional growth," he says.

But at Public Allies, his perspective took a dramatic shift.

"They put me in a position that I never [had] felt was accessible to me [before]. I never had a job where I was challenged to perform. [At Public Allies] I was given expectations that were higher than I was used to, and I was required to perform, regardless of what else was going on in my life. I was struggling to balance my personal and professional life, and it was a little rocky, but my program manager helped me realize I had to be responsible for meeting my commitments every day. I did it, and it's been immensely useful to my career."

After Public Allies, David went on to lead several youth-development programs, including five years as a youth organizer with the Sierra Club. Now he is completing his undergraduate degree in teaching at Hunter College and consulting with groups on diversity and environmental justice.[6]

We believe that leaders should uphold high and consistent standards for themselves. Leaders are role models who should adhere to the standards they set for others. That means that leaders should not ask others to do anything they wouldn't do themselves. They should not assume privileges that others don't share. They should demonstrate what they expect of others, recognize assets where others don't see them, ensure that they bring diverse people together in inclusive environments, build effective teams, and collaborate with other groups to solve problems. They should also admit their mistakes, share their struggles, ask for help, and own their need for learning and improvement. Again, we cannot be perfect practitioners, but we can do our best and be honest and accountable when we fall short.

Accountability also requires empathy. We have to put ourselves in others' shoes, understand and value others' perspectives, and not just focus on how we perceive our work or our impact on others. We are all half full and half empty. We often see things from our own perspectives and can rush to judgment before considering that others may see the situation differently, may have additional information, or may have a larger purpose that isn't ours. To make this point, Steven Covey adapts a phrase from the Catholic Prayer of St. Francis: "Seek first to understand, then to be understood."[7] For example, when I was Public Allies Milwaukee's executive director and the organization's national vice president, I had many opinions about what our CEO should do. Because I was at the table with our CEO, debating and making decisions, I thought I understood that level of responsibility. But when I became CEO, things changed. My perceptions proved wrong. Ultimate responsibility is a funny thing. You discover that you have to balance many interests and make decisions, often without all the information or support you would like.

Integrity may also be viewed through conflicting lenses. For example, as a leader, I may need to uphold the integrity of the organization by disciplining poor performance or by instituting additional monitoring requirements to ensure that we are complying with all regulations. In these circumstances, others may think that a person who has been disciplined or removed was not allowed to learn or did not have his or her assets valued. They may see the new monitoring requirements as an expression of distrust in their judgment, and they may feel that they are being forced to compromise by implementing their programs in a way that differs from their views about how best to create social change. It can be difficult for an organizational leader to find the right balance because individuals on staff may personalize organizational decisions, may not have all the necessary information, or may have other agendas.

Staff members at our local Public Allies sites also deal with conflict between upholding the integrity of the program and upholding the integrity of the Ally community. The need for integrity in the program may lead them to discipline or remove an Ally who is not meeting the program's expectations and standards. If we disregard those standards, we disrespect those who do meet them, which ultimately makes accountability optional. But there's a conflict because the integrity of the community holds that each member is a valued asset, and the Allies build a strong sense of community with each other. The dismissal of an Ally is all the more painful because our organizational integrity and our accountability to the dismissed Ally require us to be silent about the reasons for dismissal.

The Allies Organize Against Public Allies

A few months after I became CEO of Public Allies, I received a letter signed by all our Chicago Allies, with a list of demands that expressed a vote of no confidence in their local staff.

An Ally there had been arrested. He had a criminal record, and so this meant that he was in serious trouble.

The staff members had initially defended the Ally, but as the web of dishonesty he had constructed began to unravel, they felt they could no longer do so. They dismissed him from the program. The Chicago Allies became outraged that the staff members were not doing everything they could to get this young man out of jail. It seemed to them that the staff members were treating him as if he were guilty, before he had even been tried.

When I received this letter, my initial thought was that we train our Allies to be organizers, and so we shouldn't be surprised when they organize against us. The leading advocate for the group of Allies was April Méndez, a young woman whose evangelical Christian faith had inspired her service. She was passionate about Public Allies acting justly in this case. Many times, as she lobbied me about this issue, she would complain, "You're not hearing us." To which I would reply, "I'm hearing you just fine, but, given what I know, I'm not agreeing with you."

Today April is vice president for leadership at Interfaith Youth Core, which aims to make interfaith cooperation a social norm around the world, primarily by developing young leaders who learn to work together through interfaith service. She recounts this time in our lives:

> While I cringe now, looking back at the demands we made, I feel pride in my class of Allies. We took our friendships and commitment to each other seriously. The solidarity of our class was so critical! We were radically different in so many ways, but we were also radically similar, especially in terms of the values that drove us. [The Ally who had been fired] was different from anyone I had ever been in contact with before, and he had not always pulled through as a team member, but he was a member of our team. We were going to make sure he was given a fair chance because the stakes in his life were so high. I'm proud of what we did and understand that Public Allies did what should have been done, based on what it knew. Public Allies allowed our solidarity, our expression, and our use of our skills. What we did disrupted the workings of Public Allies, but we became a stronger community as a result. There is a challenge when you create the space for people to express grievances—that they will have more expectations that you will solve their grievances. Creating that space risks greater frustration but is still worth it in the end. I've learned to create that space as a leader since.[8]

I met April through a conflict, but I found her impressive. Our Chicago office awarded her the Richard Blount Spirit Award.* In addition, April served on the advisory board of Public Allies Chicago and later received an Alumni Changemaker of the Year Award for her work building a grassroots youth organization in Chicago.

"Public Allies Chicago and Paul clearly refused to see this as a black-and-white issue," she says. "They could easily have come down hard on me and threatened termination and cut me out of additional opportunities. Instead, they listened, gave the best answer they could, didn't budge on what they knew was the right move, and rewarded me for the positive aspects of what I had done."

* Richard was one of the founding staff members at Public Allies Chicago and later became an Ally during the program's second year. Sadly, he died in 1997. He had come up to Milwaukee many times to help me when I was getting started.

Along with being empathetic and putting ourselves in each other's shoes, we must be forgiving. As a leader, I've had my share of conflicts. I've learned a great deal from them and also learned the importance of forgiveness—both giving and receiving it. As leaders, we must forgive others who take responsibility for their mistakes or transgressions, and we must own up and ask others to forgive ours when we fail. Wayne, my twelve-step sponsor, once gave me a lesson that is hard to practice: "If you want inner peace, you have to admit you're wrong when you're wrong, and sometimes you even have to admit you're wrong even when you're right."

While in South Africa in 1997 in connection with a fellowship, I had the inspiring privilege of hearing Archbishop Desmond Tutu speak about forgiveness. His message was that anger, resentment, and revenge harm us and don't allow us to move forward. One must understand another's transgression fully and have empathy for the perpetrator, but one does not have to condone the transgression. When we open ourselves to forgive others, we open a door to freedom and our future.[9] Chris Kwak, a program officer at the W.K. Kellogg Foundation, puts this idea in even simpler terms: "You can either transform pain or transfer it." We can either be stubborn and resentful, which harms us and the relationship, or we can grow from the experience. We are all half full and half empty, and we all make mistakes. Leaders have to move forward and not get stuck in the past.

My friend Richard has set an inspiring and humbling example for empathy and forgiveness. Richard's two children had been hit by a drunk driver and were in the hospital, one in a coma. Richard, a recovering alcoholic, had driven drunk many times before and had the empathy to recognize that the driver was really no different from himself. While his children were still in the hospital, Richard contacted the driver and took him to a support group for alcoholics. At a terrible and tragic time, Richard was able to own his emptiness and see the drunk driver's emptiness as the same. Richard's example sets a high bar.

Being Accountable to Those We Serve

When I was the new executive director of Public Allies Milwaukee and was trying to establish myself in town, I was invited to join the board of the Milwaukee Inner City Youth Serving Agencies coalition. The board included the leaders of most of the large youth organizations in the city, and I joined just as they were going into a phase of strategic planning—Governor Tommy Thompson of Wisconsin was reforming the state's welfare system, through which single, unemployed parents in poverty received cash assistance to help them support their families, and the agencies in the coalition were determining how to respond.

To prepare for my service on the board, I met with a few people in the community who I knew had expertise in welfare reform. I asked them what a group like ours could do, and the answers were filled with possibility. People shared ideas with me that, if advocated by this group of well-respected organizations, could really help children and families. I felt well prepared for the upcoming strategy meeting.

During the meeting, I threw out some of these ideas and was greeted with a range of responses, from ambivalence to impatient hostility. My idealism and naïveté were not welcomed. I learned that the coalition was not interested in advocating to ensure that welfare reform was better for children and families. The only advocacy they would do was for more money to support their services to children and families. The coalition was concerned with its member agencies' interests, not with the community's interests. This was a disheartening lesson. I did not remain a member of that coalition's board. And, unfortunately, I have watched this scenario play out repeatedly over the years as institutional interests have often diverged from community interests.

I lead an institution, too, and know it can be a struggle to balance those interests. Sometimes the struggle is just a matter of organizational realities—legal or professional standards that limit an organization's liability and require groups to work in ways that place institutional interests first or require decisions to be made more from the head than from the heart. Sometimes organizations lack staff capacity and resources, and those deficits inhibit deeper, more inclusive engagement with the community or constituencies. In other instances, the problem is the divergence between the interests of the people who pay for services and the interests of those who receive them. For example, a doctor who led an antiviolence campaign in Milwaukee once relayed to me that he was working on a modest gun-control policy related to minors. He had visited youth organizations for support in a neighborhood where gun violence was the number one cause of youth injury and death, but the major youth agencies would not touch gun control with a ten-foot pole. Why not? They were worried that they might alienate board members and donors who were against gun control. They weighed the number one cause of harm to kids against the money of a few donors, and the donors' money won.

I think one of the challenges facing organizations is that the job of leader has changed over time. The nonprofit sector experienced a big growth spurt in the 1960s, led by activists who built organizations to empower people in poverty and to be advocates for social justice. The leaders were often social workers and activists. They had their shortcomings, especially as managers, but their hearts were in the communities they served. But today every executive director must be a fundraiser first. Executive directors must be able to attract corporate, individual, foundation, and government resources. As a result, they are often much less courageous about being advocates on issues that affect their communities, for fear of creating a controversy or upsetting donors. Too often we experience a sad silence as the nonprofit community stays out of battles that address anything beyond their direct funding.

Dorothy Stoneman

One inspiring example of a courageous, caring, and empowering leader is Dorothy Stoneman, the founder and CEO of YouthBuild USA. YouthBuild programs employ young people who have left high school without a diploma, have been incarcerated, or are otherwise disconnected from education and work. These young people earn a high school diploma or a GED while gaining skills in the trades by building affordable housing in their communities.

Since 1992, when YouthBuild USA was authorized as a federal program, over one hundred thousand youth have built more than twenty thousand units of affordable housing. There are currently 273 YouthBuild programs in forty-five states. One of YouthBuild USA's long-range goals is building leaders for low-income communities who will work for social justice throughout their lives. Dorothy sees the assets and leadership potential in all her young people, and we've been fortunate to have several YouthBuild alums join Public Allies.*

Dorothy takes her accountability to the youth and communities she serves very seriously. It begins with a deep internal commitment: "I want to shift the power relationships in our society, which is structured in ways that disempower youth and low-income people. We have to build structures of accountability to them, not just goodwill."[10]

Dorothy has structured YouthBuild USA to include five seats for alumni on its board of directors (which is also made up of a majority of people of color, many of whom are from or have experience serving low-income communities); a national policy council, which is half local-site directors and half participants or graduates, so that they have equal voice in the program's design and standards; and an elected alumni council, which advises the management of the organization. One mandatory standard for all YouthBuild USA affiliates is that each one create a youth policy council. Dorothy attends every meeting of the national youth leadership and policy councils so that the youth have access to the person with the greatest power: "I learn a lot by listening to them. I enjoy having direct feedback." She also communicates actively with her young people via e-mail and social networking sites. "So many of our young people have lacked caring adults in their lives," she says, "and we must be role models and representatives of that love, and care about them as individuals."

Dorothy grew up a white person of privilege and attended Harvard. She became active in the civil rights movement, and in 1965 she moved to Harlem to teach.

"I was the only white woman where I lived in Harlem," she recalls, "and I had made a commitment to use my privilege and skills to help

* Public Allies alumni Frank Alvarez, Robert Clark, and Ely Flores all won YouthBuild's top national alumni award. Robert founded and now leads a YouthBuild program in Newark, New Jersey. Ely is an environmental justice organizer in California. For Frank's story, see Chapter One.

those who'd been mistreated in society, and to use every opportunity to learn what the world looked like from their perspective."

She was embedded in the community and was hired at the East Harlem Block Schools, which were run by low-income parents from the neighborhood. The parents hired her and, a few years later, promoted her to executive director.

"I reported to them and was accountable to their vision and direction," she says. "I was there almost ten years and wrote my master's thesis on community control. So when I started a program for young people, I brought these same principles of accountability by the professionals to the young people being served."

Dorothy worries that too many leaders today have never embedded themselves in the communities they serve or have never been accountable to struggling communities: "They often haven't been deeply informed by removing themselves from their privilege and embracing a different world view. They don't understand how things look from an oppressed perspective. If a leader who comes from privilege hasn't done that, they should recognize their ignorance and have humility about their work in those communities. Privileged people are not educated to know we are ignorant. We are taught how to best compete with each other. So another kind of training is needed. We may do good work in communities, but if we gain that understanding and accountability, we will do better."

The challenge today for many organizations is the relentless drive of fundraising. Nonprofits effectively operate two distinct businesses. The first is a service business, in which they build services to achieve impact against needs they've identified in their communities. The second is a revenue business, in which they need third-party payers for those services. Those donors also have needs that must be served by the organization.

Ideally, these two businesses are integrated, but in many groups there is tension. The problem is that sometimes the donors have goals for the community that differ from the goals that the community or the organization's leaders or the front-line staff think are most necessary. And so organizations are pulled in various directions, driven by funders' different program and budgetary interests, but they figure that these distractions are a necessary trade-off for the resources to do their jobs.

Imagine walking into a coffee shop, ordering a $4 latte, and asking that $3 go directly to the coffee grower and that 60 cents go to the people who roasted and brewed your coffee, with only 40 cents to be used for the coffee shop's rent, machinery, furniture, marketing, management, cleaning, and so forth. And the next customer wants all $4 to go just to organic farmers in Tanzania. Absurd though that sounds, it is how nonprofits are funded. It is a very inefficient system. Executive directors spend most of their time managing their donor relationships, managing the inefficiencies that come from meeting donors' diverse program interests, and coping with donors' budgetary micromanagement. And as leaders cultivate and build relationships with the donor community, they can begin to gain distance from those they serve. Dorothy Stoneman puts it this way:

> There is a slippery slope where nonprofit leaders begin to adopt the beliefs and systems of those in power and get further removed from those who are without. And leadership salaries have grown extravagant in some instances, as they try to live like their donors and become part of that world. The first time I got federal money to employ young people, the youth questioned me: "So now a bunch of white people are going to get rich off our poverty?" It had a big impact on me. I worry that too many leaders in the sector get removed from the knowledge and interests of the community, forget whom they are being paid to benefit, and gain too much solidarity with their donors.[11]

Indeed, Barack Obama, writing as a U.S. Senator about this problem, describes how much he used to appreciate being able to take private jets from Washington back to Chicago so he could rejoin his family more quickly.[12] Obama contrasts that convenience with the transformational value of what he learned about a health care issue when a man shared personal information with him as the two of them waited in line at a small airport to board their commercial planes. Obama goes on to reflect on how comforts and conveniences can create barriers between leaders and the daily concerns of ordinary people. I believe that more people who achieve positions of power and influence should likewise reflect on how leaders can continue to connect with and understand the people they serve.

Dorothy Stoneman's thoughts echo John McKnight's concerns, reported in earlier chapters, about how the professionalization of service can disable communities, and about how two middle-class neighborhoods can be supported by a single poor one.[13] Professionals build systems that define people as empty and as having needs; they create isolated services to meet those needs, and then they decide whether the services have been successful or not. Such "care" disables communities as it removes from citizens the responsibility for building their own solutions and becoming actors, not spectators. Too often, as McKnight has argued, those who have to live with the results of such services play no role in determining what their actual needs are, how their needs will be met, and whether the services or support available to them are any good. Organizations and leaders should follow Dorothy's great example and practice the kind of integrity that puts the community's interests first.

Being Accountable to Those Who Came Before Us

One of Public Allies' original core values concerned those who came before us and those who come after us. Our logo was designed with seven rays of light, representing a Native American tradition that each action we take impacts seven generations—the three generations that came before us, our present generation, and the three that come after. It is important for our own integrity to acknowledge and be aware of those who have inspired, influenced, taught, and supported us along our journeys. As Dr. Howard Fuller says, "I am accountable to all the people who've struggled before me. When I think about my mother and grandmother, who gave up so much to ensure I would be in a better place, and those who struggled for civil rights—the unsung people who struggled to gain dignity and opportunity for me—I have an accountability to that history."[14]

Amelia Kolokihakaufisi

It was a terrible tragedy that initiated Amelia Kolokihakaufisi's leadership journey. Amelia grew up in the tough neighborhoods of East Palo Alto, a city of thirty-five thousand or so mostly Latino residents that was once the murder capital of America. The city has been bypassed by the technology wealth generated in the surrounding Silicon Valley region.

Amelia did well growing up, and she studied at San Francisco State University. But during her third year, her world was shaken. First her mother had a stroke. Amelia dropped out of college to help care for her, and she became the family's primary breadwinner. Then a second tragedy hit: Amelia's boyfriend was murdered.

At the time of her boyfriend's death, the murder rate in East Palo Alto had declined from its worst years, but shootings had increased, and the victims were now younger. Amelia, through her grief, realized that something had to be done. She helped organize the Peace and Unity March, held on February 3, 2007, which drew more than a thousand residents to demand a cease-fire in the community. "I didn't want anyone else to go through what I went through," she says.[15] For eight months afterward, there were no more murders resulting from gun violence. Amelia later attended a youth summit, where she learned about Public Allies and decided it was for her.

Amelia took her boyfriend's death as a call to better herself and her community: "It was his death that started this all. It was hard to find consolation in the tragedy. The killer was never caught. It was hard to accept. The march was a way of getting reparations for it. I didn't want him to die in vain."

She took lessons from the death of her boyfriend into her service to youth in East Palo Alto. She also learned a great deal about herself.

"I had started out thinking that leadership was about being loud and aggressive," she says, "but I learned that it could also be quiet and empathetic. I learned how to adapt to different people and situations and be versatile." But perhaps the most important lesson was to be true to herself: "I realized that I had to stop being who I thought others wanted me to be. The hardships I've experienced made me stronger and prepared me to be able to handle bigger things. I had to share that. I had felt that a part of me had died with my partner, but I realized through this work that I can live, I can grow from this experience, and I can create something worthwhile to honor those who have passed."

Today Amelia is completing college and still serving youth in East Palo Alto: "I'm applying what I learned from my boyfriend, from my life, and from Public Allies every day in my work with youth from my community."

I learned an important lesson about honoring those who come before us through a tragic combination of events during the summer of 2006. My mentor Charlie Bray died suddenly on July 23, and I spent the evening of his death grieving with his wife and friends. The next morning I was at my parents' home, where I watched my dad collapse. I took him to the emergency room, and he died three weeks later.

Reconciling my grief for these two men was quite difficult. Charlie had shown me unconditional love and had supported me more than I ever could have asked or expected. He was also a truly great exemplar of the leadership values I strive to follow. By contrast, my father and I were never close and did not have much in common. I visited him at the hospital on the day of Charlie's funeral, a funeral where I gave a eulogy about how Charlie had helped introduce me to asset-based community development and the idea that we are all half full and half empty. When I got home that night and reflected, I felt disturbed that I had always seen my dad only for his emptiness. I had never in my life really thought about or acknowledged his assets. We got along pretty well during his last fifteen years, but I realized that, for me, this relative harmony came from a place grounded in my liking him despite his deficits, not loving him for his assets.

So, that evening, I made a list of all the assets I saw in him and had learned from him—things I had never before in my life recognized. I acknowledged, for example, his work ethic, his generosity, his selflessness, his focus on solving problems instead of complaining about them, and his integrity (my oldest brother Steven's eulogy would later focus on Dad's integrity and selflessness as perhaps his greatest qualities). A few nights later, I read my dad the list while visiting him in the hospice. He was not able to respond verbally, but I sensed he heard me. It was a healing moment for both of us.

I've made the point throughout this book that leaders need to ask for help and support to sustain ourselves. I've noted that I stand on the shoulders of many giants, and I've been clear that my leadership is possible only because of their belief in and support of me. I still consult my mentors often and miss terribly those who've passed. They live in my conscience, though, and I think of them and their lessons when I'm faced with difficult situations or achieve victories. It is rare that any of us steps up to lead without the lessons and support of many around us. Even the great leaders like Martin Luther King Jr. were supported and developed along their journeys. To be true to ourselves and to others, we need to honor those who have inspired, developed, mentored, and taught us. This awareness is critical to our practice of integrity.

Bill Graustein

Bill Graustein was a geophysics researcher at Yale when his career was altered by a large and unexpected windfall. As Bill jokes, "I couldn't even spell *filanthropist,* but now I *are* one."[16]

Bill established the William Caspar Graustein Memorial Fund, named for his uncle, to inform the public policy debate in Connecticut and engage parents and the broader community in collaboratively improving education for children in the state. The fund is especially concerned with children who, like Bill's uncle and Bill's father, come from modest beginnings (Bill's grandfather was an uneducated dairy worker).

After the fund was established, Bill happened to meet Chuck Supple, then Public Allies' CEO. Chuck was immediately impressed by Bill's thoughtfulness, his interest in leadership development, and his commitment to community building, and he recruited Bill to serve on Public Allies' board of directors. As Bill began his board service, he decided to visit several Public Allies sites.

"I was struck by the consistency of values across sites," he says, "and by the expectations that all relationships should be both supporting and challenging. The values practiced inside Public Allies were those that were expected of Allies in communities. Allies were accountable to program managers, and program managers to allies. There was this combination of diversity coupled with reciprocity that formed a powerful experience in inclusion I had not seen before. Values were not just aspirational but practical. Everyone could practice them. And I saw this at each location."

Bill became Public Allies' board chair, its largest investor, and an inspiring example of Public Allies' mission and values in action. He has worked ever since to uphold these values on the board of directors and to ensure that they inform Public Allies' governance and management.

Apart from the fund and his personal philanthropy, Bill created the Community Leadership Program to help midcareer professionals reconnect to their larger purposes and values with a community of peers: "As I met with community leaders over the years, I sensed this yearning to participate in something larger than themselves, and to more clearly express their values." In this program, Bill created the same challenging and supportive environment he saw at Public Allies: "Some of the people who've taken the risk to hold me accountable are some of the most precious relationships in my life. They helped me move forward in new ways."

Bill also sponsors storytelling workshops for diverse, intergenerational groups of leaders to gain greater self-awareness and learn from others' authentic experience. A Quaker whose faith holds that the divine is accessible to everyone, and that anyone in the group can share wisdom, insight, care, and experience, Bill believes that those are the ingredients for an individual's or a community's growth. He sees "story" as the way to build bridges: "If we begin by thinking *What is something I learned that I wouldn't have learned any other way?*, it helps us move from being victims to being actors, from pain to healing and growth. It honors our human experience."

True Integrity

Integrity, in the end, is about putting all the pieces together. It is about the integration of your purpose, your values, your relationships, and your actions. It is about bringing your whole authentic self to the leadership table and to your relationships.

Public Allies' five core values are also integrated. If you are very good at being asset-based, you will be better at inclusion, and vice versa. If you are good at including people, you will be more collaborative and better at recognizing diverse assets. If you are a continuous learner, you will seek feedback and support in ways that will help you understand your fullness and your emptiness and be a better teammate. If you build self-awareness—of your story, purpose, values, assets, and shortcomings—you will work better with others and hold yourself accountable to others. And these leadership values can be practiced by anyone. Regardless of your position or level of influence, these values will make you effective at working with any group of people to solve common problems and meet common goals.

Key Ideas and Lessons

1. Integrity begins with being true to ourselves—our stories, our purposes, our values, and our moral and ethical standards.
2. Integrity is about how we hold ourselves accountable to those we work with. We leaders do not wait for others to hold us accountable. We accept responsibility for the goals we set, the commitments we make, the words we say, and the lessons we need to learn.
3. Integrity is also about how we hold ourselves accountable to those we serve. Leaders often have to balance multiple interests. We must always ensure that we are accountable to the interests of those on whose behalf we work.
4. We need to be accountable to those who have inspired, influenced, mentored, taught, and even sacrificed for us to be where we are today. Many people helped develop us as leaders, and we must honor them through our work.
5. The five core values of Public Allies are integrated. If you practice one, you will be stronger at the other four. They are a system of values that, practiced together, will make you able to engage individuals and groups to work effectively together in any community.

Reflections and Exercises

Consider the five values explored and discussed in this book.

- Which is the one that you are best at practicing in your work?
- Which one are you least adept at?
- Which value did the book approach most differently from how you've thought of it before?
- How do you see these values linked in your work? Do you believe all five are important?
- What additional values are critical to your work and leadership?
- Have you been in a situation in which you believed that your values and your group's values were not aligned? How did you deal with that? How did you manage the tension between being a good team player in the group and being true to yourself?
- Who has inspired or influenced you that you feel accountable to?

Afterword

Putting the Pieces Together to Lead

This book began with the idea that leadership is an action that many can take, not a position that only a few can hold. Leadership is about stepping up to take personal and social responsibility for working with others to achieve common goals. It is also about practicing those values that are most effective today in engaging diverse individuals and groups to work together to strengthen communities.

Our nation's history, democratic traditions, current leadership theory, and emerging trends all point to this definition. We must stop thinking of leadership only as a means of building organizations or managing people, and instead we must think about it as something that everyone can practice in his or her circle of influence to bring people and groups together to solve problems. As Robert Greenleaf wisely wrote almost thirty-five years ago, "Because so many urgent problems are the result of individual failures and leadership failures, the only way to change society [is to] produce enough people who will change it."[1] We need more people to believe in themselves, step up, and act.

To solve our most pressing and persistent challenges, we have to think about leadership, and about building community in a new way. The leadership we need is already resident in our communities. We just have to shift our lens a bit to look for potential leaders in uncommon places. There are many people ready to step up, but they don't know how. And no one organization or foundation or government official can solve a communitywide problem. It will take collective efforts that engage people and groups in moving toward common goals that can be sustained in partnership with the community. Leaders who practice these values will be able to build community capacity and collaboration, the ingredients of real and sustainable change.

Throughout this book, I've offered theory, examples, exercises, and stories that demonstrate how our approach at Public Allies can help leaders be effective in today's changing communities. I've profiled more than four dozen leaders from a diversity of backgrounds who have stepped up. Their examples inspire me, and I hope they've inspired you, too. These leaders are a small sample of the 3,800 leaders we've developed, and of the hundreds of leaders who've inspired, taught, and mentored us. The young leaders from all backgrounds who emerge through Public Allies have proved to us again and again that our approach to leadership *works*, and that there are many more people out there who can make a difference but who just don't know how yet. I hope you'll help us reach them.

We continue to face great challenges and injustices in our communities and in the larger society. There is much at stake for many of our fellow citizens. We need many more leaders ready to bend the arc of history further toward justice, as Martin Luther King Jr. put it. As the poet June Jordan wrote, "We are the ones we have been waiting for."[2]

So let me leave you with a simple question: How will *you* lead?

Notes

Acknowledgments

1. S. Wilentz, *Bob Dylan in America* (New York: Doubleday, 2010), 12.

Chapter One

1. Interview with Peter Hoeffel conducted by the author, January 10, 2011.
2. Interview with Bizunesh Talbot-Scott conducted by the author, April 19, 2010.
3. This quotation and others within this section are taken from an interview with Frank Alvarez conducted by the author, March 17, 2009.
4. D. Brooks, "Thoroughly Modern Do-Gooders," *The New York Times*, March 21, 2008.
5. J. E. Richards, "Successful Entrepreneurs Are Not Necessarily 'A' Students," *Deseret News*, January 7, 2007.
6. P. Block, *Community: The Structure of Belonging* (San Francisco: Berrett-Koehler, 2008).
7. P. Light, "In Search of Public Service," Wagner School of Public Service, New York University, June 2003; S. Cryer, "Recruiting and Retaining the Next Generation of Nonprofit Sector Leadership," Wagner School of Public Service, New York University, January 2004.

8. G. S. Davis, J. P. Kovari, and S. Percy, *Leadership Diversity in Milwaukee's Nonprofit Sector, Benchmark Study 2008* (Milwaukee: Center for Urban Initiatives and Research, University of Wisconsin–Milwaukee, 2008); P. H. Teegarden, *Change Ahead: Nonprofit Executive Leadership and Transitions Survey 2004* (Baltimore, Md.: Annie E. Casey Foundation, 2004); B. Nelson, "Nonprofits See Need for Diverse Leadership," *Daily Record*, April 16, 2010; C. J. DeVita and K. L. Roeger, *Measuring Racial-Ethnic Diversity in California's Nonprofit Sector* (Washington, D.C.: Urban Institute, 2009). The information about younger nonprofit executive directors being less diverse than older ones has been found in a few different studies, including J. Bell, R. Moyers, and T. Wolfred (with N. O'Silva), *Daring to Lead 2006: A National Study of Nonprofit Executive Leadership*, a joint project of CompassPoint Nonprofit Services and the Meyer Foundation (San Francisco and Washington, D.C.: CompassPoint Nonprofit Services and the Eugene and Agnes E. Meyer Foundation, 2006), 27–28.
9. M. Gibelman, "So How Far Have We Come? Pestilent and Persistent Gender Gap in Pay," *Social Work* 48:1 (2003), 22–32; M. Gibelman, "The Nonprofit Sector and Gender Discrimination: A Preliminary Investigation into the Glass Ceiling," *Nonprofit Leadership and Management* 10:3 (2009), 251–269; H. Joslyn, "A Man's World: Big Charities Overwhelmingly Run by White Males, a *Chronicle* Survey Finds," *Chronicle of Philanthropy*, September 17, 2009, n.p.
10. M. D. Hais and M. Winograd, *Millennial Makeover: MySpace, YouTube, and the Future of American Politics* (Piscataway, N.J.: Rutgers University Press, 2008), 2.
11. U.S. Census Bureau, "Educational Attainment in the United States: 2009 (CPS 2009)," 2009 (http://www.census.gov/hhes/socdemo/education).
12. Office of the Assistant Secretary for Planning and Evaluation (ASPE), *Vulnerable Youth and the Transition to Adulthood,*

ASPE Research Brief (Washington, D.C.: Office of Human Services Policy, U.S. Department of Health and Human Services, 2009), 1–2.

13. P. Block and J. McKnight, *The Abundant Community* (San Francisco: Berrett-Koehler, 2010), xiii.
14. H. Boyte, *Civic Agency and the Cult of the Expert* (Dayton, Ohio: Kettering Foundation, 2009); J. McKnight and C. Pandak, *New Community Tools for Improving Child Health: A Pediatrician's Guide to Local Associations* (Evanston, Ill.: ABCD Institute, 1999); United States Department of Health and Human Services, "Healthy People 2020," 2010 (http://healthypeople.gov/2020/about/DOHAbout.aspx).
15. P. Hoeffel, "It's Everyone's Problem to Solve," *Milwaukee Journal Sentinel*, August 28, 2010.
16. R. Putnam, *Bowling Alone: The Collapse and Revival of American Community* (New York: Simon & Schuster, 2000).
17. Interview with Jeff Edmondson conducted by the author, December 13, 2010.
18. Interview with Katrina Browne conducted by the author, October 13, 2010.
19. Interview with Vanessa Kirsch conducted by the author, April 3, 2011.
20. Richard Wolfe, "Barack's Rock," *Newsweek*, February 16, 2008, 5.
21. Michelle Obama, remarks at an event sponsored by the Corporation for National and Community Service, Ronald Reagan Building, Washington, D.C., May 12, 2009.
22. Interview with David Eisner conducted by the author, January 6, 2011.
23. Interview with José Rico conducted by the author, March 30, 2011.
24. This quotation and others within this section are taken from an interview with Tanisha Brown conducted by Diane Bacha, Public Allies' director of marketing and communications, January 26 and March 21, 2011.

25. This quotation and others within this section are taken from an interview with Nigel Okunubi conducted by Diane Bacha, November 30, 2010.
26. This quotation and others within this section are taken from an interview with Milo Neild conducted by Diane Bacha, February 2, 2011.
27. This quotation and others within this section are taken from an interview with Giselle John conducted by the author, September 12, 2008.
28. "There Is Life After Abuse," in Martha Shirk and Gary Stangler, *On Their Own: What Happens to Kids When They Age Out of the Foster Care System* (Boulder, Colo.: Westview, 2004), 215–244.

Chapter Two

1. R. N. Bellah and others, *Habits of the Heart: Individualism and Commitment in American Life* (Berkeley: University of California Press, 1985).
2. J. P. Kretzmann and J. L. McKnight, *Building Communities from the Inside Out: A Path Toward Finding and Mobilizing a Community's Assets* (Skokie, Ill.: ACTA Publications, 1993).
3. W. Kopp, *One Day, All Children: The Unlikely Triumph of Teach for America and What I Learned Along the Way* (New York: PublicAffairs, 2001).

Chapter Three

1. A. de Tocqueville, *Democracy in America*, vol. 2, trans. H. Reeve (New York: Random House/Modern Library College Edition, 1981 [1840]), 403–404.
2. D. Garrow, "Commentary," in C. Eagles, ed., *The Civil Rights Movement in America* (Oxford: University Press of Mississippi, 1986), 57, cited in C. M. Payne, *I've Got the Light of Freedom: The Organizing Tradition and the Mississippi Freedom Struggle* (Berkeley: University of California Press, 1995), 3.

3. H. Boyte, *Civic Agency and the Cult of the Expert* (Dayton, Ohio: Kettering Foundation, 2009), 18.
4. Payne, *I've Got the Light of Freedom*.
5. J. Anderson, *Bayard Rustin: Troubles I've Seen* (Berkeley: University of California Press, 1998), 249–250.
6. Interview with Charles McKinney conducted by the author, July 10, 2010.
7. R. Dunbar, "You've Got to Have (150) Friends," *The New York Times*, December 25, 2010; see also R. Dunbar, *How Many Friends Does One Person Need? Dunbar's Number and Other Evolutionary Quirks* (Cambridge, Mass.: Harvard University Press, 2010).
8. N. Howe and W. Straus, *Millennials Rising: The Next Great Generation* (New York: Vintage, 2000); see also M. D. Hais and M. Winograd, *Millennial Makeover: MySpace, YouTube, and the Future of American Politics* (Piscataway, N.J.: Rutgers University Press, 2008), 2.
9. Hais and Winograd, *Millennial Makeover*, xi, 1–2.
10. C. Dougherty, "US Nears Racial Milestone," *The Wall Street Journal*, June 11, 2010.
11. R. D. Putnam, "E Pluribus Unum: Diversity and Community in the Twenty-first Century," *Journal of Scandinavian Political Studies* 30:2 (2007), 137.
12. J. Jordan, "Poem for South African Women," *Passion: New Poems* (Boston: Beacon Press, 1980).
13. See M. Ganz, "Organizing," Hauser Center for Nonprofit Organizations, Harvard University, n.d. (http://isites.harvard.edu/icb/icb.do?keyword=k2139); R. Greenleaf, *Servant Leadership: A Journey into the Nature of Legitimate Power and Greatness* (Mahwah, N.J.: Paulist Press, 1977); J. M. Kouzes and B. Z. Posner, *The Leadership Challenge* (San Francisco: Jossey-Bass, 1995; adapted with permission of John Wiley & Sons, Inc.); F. Hesselbein and E. K. Shinseki, *Be Know Do: Leadership the Army Way* (San Francisco: Jossey-Bass, 2004); B. George, *Authentic Leadership: Rediscovering the Secrets to*

Creating Lasting Value (San Francisco: Jossey-Bass, 2003); B. George with P. Sims, *True North: Discover Your Authentic Leadership* (San Francisco: Jossey-Bass, 2007); S. Komives and W. Wagner, *Leadership for a Better World: Understanding the Social Change Model of Leadership Development* (San Francisco: Jossey-Bass, 2009; adapted with permission of John Wiley & Sons, Inc.).

14. See S. Alinsky, *Rules for Radicals: A Practical Primer for Realistic Radicals* (New York: Random House, 1971).
15. The difference between mobilizing and organizing is cogently addressed by Boyte, *Civic Agency and the Cult of the Expert.*
16. M. Ganz, *Why David Sometimes Wins: Leadership, Organization, and Strategy in the California Farm Worker Movement* (New York: Oxford University Press, 2009).
17. Ganz, "Organizing."
18. Greenleaf, *Servant Leadership*, 49.
19. Ibid., 46.
20. Ibid., 15.
21. Ibid., 35.
22. Kouzes and Posner, *The Leadership Challenge*, xx.
23. Ibid., 30.
24. Ibid.
25. Ibid., 18 (adapted with permission of John Wiley & Sons, Inc.).
26. Hesselbein and Shinseki, *Be Know Do*, xiv.
27. Ibid., 5–6.
28. Ibid., 25.
29. Ibid., 8–16.
30. George, *Authentic Leadership*, 18–25.
31. George and Sims, *True North*, 66.
32. Komives and Wagner, *Leadership for a Better World*, xvi.
33. Ibid., xii.
34. Ibid., 24–25.
35. Ibid., xiii.
36. Ibid., 101.

37. Ibid., 54.
38. J. C. Collins, *Good to Great: Why Some Companies Make the Leap—and Others Don't* (New York: HarperBusiness, 2001).
39. T. Johns, opening remarks, "Skills for the 21st Century" knowledge track, Ashoka Future Forum, sponsored by Manpower, Inc., Washington, D.C., April 6, 2010. Tammy Johns is senior vice president of global workforce strategy, Manpower, Inc.

Chapter Four

1. J. Jordan, "Poem for South African Women," *Passion: New Poems* (Boston: Beacon Press, 1980).
2. R. Putnam, *Bowling Alone: The Collapse and Revival of American Community* (New York: Simon & Schuster, 2000).
3. J. Wallis, *God's Politics: Why the Right Gets it Wrong and the Left Doesn't Get It* (New York: HarperCollins, 2005), 373–374.
4. L. Sullivan, "Ella Baker," *Social Policy* 30:2 (1999), n.p.
5. F. Hesselbein and E. K. Shinseki, *Be Know Do: Leadership the Army Way* (San Francisco: Jossey-Bass, 2004).
6. Interview with Paul Griffin conducted by the author, August 6, 2010.
7. S. Komives and W. Wagner, *Leadership for a Better World: Understanding the Social Change Model of Leadership Development* (San Francisco: Jossey-Bass, 2009; adapted with permission of John Wiley & Sons, Inc.).
8. P. Block, *Community: The Structure of Belonging* (San Francisco: Berrett-Koehler, 2008), 41.
9. Ibid., 65.
10. J. M. Kouzes and B. Z. Posner, *The Leadership Challenge* (San Francisco: Jossey-Bass, 1995), 26.
11. This quotation and others within this section are taken from an interview with Reggie Moore and Sharlen Bowen Moore conducted by the author, August 20, 2010.

12. Kouzes and Posner, *The Leadership Challenge*, 11–12.
13. Ibid., 11.
14. R. Greenleaf, *Servant Leadership: A Journey into the Nature of Legitimate Power and Greatness* (Mahwah, N.J.: Paulist Press, 1977).
15. Komives and Wagner, *Leadership for a Better World*, 46. The work on which Komives and Wagner are commenting is J. M. Burns, *Transforming Leadership: A New Pursuit of Happiness* (New York: Atlantic Monthly Press, 2003).
16. Kouzes and Posner, *The Leadership Challenge*, 30.
17. Lao-tzu, *Tao Te Ching*, verse 17, cited by D. Dreher, *The Tao of Personal Leadership* (New York: Harper Paperbacks, 1996), 122.
18. Komives and Wagner, *Leadership for a Better World*, 31–32 (adapted with permission of John Wiley & Sons, Inc.).
19. Ibid., 32.
20. R. Martin, "To the Rescue: Beating the Heroic Leadership Trap," *Stanford Social Innovation Review*, January 2003, 38, available online at http://www.rotman.utoronto.ca/rogermartin/ToTheRescue.pdf. See also R. Martin, *The Responsibility Virus: How Control Freaks, Shrinking Violets—and the Rest of Us—Can Harness the Power of True Partnership* (New York: Basic Books, 2002).
21. Martin, "To the Rescue," 38.
22. Ibid.
23. Ibid., 39.
24. Jesse Kornbluth, "An Interview with Ms. Dove," *The Book Report*, April 8, 1997, available online at http://www.math.buffalo.edu/~sww/dove/dove-interview.html#interviewRita.
25. Block, *Community*, 70.
26. Ibid., 21.
27. Interview with David McKinney conducted by the author, November 17, 2010.

28. J. McKnight, "Professionalized Service and Disabling Help," *The Careless Society: Community and Its Counterfeits* (New York: Basic Books, 1996), 36–52.
29. Ibid., 45–52.
30. Ibid., 46.
31. Ibid., 48.
32. Ibid., 49.
33. C. Gibson, *Citizens at the Center: A New Approach to Civic Engagement* (Washington, D.C.: Case Foundation, 2006), 1.
34. Ibid., 7.
35. H. Boyte, *Civic Agency and the Cult of the Expert* (Dayton, Ohio: Kettering Foundation, 2009), 2.
36. P. Schmitz and L. Sullivan, "Practicing What We Preach: Creating Transforming Organizations," *Wingspread Journal* 19:4 (1997), n.p.

Chapter Five

1. Interview with Steve Ramos conducted by Diane Bacha, Public Allies' director of marketing and communications, March 16, 2010.
2. J. P. Kretzmann and J. L. McKnight, *Building Communities from the Inside Out: A Path Toward Finding and Mobilizing a Community's Assets* (Skokie, Ill.: ACTA Publications, 1993).
3. P. Block, *Community: The Structure of Belonging* (San Francisco: Berrett-Koehler, 2008), 48.
4. Two studies conducted in the 1980s found that one poor neighborhood could support two middle-class neighborhoods; see J. McKnight, *The Careless Society: Community and Its Counterfeits* (New York: Basic Books, 1996), 72, 164. If the public and philanthropic resources spent per capita to "fix" the people in the poor neighborhood had been given directly to the residents, those resources would have lifted them out of poverty; instead, the resources were paid to professional "helpers," who mostly lived outside the community. The results of these studies are probably still relevant today.

5. See also ibid., 36–52.
6. A. de Tocqueville, cited in ibid., 113–117.
7. R. Putnam, *Bowling Alone: The Collapse and Revival of American Community* (New York: Simon & Schuster, 2000).
8. J. Jacobs, *The Death and Life of Great American Cities* (New York: Modern Library, 1993 [1961]). See also S. Saegert and G. Winkel, "Crime, Social Capital, and Community Participation," *American Journal of Community Psychology* 34:3 (2004), 219–233; R. L. Sampson, S. W. Raudenbush, and F. Earls, "Neighborhoods and Violent Crime: A Multilevel Study of Collective Efficacy," *Science* 277 (1997), 918–924.
9. H. Boyte, *Civic Agency and the Cult of the Expert* (Dayton, Ohio: Kettering Foundation, 2009), 7.
10. P. L. Benson, P. C. Scales, S. F. Hamilton, and A. Sesma Jr., with K. L. Hong and E. C. Roehlkepartain, "Positive Youth Development So Far: Core Hypotheses and Their Implications for Policy and Practice," *Search Institute Insights & Evidence* 3:1 (2006), 1–13.
11. Block, *Community*, 33.
12. Interview with Jeff Edmondson conducted by the author, December 13, 2010.
13. Benson and others, "Positive Youth Development So Far."
14. This quotation and others within this section are taken from an interview with Marc McAleavey conducted by the author, January 7, 2011.
15. P. Block and J. McKnight, *The Abundant Community* (San Francisco: Berrett-Koehler, 2010), xiii.
16. Ibid., 43.
17. Ibid., 43–44.
18. McKnight, *The Careless Society*.
19. Block and McKnight, *The Abundant Community*, 108.
20. This quotation and others within this section are taken from interviews with Lori Deus conducted by Diane Bacha, September 29, 2010, and by the author, February 11, 2011.

Chapter Six

1. This quotation and others within this section are taken from an interview with Susan Edwards conducted by the author, December 17, 2010.
2. R. D. Putnam, "E Pluribus Unum: Diversity and Community in the Twenty-first Century," *Journal of Scandinavian Political Studies* 30:2 (2007), 137.
3. Interview with Liz Hollander conducted by the author, January 4, 2011.
4. K. Cramer and others, *Volunteering in America Survey 2010* (Washington, D.C.: Office of Research and Policy Development, Corporation for National and Community Service, 2010).
5. National Conference on Citizenship, *America's Civic Health Index* (Washington, D.C.: National Conference on Citizenship, 2008).
6. D. Pager, *Marked: Race, Class, and Finding Work in an Era of Mass Incarceration* (Chicago: University of Chicago Press, 2007).
7. C. Dougherty, "US Nears Racial Milestone," *The Wall Street Journal*, June 11, 2010.
8. S. Page, *The Difference: How the Power of Diversity Creates Better Groups, Firms, Schools, and Societies* (Princeton, N.J.: Princeton University Press, 2007), xxv.
9. This quotation and others within this section are taken from an interview with Ava Hernandez conducted by the author, December 9, 2010.
10. Martin Niemöller, cited in Milton Mayer, *They Thought They Were Free: The Germans, 1933–45* (Chicago: University of Chicago Press, 1961).
11. For a diagram (adapted from the work of Bailey Jackson, Rita Hardiman, and others) depicting the cycle of prejudice and oppression, see www.library.wisc.edu/edvrc/docs/public/pdfs/SEED Readings/CyclePrejudiceOppression.pdf.

12. See http://www.tracingcenter.org.
13. Katrina Browne, unpublished paper, 2006.
14. Interview with Laura Bumiller conducted by the author, October 14, 2010.
15. Interview with Ebony Scott conducted by the author, December 16, 2010.
16. Interview with Ava Hernandez.
17. Interview with David Weaver conducted by the author, October 18, 2010.
18. Interview with David McKinney conducted by the author, October 18, 2010.
19. Interview with Katrina Browne conducted by the author, October 13, 2010; see also *Traces of the Trade: A Story from the Deep North*, a DVD by Browne available at www.tracesofthetrade.org.
20. This quotation and others within this section are taken from an interview with Hez Norton conducted by Diane Bacha, Public Allies' director of marketing and communications, October 20, 2010.
21. This quotation and others within this section are taken from an interview with Nelly Nieblas conducted by the author, December 20, 2010.
22. Interview with Ebony Scott.
23. Michelle Obama, remarks at an event sponsored by Greater DC Cares, Washington, D.C., June 16, 2009.
24. G. Orfield, *Revisiting the Goal of an Integrated Society: A 21st Century Challenge* (Los Angeles: The Civil Rights Project/Proyecto Derechos Civiles at UCLA, 2009).
25. Interview with David Weaver.

Chapter Seven

1. This quotation and others within this section are taken from interviews with Fred Brown (January 13, 2011), Cynthia James (January 12, 2011), and Matt Bartko (January 12, 2011), all conducted by the author.

2. J. M. Kouzes and B. Z. Posner, *The Leadership Challenge* (San Francisco: Jossey-Bass, 1995).
3. I later found that Patrick Lencioni had published a similar exercise; see P. Lencioni, *The Five Dysfunctions of a Team* (San Francisco: Jossey-Bass, 2002; adapted with permission of John Wiley & Sons, Inc.). I'm not sure whether our facilitator drew this exercise from Lencioni's parable or whether that was just a coincidence.
4. The Myers & Briggs Foundation offers detailed descriptions of the strengths and weaknesses of all sixteen personality types; see http://www.myersbriggs.org/my-mbti-personality-type/mbti-basics/the-16-mbti-types.asp.
5. Interview with Tina Morrow conducted by the author, January 19, 2011.
6. Interview with Darren Thompson conducted by the author, January 18, 2011.
7. D. Goleman, *Emotional Intelligence* (New York: Bantam Books, 1995), 43, 28.
8. Interview with Tina Morrow.
9. M. S. Peck, *The Different Drum: Community Making and Peace* (New York: Simon & Schuster, 1987), 95–99, 171.
10. Ibid., 104.
11. Interview with Kate Flynn conducted by the author, January 27, 2011.
12. Interview with Alisha Klapps conducted by Diane Bacha, Public Allies' director of marketing and communications, January 27, 2011.
13. Interview with Nelson Rivera conducted by Diane Bacha, January 27, 2011.
14. Interview with Vanessa L. Llanas conducted by Diane Bacha, January 27, 2011.
15. D. Stone, B. Patton, and S. Heen, *Difficult Conversations: How to Discuss What Matters Most* (New York: Penguin, 1999), 233–234.

16. Lencioni, *The Five Dysfunctions of a Team*, reflects our experience with common team challenges. The five dysfunctions are to lack trust and vulnerability; to focus on individual recognition rather than on team results; to fear conflict and exist in artificial harmony; to fail to ensure buy-in by failing to ensure that all are heard, if not agreed with; and to hold low standards and avoid accountability.
17. A. Hetzner, "State's Black Fourth-Graders Post Worst Reading Scores in U.S.," *Milwaukee Journal Sentinel*, March 24, 2010, available online at http://www.jsonline.com/news/education/89007417.html.
18. J. Hagedorn, *Forsaking Our Children: Bureaucracy and Reform in the Child Welfare System* (Chicago: Lake View Press, 1995).
19. Ibid., 124, 7. The latter point is also a perfect illustration of John McKnight's observation that a single poor neighborhood can support two middle-class neighborhoods; see J. McKnight, *The Careless Society: Community and Its Counterfeits* (New York: Basic Books, 1996), 72, 164.
20. Ibid., 39–40.
21. J. Kania and M. Kramer, "Collective Impact," *Stanford Social Innovation Review* 9:1 (2011), 38.
22. Ibid.
23. Ibid., 36.
24. Interview with Jeff Edmondson conducted by the author, December 13, 2010.
25. Interview with Khalilah Slater-Harrington conducted by the author, January 19, 2011.
26. Interview with Jeff Edmondson.
27. D. D. Chrislip and C. E. Larson, *Collaborative Leadership: How Citizens and Civic Leaders Can Make a Difference* (San Francisco: Jossey-Bass, 1994), 129.
28. Ibid., 14.
29. Ibid., 31.
30. Ibid., 64, 108, 138.

Chapter Eight

1. This quotation and others within this section are taken from an interview with Melia Dicker conducted by the author, February 1, 2011.
2. H. Gardner, *Multiple Intelligences: The Theory and Practice* (New York: Basic Books, 1993), xx.
3. See http://www.accelerated-learning.info.
4. P. Senge, *The Fifth Discipline: The Art and Practice of the Learning Organization* (New York: Currency/Doubleday, 1990), 6–10.
5. J. Whitmore, *Coaching for Performance: The New Edition of the Practical Guide* (London: Nicholas Brealey, 1992), 18.
6. Interview with Todd Wellman conducted by the author, October 12, 2010.
7. Interview with Robert Burkhardt conducted by the author, March 1, 2011.
8. Interview with Dan Condon conducted by the author, March 1, 2011.
9. Whitmore, *Coaching for Performance*, 8.
10. Interview with Danise Sugita conducted by the author, January 13, 2011.
11. Interview with Melissa Aguilar conducted by Diane Bacha, Public Allies' director of marketing and communications, January 25, 2011.
12. Interview with Carson Henry conducted by Diane Bacha, January 26, 2011.
13. This quotation and others within this section are taken from my real-time notes on the Presentations of Learning.
14. See the Bridgespan Group, "Growth of Youth-Serving Organizations: A White Paper Commissioned by the Edna McConnell Clark Foundation," March 1, 2005, available online at http://www.bridgespan.org/LearningCenter/ResourceDetail.aspx?id=314&itemid=314&linkidentifier=id.
    Public Allies is one of the organizations whose case study contributed to the findings.

Chapter Nine

1. This quotation and others within this section are taken from an interview with Leif Elsmo conducted by the author, March 14, 2011.
2. S. R. Covey, *The 7 Habits of Highly Effective People: Restoring the Character Ethic* (New York: Fireside, 1989), 106.
3. Interview with Dr. Howard Fuller conducted by the author, February 23, 2011.
4. Interview with Cris Ros-Dukler conducted by the author, March 21, 2011.
5. P. Block, *Community: The Structure of Belonging* (San Francisco: Berrett-Koehler, 2008), 21.
6. This quotation and others within this section are taken from an interview with David Veliz conducted by Diane Bacha, Public Allies' director of marketing and communications, November 19, 2010.
7. Covey, *The 7 Habits of Highly Effective People.*
8. This quotation and others within this section are taken from an interview with April Méndez conducted by Diane Bacha, February 1, 2011.
9. A book by Archbishop Tutu expands on what I heard that day; see D. Tutu, *No Future Without Forgiveness* (New York: Doubleday, 1999), especially 35, 271.
10. This quotation and others within this section are taken from an interview with Dorothy Stoneman conducted by the author, March 16, 2011.
11. Ibid.
12. B. Obama, *The Audacity of Hope: Thoughts on Reclaiming the American Dream* (New York: Vintage Books, 2008 [2006]), 230.
13. See J. McKnight, *The Careless Society: Community and Its Counterfeits* (New York: Basic Books, 1996), 72, 164.
14. Interview with Dr. Howard Fuller.

15. This quotation and others within this section are taken from an interview with Amelia Kolokihakaufisi conducted by the author, January 25, 2011.
16. This quotation and others within this section are taken from an interview with Bill Graustein conducted by the author, March 7, 2011.

Afterword

1. R. Greenleaf, *Servant Leadership: A Journey into the Nature of Legitimate Power and Greatness* (Mahwah, N.J.: Paulist Press, 1977), 46.
2. J. Jordan, "Poem for South African Women," *Passion: New Poems* (Boston: Beacon Press, 1980).

The Author

Paul Schmitz founded Public Allies Milwaukee in 1993, served as vice president and chief strategist from 1997 to 1999, and was appointed national CEO of Public Allies in 2000. In addition, Paul serves as co-chair of Voices for National Service, serves on the board of Independent Sector, blogs on leadership for *The Washington Post*, and is a faculty member of the Asset-Based Community Development Institute in the School of Education and Social Policy at Northwestern University.

As a private volunteer, Paul co-chaired the 2008 Obama presidential campaign's civic engagement policy group, was a member of the Obama-Biden Transition Team, and was appointed by President Barack Obama to the White House Council on Community Solutions.

Paul graduated from the University of Wisconsin–Milwaukee in 1994 with a degree in political science and received the university's Graduate of the Last Decade alumni award. He was selected as a Next Generation Leadership Fellow by the Rockefeller Foundation, was recognized by *The Nonprofit Times* as one of the fifty most powerful and influential nonprofit leaders in the country, and is a recipient of *Fast Company* magazine's Social Capitalist Award for innovation. He lives in Milwaukee with his three children, Maxwell, Maya, and Olivia.

Public Allies

Learn about Public Allies, find more about the stories and the people featured in this book (including photos and videos), look at exercises from our program and more at www.everyoneleads.com. You can also connect to our local programs, where you can get involved in the work we do every day. What follows is the site list as of 2011; new sites are announced each spring.

Public Allies Arizona

Lodestar Center for Philanthropy and Nonprofit Innovation, Arizona State University
www.publicallies.org/Arizona

Public Allies Central Florida

Community Based Care of Central Florida
www.publicallies.org/centralflorida

Public Allies Chicago

www.publicallies.org/chicago

Public Allies Cincinnati

Bridges for a Just Community
www.publicallies.org/cincinnati

Public Allies Connecticut

RYASAP
www.publicallies.org/connecticut

Public Allies Delaware

Center for Community Research and Service, University of Delaware
www.publicallies.org/delaware

Public Allies Eagle Rock (Colorado)

Eagle Rock School
www.publicallies.org/eaglerock

Public Allies Indianapolis

Indianapolis Neighborhood Resource Center
www.publicallies.org/indianapolis

Public Allies Los Angeles

Community Development Technologies Center
www.publicallies.org/losangeles

Public Allies Maryland

School of Social Work, University of Maryland
www.publicallies.org/maryland

Public Allies Miami

Catalyst Miami
www.publicallies.org/miami

Public Allies Milwaukee

School of Continuing Education, University of Wisconsin–Milwaukee
www.publicallies.org/milwaukee

Public Allies New Mexico

New Mexico Forum for Youth in Community
www.publicallies.org/newmexico

Public Allies New York

www.publicallies.org/newyork

Public Allies North Carolina

North Carolina Institute of Minority Economic Development
www.publicallies.org/northcarolina

Public Allies Pittsburgh

CORO Pittsburgh
www.publicallies.org/pittsburgh

Public Allies San Antonio

Alamo Colleges, Economic and Workforce Development Division
www.publicallies.org/sanantonio

Public Allies Silicon Valley/San Francisco

Bay Area Community Resources
www.publicallies.org/sanfrancisco

Public Allies Twin Cities

Pillsbury United Communities
www.publicallies.org/twincities

Public Allies Washington, D.C.

www.publicallies.org/washingtondc

Index

M

N

O

P